Seamus Heaney as Aesthetic Thinker

Irish Studies
James MacKillop, *Series Editor*

Other titles from Irish Studies

Compassionate Stranger: Asenath Nicholson and the Great Irish Famine
Maureen O'Rourke Murphy

Irish Women Dramatists, 1908–2001
Eileen Kearney and Charlotte Headrick, eds.

Israelites in Erin: Exodus, Revolution, and the Irish Revival
Abby Bender

Joyce/Shakespeare
Laura Pelaschiar, ed.

Postcolonial Overtures: The Politics of Sound in Contemporary Northern Irish Poetry
Julia C. Obert

Representing the National Landscape in Irish Romanticism
Julia M. Wright

The Snake's Pass: A Critical Edition
Bram Stoker; Lisabeth C. Buchelt, ed.

Writing Lough Derg: From William Carleton to Seamus Heaney
Peggy O'Brien

Seamus Heaney as Aesthetic Thinker

A Study of the Prose

Eugene O'Brien

Syracuse University Press

First Edition 2016

16 17 18 19 20 21 6 5 4 3 2 1

∞ The paper used in this publication meets the minimum requirements of the American National Standard for Information Sciences—Permanence of Paper for Printed Library Materials, ANSI Z39.48-1992.

For a listing of books published and distributed by Syracuse University Press, visit www.SyracuseUniversityPress.syr.edu.

ISBN: 978-0-8156-3460-7 (cloth)
978-0-8156-3448-5 (paperback)
978-0-8156-5372-1 (e-book)

Library of Congress Cataloging-in-Publication Data

Available from the publisher upon request.

Manufactured in the United States of America

To the loves of my life, Áine, Eoin, Dara, and Sinéad,
and in memory of Noreen Brophy-McElhinney,
who has left a luminous emptiness in all our lives

If it were not for the Poetic or Prophetic character, the Philosophic & Experimental would soon be at the ratio of all things, & stand still unable to do other than repeat the same dull round over again.

—William Blake, *There Is No Natural Religion*

Contents

Acknowledgments

In a work of this length, a number of people have been involved from the beginning to the end, and I would like to take this opportunity to thank them. Áine McElhinney read this book critically as a final draft, and her observations and pertinent questions, some of which I struggled to answer, have made the argument stronger and the expression clearer. Tony and Sinéad Corbett both read and commented on the manuscript, and their input, as well as their friendship over the years, has made the book better.

Eamon Maher, through phone calls, e-mails, and a careful reading of the book, participated in all stages of its gestation. Our discussions on literature, and on the role of the literary in culture, have sharpened many of my own ideas, and I thank him for his collegiality and his friendship. My colleagues in the Department of English Language and Literature at Mary Immaculate College (MIC), both academic and administrative, through their hard work and professionalism, have made my job as head of the department easier and have helped to provide the time during which this book was written, and I would like to thank them most sincerely: Linda McGrath, John McDonagh, Maria Beville, Marita Ryan, Anne O'Keeffe, Kathryn Laing, Margaret Healy, and more recently Joan O'Sullivan, Donna Mitchell, and Eóin Flannery.

The undergraduate and postgraduate students who study Heaney with me in different courses in Mary Immaculate College have enriched this book by their questions and by their discussions. Without computer assistance and financial assistance, this book could not have been completed, and I would like to thank Niall Sheehy, John

Spencer, and John Coady at MIC for their invaluable assistance. Mary Immaculate College is a very supportive working environment for the kind of research that I pursue, and I would like to thank the college for this productive and affirming environment and for the good coffee that has always been a source of inspiration.

I would like to thank Faber and Faber, Farrar, Straus and Giroux, and W. W. Norton and Company for permission to quote from the works of Seamus Heaney. I would also like to thank Catherine Heaney and the Heaney estate for their kind permission and support.

The cover photograph was taken by Press 22 at the Kate O'Brien Weekend in Mary Immaculate College, on February 26, 2012. It was a very special occasion, and I would like to thank Grace Cameron for sourcing this photograph for me. It captures Heaney as poet and aesthetic thinker at the height of his powers.

The two anonymous peer reviewers for Syracuse University Press offered genuine and insightful comments, critiques, and suggestions on the original draft of this book, which added significantly to its intellectual argument, and for these contributions, and for their open minds to what is a new departure in Heaney studies, I would like to thank them most sincerely. Annette Wenda was a punctilious and helpful copy editor, and I thank her for the care with which she read my work; it is the better for her input. Deborah Manion, Kelly Balenske, and others at Syracuse University Press have been a pleasure to work with, and I thank them for their efficiency and support in the gestation of this book.

In terms of academic acknowledgments, the work of Seamus Heaney has been a constant presence in my life for the past thirty years, and I would like to acknowledge the privilege it has been to engage with his work on a sustained level. I met him only three times, but he has been an enabling presence in my intellectual life, and his loss has been keenly felt. I would also like to thank Catherine Heaney most sincerely for her kindness and courtesy in responding to my queries and questions.

Finally, sincere appreciation to my family for all of their help. My parents, Bill and Alice O'Brien, set me on this path with a lot of books in the house, and for that, and much else, I thank them. My three children, Eoin, Dara, and Sinéad, were great sources of support, questions, and encouragement (and fun) in the writing of this book. Their ongoing inquiries as to the progress of the book kept me going, and their ongoing interest in my work has been a huge support to me. They are also great fun. Paul and Katie, as ever, were in my mind throughout the process. Finally, I would like to thank my wife and partner, Áine, my first reader and ideal audience, for support that touches the Lacanian real—necessary, sustaining, constitutive—but impossible to put into words.

Seamus Heaney as Aesthetic Thinker

Introduction

The Structure of Poetic Thinking

In an ever-growing list of studies on the work of Seamus Heaney, this book will attempt something different. His poetry will not be the focus of analysis, except where it is relevant to the main theme, which is an outline of Heaney as an aesthetic thinker in the European intellectual tradition. This tradition, generally located in the sphere of Continental philosophy and cultural theory, sees the aesthetic as a valid epistemological mode of thinking. From Plato through Immanuel Kant and Georg Wilhelm Friedrich Hegel to contemporary philosophical and theoretical writers such as Martin Heidegger, Theodor Adorno, Jacques Lacan, Jacques Derrida, and Giorgio Agamben, the aesthetic has been studied as an area that offers a supplementary mode of knowing to the paradigm of rational discourse and philosophical or scientific inquiry. This notion is in no way to decry such rational philosophical and theoretical inquiry; however, it cannot be denied that not everything can be expressed in such discourses. The aesthetic, as a mode of thinking, has value because it can address aspects of the human being that are not voiced by the discourse of rational intellectual inquiry, and in this book the mode of knowledge expressed in a particular area of aesthetic practice, namely, poetry, is the focus of attention. So rather than being about Heaney as a poet, or about his poetry itself, this book will focus on Heaney as a thinker about poetry, or, to put it another way, on Heaney as an aesthetic thinker.

In an interesting book on the poetry of Wallace Stevens, Simon Critchley outlines twenty-one propositions about poetry, and numbers eight and nine are germane to the point that I am making here:

> Philosophically expressed, all poetry is idealistic, at least in ambition. However, the *material poetica*, the raw stuff out of which poetry makes its radiant atmospheres, is the real, real particulars, actual stuff, the incorrigible plurality of things. Poetry is the imagination touching reality.
>
> Poetry allows us to see things *as* they are. It lets us see particulars being various. Nevertheless, and this is its peculiarity, poetry lets us see things as they are anew, under a new aspect, transfigured, subject to a felt variation. The poet sings a song that is both beyond us yet ourselves. Things change when the poet sings them, but they are still our things: recognizable, common, near, low. We hear the poet sing and press back against the pressure of reality. (2005, 11)

There is a level of knowledge enunciated here that can only be expressed by poetry, by a discourse wherein the sound, shape, placement, and connections across sense and meaning are all valued signifiers of the complexity and scope of poetry as a mode of thinking. In poetry, "language does not simply efface itself in delivering us over to that of which it speaks, but rather the tonality of the word is brought to resonate" (Sinclair 2006, 141). It will be my contention that Heaney's prose as a genre can be situated as part of such an ongoing aesthetic and linguistic exploration of the world, and of our knowledge of that world, and of the nature of the human being. The final term is especially significant, as poetry attempts to express and understand how we *are* in the world—and here one can immediately see connections with Heidegger's terms *Dasein* (being) and *In-der-Welt-sein* (being in the world). Part of the project of this book will be to look at the correlations between Heaney and Heidegger as both poets and thinkers. I would feel that Heaney would agree with the Heideggerian notion that "all philosophical thinking, even the severest and most prosaic, is in itself poetic, yet never is poetry"

(Mugerauer 1990, ix). This understanding is especially strong when one looks at the place of the real world, of emotions and of actual things in their work. For both men, knowledge and truth are complex and involve both the body and the mind, the emotional and the rational, touch as well as thought. For both Heidegger and Heaney, poetry is a form of thinking.

This idea of poetry as an epistemological discourse is one that has been gradually attenuated over time. The grand narratives that have guided intellectual inquiry in the Western world, namely, religion and philosophy, have tended to adopt a Cartesian dualism that values the mind, the intellect, and the soul, at the expense of the body, the emotions, and the heart. I would suggest that aesthetic thinking, especially thinking that is informed by psychoanalytic theory, brings to the fore occluded unconscious dimensions of language and signification. Heaney, like Heidegger, sees the aesthetic as a necessary element of any search for knowledge and as a valuable mode of thinking that can access the very complex reality of language and the individual.

This study will focus on Heaney's essays, book chapters, interviews, and lectures. It will analyze texts wherein Heaney sets out a complex examination of the power of poetic language to access the seemingly occluded elements of experience—elements that have been variously labeled as the real, the unconscious, the somatic, and the emotional—and to include these elements in a complex structure that investigates the effect, and affect, of the aesthetic on issues of politics, identity, ethics, and epistemology. He also sets out a strong argument for the value of the aesthetic as an emancipatory discourse in the public sphere. His writing will be seen to cohere around the attempt to answer a series of "central preoccupying questions" posed in *Preoccupations* about the role of a poet in the contemporary world: "how should a poet properly live and write" (Heaney 1980, 13). Here, the relationship between text and context is a central aspect of Heaney's ongoing epistemological preoccupations, and he sees this relationship as a very complicated one. The role of literature is of value in itself, as an autotelic discourse, but it is also of value as an enabling lens through which to view political and ethical issues in a different light; as he puts it, "I credit poetry, in other words, both for being itself and for being a help" (1995a, 11).

Heaney suggests that poetry and poetic writing can act as a mode of thinking within a Habermasian sense of the public sphere. In this endeavor, he is part of a long line of poets who saw poetry as an essential component of thought. Arthur Rimbaud, for example, felt that the "unnameable of poetic thinking is basically this thinking itself, considered *in its opening out*, in its coming" (Badiou and Toscano 2005, 25), and Heaney will undergo a parallel process of opening out as he writes about the nature and value of the aesthetic. A significant portion of his work refers to his ongoing focus on his home place and of his gradual opening out of this place by situating it within an ever-broadening cultural and linguistic context in order to locate it imaginatively within the European and Greco-Roman intellectual tradition. Generally, his focus on "Mossbawn" is viewed as an index of his groundedness in the local; I will argue precisely the opposite, namely, that what he is doing is reading his home place in a broader temporal, spatial, and imaginative context, which will allow new meanings of that place to emerge. These meanings are both mythic and unconscious, and both of these discourses will permeate and penetrate the given associations of Mossbawn as a location in County Derry, Ireland. Poetic thinking can validate such interanimations. Poetry has a life and reality of its own, but it also has access to the realm of the repressed emotions, unconscious desires, and unvoiced prejudices. Post-Freudian theory, and especially the work of Jacques Lacan, sees the unconscious as an area that is significant for all of our motivations, but as something that the language of the public sphere is largely unable to access or express. The same is true of the body and the realm of emotions, feelings, and drives, which are often seen to be unimportant with respect to knowledge and rational thinking.

What makes Heaney an especially valuable writer, in both poetry and prose, is that he is able to write in a way that includes the body, in all its somatic and haptic dimensions, in his thinking. I will examine his prose essays regarding how they both analyze and embody this sense of poetry as a form of knowledge, and I will also recontextualize this work by reading Heaney within the milieu of a broader European intellectual tradition, as I feel that it is an aspect of Heaney's work that has been overlooked in the critical discussion of his writing. By this tradition, I mean that line of aesthetic thinking that traces itself back to Greek ideas of ethics, politics, and language. In other words, I hope to read these texts against a new critical and intellectual context, a context of some aspects of Continental philosophy. I see Heaney as a poet-thinker in a strong line of such poet-thinkers and as someone whose work resonates with the work of a number of European philosophers and thinkers, writers who will be set out comparatively in this book. He has generally been seen as part of the Anglophone and Irish traditions, and I will argue that by relocating him as a European thinker, and a self-conscious one in terms of his use of etymologies, more nuanced levels of meaning can be derived from his work.

Reading Heaney's work with the aid of literary theory, or through the lens of literary theorists, has become an accepted hermeneutic approach. That Heaney was familiar with philosophy and theory is clear from his essays and interviews, and in his essay on Auden in *The Government of the Tongue* he makes the specific point that "deconstructionist tools" have yielded "many excellent insights" (1988, 120). One of his earliest critics, Blake Morrison, situated Heaney against the grain of his general early reception, which he sees as a "simplified version of his achievement" (1982, 12). He cites the views of A. Alvarez as exemplary of this perspective, before replacing them with a different understanding of Heaney's poetic endeavor. Alvarez had suggested that Heaney's poetry "works comfortably in a recognized tradition," "challenges no presuppositions," and "does not advance into unknown territory" (1980, 16–17). Morrison continues: "This I fear is the logical culmination of the established line on Heaney: he has a safe reputation but also a reputation for being safe. We are encouraged to enjoy his work but not to see it as part of a world that includes Ashbery, Ammons, Pynchon, Grass, Stoppard,

Fowles, Barthes, Derrida, and Foucault" (1982, 12). The inclusion of three philosophers or literary theorists among the novelists and poets who are seen as more conceptually challenging is interesting and proleptic of future directions in Heaney studies, as it gestures toward a depth of thinking in Heaney's work, a depth that has associations with other contemporary thinkers, working in different genres. Other critics have seen the connections between Heaney and such thinkers.

Daniel Tobin has written that Heaney had noted Gaston Bachelard's warning that the source of our first suffering "lies in the fact that we hesitated to speak" in his notebook (Clines 1983, 43) and suggests that this phrase could "act as a motto for Heaney's early work" (Tobin 1998, 68), before going on to explore that poetry through the concepts of speech and silence. Tobin has also used the thinking of Emmanuel Levinas to contextualize productively some of Heaney's attitudes, seeing some of the "Squarings" poems of *Seeing Things* as redolent of Levinas's view of alterity, as a "going outward toward the other" (ibid., 258). He has also read "Squarings vi" (Heaney 1991, 20) as enunciating Martin Heidegger's idea of being toward death (Tobin 1998, 259), while he sees "To a Dutch Potter in Ireland (Heaney 1996, 2–4), in *The Spirit Level*, as being in dialogue with Adorno's view that there can be no art after Auschwitz: "Heaney affirms that art can indeed be raised from the inferno" (Tobin 1998, 278).

Henry Hart in his book *Seamus Heaney: Poet of Contrary Progressions* uses deconstruction and the work of Jacques Derrida to offer new hermeneutic perspectives on Heaney's poetry. He compares Heaney's "sustained attack on the binary oppositions that have stratified and oppressed his society in the past" to the thinking of Jacques Derrida, and he goes on to see Heaney, especially in *The Haw Lantern*, as applying "deconstructive manoeuvres" that have "ethical relevance for the reorganization of all aspects of culture" (1992, 7). He also uses the work of Jacques Lacan to shed further light on Heaney, suggesting that if, as Lacan has argued, the unconscious is structured like a language, then "Heaney's project will be to make the linguistic unconscious speak more candidly of its hierarchical structures" (ibid., 31). Later in the work, Hart speaks of Heaney's deconstructionist slant (ibid., 179) when discussing his mode of unpacking the sociopolitical givens of his society. Similarly, Michael Molino looks at Heaney's use of his own traditions as a context for the speakers of his poems in light of Derrida's ideas: "Each time the speaker in one of Heaney's poems forges a new utterance that excavates tradition that speaker both regenerates and subverts tradition in a complex interplay of sameness and difference—what Derrida calls 'originary repetition'" (1994, 5). He also examines Heaney's own probing of the past in a new way, in his poem "Bogland" (Heaney 1966, 55–56), through the lens of Derrida's notion of inaugural writing (Molino 1994, 48–50). Irene Gilsenan Nordin (1999) has published an extensive study of Heaney's collection *Seeing Things*, using the phenomenology of Maurice Merleau-Ponty and the philosophy of Martin Heidegger as critical and theoretical lenses, while Elmer Kennedy Andrews (1998) has published a guide to Heaney's poetry that includes feminist, deconstructive, psychoanalytic, postcolonial, and linguistic analyses of Heaney's work.

My own previous work has also foregrounded literary theoretical perspectives on Heaney's poetry to a large degree, focusing on issues of ethics, aesthetics, and identity as well as his ability to access aspects of the unconscious in his writing. My point here is that there is a strand of critical work on Heaney that makes connections between his poetry and the discourses of literary theory and Continental philosophy. This study will take that connection to another level. I feel that, despite some fifty books on his work, Heaney's critical and aesthetic prose is an area that has not been given sufficient scholarly attention. In a previous publication, *Seamus Heaney's Searches for Answers*, I devoted a chapter to a brief overview of Heaney's prose, which I entitled "Preoccupying Questions" (2003, 9–27). In this chapter, I looked at the underlying ideas that were gathered in his early prose books and suggested that there were connections to be found between his thinking on poetry and the thinking of Continental European thinkers and critics. I also suggested that his work had an underlying focus on issues of ethics, politics, and identity. Of course, in nineteen pages, this chapter was only a survey of his prose writing, and a book-length story of the prose would not be written until 2009. The only full-length study of his prose is by Michael Cavanagh, entitled *Professing Poetry: Seamus Heaney's Poetics.* I would fully agree with Cavanagh when he writes about the valuable insights that the prose can bring to Heaney's own poetry, and indeed to the poetry of others. His chapter titles make clear that what is at stake in his book is what he terms "Heaney's poetics" (2009, ix) and the value of the prose as an analytical tool that can shed light on Heaney's own poetry as well as his criticism of other poets:

> *Professing Poetry* is written for readers who wish to learn something about Heaney's prose criticism—in my opinion the best written by a poet since T. S. Eliot's. But it is not an enchiridion or handbook for that criticism. It is heavily thematic, returning persistently to Heaney's troubled, not wholly consistent, and yet ultimately profound and satisfying meditation on poetry's justification, its "redress." Although the work deals with theoretical matters, it is everywhere as concrete as the subject will permit, and it isn't a work of literary theory as that term is commonly understood. (ibid., ix–x)

The titles of Cavanagh's chapters embody his aim, as we see Heaney connected to a number of other poets: "T. S. Eliot and Seamus Heaney," "Seamus Heaney and Robert Lowell," "Dante and Seamus Heaney's Second Life," "Fighting Off Larkin," and "Yeats and Seamus Heaney" (ibid., vii). This book encapsulates, *in extenso*, what many other articles and essays have expressed *in parvo*, namely, that Heaney's prose is a second-order discourse to his poetry. It is a fine and detailed study and one to which I will be referring in the course of this book; its concerns, however, are different from my own.

Neil Corcoran was one of the first critics to devote a full chapter to the prose, entitled "Heaney's Literary Criticism" (1998, 209–33), in which he sees Heaney's second collection of essays, *The Government of the Tongue* (1988), as a companion to some of the poems in *The Haw Lantern* (1987), with "the essays sometimes fleshing out in discursive terms what the poems encode more obliquely" (1998, 138). It is a significant exploration of Heaney's essays, which deals mostly with *The Government of the Tongue* and *The Redress of Poetry*, with *Preoccupations* being covered incidentally. He studies the books thematically, as opposed to chronologically, and this approach strengthens the analysis. He uses the headings "Exemplars," "Unspoken Background," "Home," and "Listening" as rubrics through which to focus on the major themes and on what he sees as Heaney's "critical admiration" of other writers (ibid., 231).

In *The Cambridge Companion to Seamus Heaney*, David Wheatley plows the same furrow in a chapter entitled "Professing Poetry: Heaney as Critic," where he, too, speaks of the value of Heaney's prose as critical metacommentary, noting that he has written on Irish poetry in both Irish and English, with particular attention to Kavanagh and Yeats, and English poetry from "*Beowulf* and Christopher Marlowe to Ted Hughes, Geoffrey Hill and Philip Larkin" (O'Donoghue 2009, 122–23). Wheatley makes some very relevant comparisons, and the result of his work is to locate Heaney within a broader Anglophone tradition; however, once again, the focus of the analysis is confined to the study of poetry, with his prose being seen as a metacommentary on that poetry.

I think this brief excursus through the work on his prose makes clear that, for most critics, Heaney is a poet first and foremost, and his prose comes into the audit very much as secondary work; when it is studied, it is contextualized either as a metacommentary on his own writing or within a British and Irish framework through connections of theme and poetic technique. In many of the chapters and essays, this account of Heaney's criticism is accurate and incisive, and it is not my purpose here to set up Corcoran, O'Donoghue, Cavanagh, or Wheatley as straw men against whom I will set out my own argument. Instead, I cite their works to show the general agreement that exists around the study and examination of Heaney's prose and to show that there has been, to date, no analysis of the prose in terms of its ideas and in terms of its attempt to search for forms of truth through writing and thinking about the broader nexus between the aesthetic, the ethical, and the political in the tradition of aesthetic thinking.

Hannah Arendt, in her introduction to *Illuminations*, makes the point that, in the work of Walter Benjamin, "we are dealing . . . with something which may not be unique but is certainly extremely rare: the gift of thinking poetically" (Benjamin 1968, 50); I would contend that in the work of Seamus Heaney, we are dealing with a comparable phenomenon. In his prose writing, we see a nuanced attention to language and to how it achieves its aims both consciously and unconsciously. Heaney, like Heidegger, forces us to recognize the "complicity between the matter and the manner of thinking as the presence of figurality itself, as the folding or thickening of the limits of language" (W. Allen 2007, 95). Language, while it can be logical, must also be necessarily more than logical as it enunciates, albeit in slanted form, the unconscious; for Heaney as well as Heidegger, "buried in all language is the rift between world and earth. Poetry reveals that rift. Revealing that rift poetry lets words speak" (Harries 2009, 116).

One of the very few critics to suggest that Heaney's language works at a higher than normal level is Harry White, whose book *Music and the Irish Literary Imagination* is a significant piece of work. He uses the term *omphalos* from Heaney's work and transposes it into a generic symbol of the connection between music and literature. His argument suggests that "the quest for the Irish Omphalos entails a consideration of music not simply as a striking absence but as a vital presence in the Literary Revival and in contemporary Irish literature" (2008, 3). White grasps the poetizing and inclusive attitude that Heaney has to the "Shakespearean-local-associative" level of language (Heaney 2002, 174). He grasps that, in Heaney's writing, the "pulse and cadence of the verse transmit this fundamental synonymity of experience and expression" and also that the blunt and falling music of the quotation stands in metonymy for the "music which Heaney can hear inside language and through which he orders his experience" (H. White 2008, 33).

For White, music allows for this unconscious, associative, and suggestive aspect of language to be enabled. He does not focus on the working of the unconscious, as it is not within the remit of his fine study. However, in the chapter on Joyce, where he is speaking about the phrase "gone beyond recall," he points out in a footnote that this "phrase seems to be an unconscious echo of 'Love's Old Sweet Song,'" which begins, "Once in the dear dead days beyond recall" (ibid., 159). Given Joyce's recourse to this song in *Ulysses*, the allusion here seems plausible. I would argue that this example is exactly the associative process that is central to Heaney's poetizing intelligence, and it also demonstrates the value of reading Heaney against a different cultural context.

For example, when talking of Robert Frost, Heaney notes that "Frost is a highly literary poet but he allows the world as it is to have its say" (Heaney and O'Driscoll 2008, 453), and Heaney sees it as a necessary part of poetized thinking: allowing language to be operative in both immanent and transcendent modes of signification. As so often happens, what a poet admires in another writer is in many ways what he strives to achieve himself, and this point is very true of his sense that Frost, while being at home in the "high cultural context of university courses," also had a sense "of 'this-worldness,' the subject matter, the dead-on and the head-on-ness" (ibid.). It is this fusion of the background and the foreground, of the rational and the emotional, of the conscious and the unconscious in Frost's life and work that attracts Heaney, and we can see the connections with his own thought and commentary on art and politics. There are a challenge and a depth in Frost's approach that are echoed in Heaney. Poetic thinking is intimately connected with that sense of "this-worldness" and with its importance to any form of knowledge or truth. To see Frost as an exemplar would be normal given that both writers are part of an Anglophone canon; however, he has looked further afield in search of such influences.

Speaking of what he sees as a "mutually fortifying alliance" between Dante and Eliot, Heaney admires the way in which "the figure of the poet as thinker and teacher merged into the figure of the poet as expresser of a universal myth that could unify the abundance of the inner world and the confusion of the outer" (2002, 174–75). Once again, it is the poetizing synthesis that he values here, as thinking and teaching are merged into an expression of a myth that allows the inner and outer worlds to be mutually expressed. Only a specific poetizing vision can achieve this synthesis, as it is this vision that is able to grasp those moments of the Lacanian real, which cannot be directly encountered or grasped. This real, or what Heidegger has termed the "unaccustomed," only "opens itself up and opens up the open only in poetizing (or, separated from it by an abyss and in its time, in 'thinking')" (2000, 126). This real is what Heaney achieves as a poetizing thinker in his own work.

I will maintain that his poetry is intimately connected with his prose and that the prose itself is driven by an intellectual desire to probe the interstices of epistemology, politics, ethics, and the aesthetic in an attempt to come to a fuller understanding of what it means to be fully human in a "world of meditated meaning" by attempting to fill "a knowledge-need." He uses this phrase in an essay about the poetry of Elizabeth Bishop, and it can serve as a synecdoche of his role as an aesthetic thinker who understands the need to access the emotional, irrational, and somatic realms of awareness that often motivate our more rational utterances. He is speaking about her poem "At the Fishhouses" and noting the descriptive power of the text. He suggests that the descriptions are so accurate that they could be part of "a geography text book." However, he goes on to explain that these lines are "poetry, not geography," which means that they have a "dream truth as well as a daylight truth about them, they are as hallucinatory as they are accurate" (1988, 106). Heaney's use of "hallucinatory" here is instructive, as knowledge, while related to the rational, is also related to the unconscious and to the emotional: hence the phrase "knowledge need" that relates the rational world of knowledge to the world of desire as outlined in the works of Sigmund Freud and Jacques Lacan, who both see "need" as a precursor to desire, something that, for both of these thinkers, is at the core of human existence. For Freud and Lacan, knowledge is a syncretism of conscious and unconscious discourses. As we will see, much of Heaney's own work probes the interstices of the rational and the irrational, the logical and the emotional, the conscious and the unconscious.

It is the unconscious that connects so much of contemporary aesthetic thinking and philosophy in the European public sphere. I would further suggest that this focus on poetry as a form of thought is one that situates Heaney within the realms of contemporary Continental philosophical and theoretical discourse. In this introduction, I will suggest in what ways Heaney is seen to be connected to this intellectual tradition and how this study attempts to develop this connection. However, it is also important to say what this book is not going to do. It does not set out a programmatic assessment of Heaney's prose in chronological or thematic manner. It does not see Heaney as a Heideggerian, a Derridean, or a Lacanian; it will not offer Derridean or Agambenian readings of his work; it will not see him as a thwarted philosopher, nor will it attempt to set out some arborescent, structured, formal aesthetic philosophy from his works. That was not his mode of intellectual operation, and this book will not attempt to impose retrospectively such a structure on his work. Just as Heaney focused on a specific text and then gradually widened the optic to demonstrate how the individual text influenced and critiqued its context, so this study will follow the same rhizomatic method, with choices motivated at all times by a focus on Heaney's reading of specific texts and the contextual associations of these readings with regard to theme and approach.

Instead, Heaney's mode of thinking on these matters, and his connections with the other thinkers mentioned, can best be categorized as rhizomatic, to use a term coined by Gilles Deleuze and Félix Guattari in their seminal work, *A Thousand Plateaus* (1987). They are attempting to describe a mode of thinking that allows for the associative logic of the unconscious and for areas of language and thought that are normally elided from theoretical and philosophical thinking. In contrast to the architectonic and structured style of Hegel and Kant, Deleuze and Guattari argue for a more associative structure to thinking. Contrasting with what they call the "root-book" that embodies "subjective organic interiority" (1987, 5), they suggest an alternative in terms of "the rhizome in opposition to the tree, a rhizome-thought instead of an arborescent thought" (Deleuze 2001, xvii). The importance of this thought process is that linkage is plural in a rhizome. There is no hierarchical structure; instead, there are connections between singularities as "any point of a rhizome can be connected to anything other, and must be. This is very different from the tree or root, which plots a point, fixes an order" (Deleuze and Guattari 1987, 7). Poetic and aesthetic thinking, I will contend, is more associatively than hierarchically structured. Unlike the arborescent mode of thought that follows a single theme with a single root through a single structure, the type of thinking that Deleuze and Guattari are endorsing is one that allows for diverse and plural connections at the level of the signifier, at the level of the sound of the word, as well as at the level of unconscious associations and connections. Significantly, as I hope to show, poetic thinking can focus on a thing, on a singularity in the world, and then use it as a starting point for the posing of a series of rhizomatic connections that shed more light on the meaning of the thing in question. The same is true of the interaction of text and context.

The points made by Simon Critchley about poetry have already been noted, but one of the most important ones is that "poetry is the description of a particular thing," but, significantly, this description is enacted in "the radiant atmosphere produced by the imagination." Thus, poetic acts are "acts of the mind, which describe recognizable things," but they "vary the appearance of those things, changing the aspect under which they are seen," and this poetry brings about "*felt* variations in the appearance of things. What is most miraculous is that poetry does this simply by the sound of words" (2005, 9). Interestingly here, Critchley sees poetry as combining reason's "acts of the mind" and emotion's "*felt* variations," and perhaps here we come to the core of the poetic and aesthetic thinking of which Heaney's work is a singular example. Thought, in this type of aesthetic epistemology, is imbricated with feeling; thought is no longer purely abstract, but is connected to the world of things through a specific use of words. This specific use of words is both a form of thought as well as an agent of thought. As Deleuze has suggested, "Literature is a constant source of thought experiments, it is one of the fields in which thought is at work, perhaps even in an exemplary fashion, as the literary text is a locus where the shift between interpretation . . . and experiment" (Lecercle 2010, 3), and it is this connection between the aesthetic and the epistemological that is the locus of Seamus Heaney's poetic thinking.

It is important to stress the particularity of such aesthetic thinking and to contrast it with the abstract thought-systems of philosophers such as Kant and Hegel. Heaney, like Deleuze, feels that "there are no universals, only singularities. Concepts aren't universals but sets of singularities that each extend into the neighbourhood of one of the other singularities" (Deleuze 1995, 146). Thus, when Heaney speaks about the unconscious, it is in the context not of abstract inquiry but of Bishop's poem, which is connected rhizomatically to a discussion of the hallucinatory and the unconscious: "The fabric of the rhizome is the conjunction, 'and . . . and . . . and . . .'" (Deleuze and Guattari 1987, 25). This paratactic connection between different ideas is at the core of aesthetic thinking; it is an associative process, which has multiple points of entry and multiple points of exit. Deleuze speaks of there being "centres everywhere" in rhizomatic thinking; he speaks of "lines which do not amount to the path of a point, which break free from structure—lines of flight, becomings." For Deleuze, it is a process of "thinking in things" and "among things" (Deleuze and Parnet 1977, 26), and it is a very good way of explaining the type of aesthetic and poetic thinking in which Heaney engages.

He finds an image or an event from a poem, from a story, from political life, or from history and gradually connects it, through imaginative and unconscious association, into a web of thought within which the original event is seen in a new light as it is being viewed from a very different perspective or indeed from different perspectives. In his work, the words themselves have a value as signifieds: "The letters are a rhizome, a network, a spider's web" (Deleuze and Guattari 1986, 29), and just as the materiality of a spider's web can disrupt our passage from one place to the next as we attempt to sweep it out of our way, so poetic language can interrupt "the dialectical movement in which things are conceptually determined" (Bruns 2006, 190). It carves out a space for the unconscious, for emotions, and for feelings in the network of thought about the significant issues of life: ethics, politics, and the lived nature of the human being. Through this web of connections between different ideas and feelings, poetic thought offers the thinker greater depth perception on issues and more of a sense of purchase on the real world.

The rhizome is active at another level in this study of Heaney's thought, as it is the structure through which Heaney's thinking can be connected to the other aesthetic thinkers who are the subject of this book. His work can be rhizomatically connected to aspects of the thinking of Jacques Lacan, Jacques Derrida, Martin Heidegger, Theodor Adorno, and Giorgio Agamben. Again, I am not attempting to suggest that Heaney read any or all of these writers, nor is there any attempt being made to squeeze these very different thinkers into a "one-size-fits-all" structure. Instead, lines of connection are traced between aspects of their thought, and aspects of Heaney's own thinking, in order to demonstrate that an appropriate and revealing context for his own writings on poetry and the aesthetic can be found in the work of these thinkers. Generally, studies of Heaney are situated in the Anglophone world, and his literary and intellectual context is demarcated through the work of T. S. Eliot and Ted Hughes, as well as the Irish tradition, and of course this point is valid. However, in a rhizomatic approach, these two areas of influence can be seen as just two of many associated contexts for his work. He is also steeped in the European literary tradition of Homer, Virgil, and Dante and has had an abiding and ever-deepening interest in poets from eastern

Europe, like Czesław Miłosz, Zbigniew Herbert, Joseph Brodsky, and Osip Mandelstam, in terms of both their lives and their work.

My approach will not be driven by any need to decry or attenuate the other contexts of Heaney's reading, but rather to develop these new ones. His connections to this tradition of European poetic thinking are, I maintain, rhizomatic, as, "unlike a structure, which is defined by a set of points and positions, with binary relations between the points and biunivocal relationships between the positions," a structure that of necessity elides or silences aspects that are not part of these fixed positions, the rhizome "is made only of lines . . . lines of flight or deterritorialisation" (Deleuze and Guattari 1987, 21), and this book will trace some of those lines of flight between Heaney and these European figures in a way that will hopefully illuminate the thinking of all of those individuals involved. In terms of deterritorialization, I would strongly suggest that Heaney's prose demonstrates an increasing movement outward from his own early preoccupations with Ireland and the matter of Ireland, but not in a way that ever left these concerns behind. It will be suggested that his first place, "Mossbawn," standing in synecdoche for Ireland and its sociopolitical and historical contexts, becomes altered owing to a more Pan-European perspective, a perspective that I will argue was there from the beginning. There will be elements of deterritorialization at work throughout his thinking, as he is willing to engage with the visceral and atavistic emotions of sectarian and political hatred, what John Montague has called in a memorable phrase "the vomit surge / of race hatred" (1972, 45), in order to understand them and to grant their validity. In this sense, his work attempts to "touch the base of our sympathetic nature while taking in at the same time the unsympathetic nature of the world to which that nature is constantly exposed" (Heaney 1995a, 29). I would suggest that this location of poetry within real-world situations, and his sense of it as a discourse that can help to reach some form of real-world truth, locates him within a constellation of the European aesthetic thinkers who are also part of this study.

The argumentative mode of this book also needs to be set out at this stage. It will not look at biographical connections between Heaney and these thinkers. That he read them, or was aware of their work, is not central to my argument, though given their prevalence in academic discourse on poetry, and given his own immense reading on poetry and literature, it is probable that he was at the very least aware of their work. Correspondingly, I am not looking to set out a philosophical aesthetic theory on Heaney's behalf; rather, I am attempting to trace the rhizomatic connections between his work and the work of these writers and to show how, in their parallel approaches to different themes and issues, they can all shed light on each other's work in a mutually revealing context.

Heaney has spoken, as we saw in the case of his discussion of Bishop, of a "dream truth" and of a sense of hallucination, and in this context there are significant connections to be made with the linguistic psychoanalytic theory of Jacques Lacan and the thinking of Heaney. Initially, both writers see the importance of poetry: "Most psychoanalysts explain poetry by means of psychoanalysis; for many years, Lacan explained psychoanalysis by means of poetry" (Chaitin 1996, 1), and while this statement may be a slight exaggeration on the part of Chaitin, it has a measure of truth to it. Lacan has often cited poets to explain his psychoanalytic theories, especially the theory of the unconscious. Noting that, very often, "poets don't know what they're saying, yet they still manage to say things before anyone else," he cites Rimbaud's formula "I is an other" (1991, 8) as an example of how parts of language exceed conscious intention and how the unconscious, through phonetic associations, rhymes, and connections and through "associative series of contrasts and likenesses, oppositions and concurrences between the manifest and latent signifiers" (Grigg 2008, 164), can speak through poetry. Freud too saw poetry and metaphor as crucial to explaining the workings of the human psyche, using the poetic stories of Oedipus and Electra, for example, to make his points.

This factor is significant for Lacan, as he has often spoken about the aspect of reality that escapes signification in language, which he termed the "real." It, like the unconscious, can be accessed in only oblique ways by language, and his notion of "full speech" is a type of speech that will in some way enunciate aspects of this real: "this full speech in which its base in the unconscious should be revealed" (1991, 52), and the language of poetry is a possible source of such revelation. As Michael Lewis asks, "Would full speech be speech that did not elide or ignore the material density of language, something like poetry?" (2008, 41).

Thus, for Lacan, poetry as a way of facilitating psychoanalytic knowledge has long been central to his own writing and theoretical position, as it "exploits the poetic function of language to give desire its symbolic mediation" (2006, 264). This view of language is not confined to a rational relationship between words and ideas, but it includes and encompasses all aspects of language, with poetry given a special position. Listening to poetry allows for "a polyphony to be heard and for it to become clear that all discourse is aligned along the several staves of a musical score," as associative and phonetic strands of meaning tend to haunt the signifying chain, as they are "vertically linked" to each point of the chain (ibid., 419). In this sense, the chain of language is always haunted by other words that could be substituted along the vertical and indeed horizontal axes of the signifying chain, and poetry allows this polyphony to be heard, and to be used as part of psychoanalytic knowledge, as it attempts to access aspects of the unconscious. We have already seen Heaney refer to hallucination and dream truth as ways of accessing aspects of situations that rational language cannot express, and the connections between his work on the unconscious aspects of language and the work of Lacan will be teased out in this study, as both thinkers search for the truth of specific situations. In this sense, Lacan sees that "truth shows itself [*s'avere*] in a fictional structure" (ibid., 625), and Heaney's writing reinforces the idea that poetry and literature are parallel keys to truth.

Derrida, like Lacan, also focuses on the fictional structures of literature and of poetry. In a lecture on Heidegger, he approvingly cites the latter's idea that "all the arts unfold in the space of the poem, which is 'the essence of art,'" and goes on to explain that Heidegger saw poetic speech (*Dichtung*) as seminal to the articulation of truth and felt that it needed to be "liberated from literature" (Derrida, Bass, and Ronse 1981, 11). Like Lacan and Heaney, Derrida prioritized the importance of poetic thinking. In a letter to Didier Cahen, where he is talking about a celebration to honor Edmond Jabès, Derrida notes that he is pleased that this commemoration is taking place at the College International de Philosophie, because "from the very beginning we wished it to be a place that would welcome and encourage poetic thinking, and it is in precisely these terms that you have chosen to mark this anniversary" (Derrida, Brault, and Naas 2001, 122). Poetic thinking is a mode of thought that takes into account emotions, feelings, and the mortality and lived life of the individual; it allows for the body and the unconscious as dimensions of knowledge. Derrida notes that thinking concerning the animal "derives from poetry," as this dimension of human existence, the connection with the world through our physical and animal being, is very much what has been bracketed in traditional rational discourses, and it is a dimension of knowledge that is not fully incorporated into philosophical critique (though there are some exceptions), which Derrida views as "the difference between philosophical knowledge and poetic thinking" (2008, 377).

Through this focus on the aesthetic, which derives from *aisthanesthai*, meaning "to perceive (by the senses or by the mind)," or "to feel," this somatic aspect of our being in the world becomes a constituent factor in driving knowledge about aspects of that being. Poetic thinking can thus act as a supplement to a more formalized rational critique, as through its particularistic focus on a single parole; it can offer significant insights into aspects of the broader langue. Poetic experience brings aspects of the felt world into the realm of knowledge: there is "something irreducible in poetic or literary experience" (Derrida and Attridge 1992, 50). Derrida sees poetics as central to politics and ethics as discourses. Given the importance of concepts of home to Heaney's aesthetic thought, it is interesting that Derrida too sees ideas of home as both central and problematic to issues of ethics and politics. For Derrida, his sense of "hospitality" is essentially poetic in that it consists of an address to the "other" and of doing "everything possible to address the other, to grant or ask them their name," in order to interact with the complexity of the other, while never reverting to some form of "frontier control" (2005b, 67).

Derrida sees this sense of home as something that involves an address to the other from the self, but in a way that leaves that self in some way accessible to influences of the other and to resultant elements of transformation, while still retaining aspects of the self. He speaks of "a question that arises on the threshold of 'home,' and on the threshold between two inflections. An art and a poetics, but an entire politics depends on it, an entire ethics is decided by it" (ibid.). The reason that poetic thinking is so central to Derrida is that its use of associative aspects of language to express feelings, sensations, and intuitions is unable to be cross-checked against any rational, binary basis. As he puts it, "At each moment of poetic experience," the "decision must arise against a background of the undecidable" (1998, 62), and it is an exemplary process in the search for a form of epistemology that takes into account feeling, sensation, the unconscious, and the somatic. Poetic thinking, while singular, idiosyncratic, and asystematic, nevertheless grants access to aspects of experience that other discourses attenuate or occlude. Thus, a poetic sense of "home" would focus on the liminal points between "home" and "not home," as well as on the nature of belonging in the home: it would look on the *Unheimlich* as well as the *Heimlich*, to use Freudian terms, and would see home as a complex and fluid construct. Poetic thinking opens a space for the other of philosophy, and this space is crucial if philosophy is to interrogate itself. In this sense, it is redolent of Derrida's idea of a *non-lieu*, a nonsite, from which "philosophy as such appear to itself as other than itself, so that it can interrogate and reflect upon itself" (1995, 159). This space, which I would equate with the space of poetic thinking, "gives *in principle* the power to say everything, to break free of the rules, to displace them, and thereby to institute, to invent and even to suspect the traditional difference between nature and institution, nature and conventional law, nature and history," and it is in this space that "we should ask juridical and political questions" (Derrida and Attridge 1992, 17). The connections between Derrida's view of home and Heaney's view will become clear later in this study.

Derrida's connection with Heidegger is another aspect of the rhizomatic nexus that connects these thinkers to Heaney. Heaney's association with Heidegger is strong in that both wrote about the value of poetry as a mode of knowledge and as a mode of thinking. Heidegger saw the poetic as a way of connecting with the things of the world and of including the lived life in the world within the search for knowledge and truth. Literature could present what he calls a clearing, a conceptual space that "grants and guarantees to us humans a passage to those beings that we ourselves are not, and access to the being that we ourselves are" (Heidegger 1971, 51). For Heidegger, art, and especially poetry, is a gateway toward this access to the truth of being fully human, and truth, "*all art* as the letting happen of the advent of the truth of what is, is, as such, *essentially poetry*" (ibid., 70).

That there is a parallel between this view of poetry as a way of achieving knowledge and truth and Heaney's own work is clear from a number of examples, but we need look back only at Heaney's comments on Bishop's poem, which has access to both a "dream truth" and a "daylight truth," to see that poetry as a revelation of truth is a significant factor in his thinking. He makes this overt in his comments on W. H. Auden, who was "deeply, deeply worried about truth-telling in poetry" (Cole 1997, 124). This connection with truth and with Heidegger is one to which our discussion will return, and there are other similarities in thematic and formal focus on the value of poetry as a form of thinking between the two writers.

It is fair to say that Theodor Adorno, while critiquing Heidegger in much of his work, nevertheless shared with him the view that the aesthetic is a significant aspect of epistemology. Indeed, one of his most important works, *Aesthetic Theory* (1997), makes this very point in an extended manner. Although there are many areas on which they disagree, Heidegger and Adorno form part of the rhizomatic context of this study because of their parallel views on the importance of the aesthetic as a form of inquiry. Indeed, Adorno's conception of "truth content" (*Wahrheitsgehalt*) "indicates the crux of artistic knowledge and of philosophical interpretation in *Aesthetic Theory*" (Zuidervaart 1991, xxii). Like Heaney, and Heidegger, Adorno sees the aesthetic as a form of thinking: "The truth content of artworks is fused with their critical content" (1997, 35). He also sees the aesthetic as composed of a dialectic between form and content, a parallel that we will also find in Heaney's own teasing out of the value of poetry in the social and political realm. Adorno notes that aesthetic truth content and history are "deeply meshed" (ibid., 41), and he is distrustful of pan-generic appeals to concepts of "spirit," as his is a particularist perspective that foregrounds the necessity of "critique" if the truth content of the aesthetic is to be revealed, and it is in this sense of critique "that art and philosophy converge" (ibid., 88). That correlation is to be found in Heaney's writing, a writing that is often focused on a very specific interpretation of a poet or poem, as opposed to generic and more systemic statements, and for Adorno this connection between the aesthetic and thought is central to its meaning as artworks "await their interpretation" (ibid., 128).

The area of interpretation, and of a form of critique of the aesthetic, also connects these thinkers with the work of Giorgio Agamben, who was something of an early admirer of the work of Heidegger, so it is no surprise that poetry and the aesthetic are important areas of study for him. Like the other writers, and Heaney, he sees poetry as providing access to aspects of knowledge and truth that are not normally accessible to language. Agamben sees poetry as a central point of differentiation between biological life, "which lives only to maintain itself, and human poetic life, which lives in order to create forms" (Colebrook 2008, 109). In other words, Agamben sees poetry as a central defining human characteristic, speaking about "the poetic status of man [*sic*] on earth" (1999b, 42). In a philosophical swerve, which echoes the thinking of Heidegger, he says that man has a poetic status because "it is *poiesis* that founds for him the original space of his world" (ibid., 63). Poetry, for Agamben, is deeply imbricated with thinking, making, and form, all of which are central human attributes, and his work will resonate with Heaney's own, both in terms of poetry as a form of thinking and in terms of poetry as a mode of access to the unconscious.

Agamben sees "the harmony between sound and sense" as what "defines the very site of poetry" (1999a, 28). He makes a case for a poeticized form of thinking that exists at the crossing between the semantic and the phonetic, where "language's movement toward sense is as if traversed by another discourse, one moving from comprehension to sound," and as they meet each other: "*Each of the two movements then followed the others tracks, such that language found itself led back in the end to language, and comprehension to comprehension.*" This process is what we call poetry, and Agamben stresses time and time again this complicated imbrication between poetry and a form of thinking: "*poetry crossing with thought, the thinking essence of poetry and the poeticizing essence of thought*" (ibid., 33; emphasis in the original). The fact that he puts it in italics in the original essay underscores its importance to him, as well as embodying the power of the visual aspects of language to underscore meaning.

In Agamben's thinking, poetry is central to our human being; it is a defining attribute of our achievement of knowledge and of our desire for truth. Looking back at the Greeks, another connection with Heaney who also privileges Greek origins, Agamben argues that for them, the essence of a work of art was that "in it something passed from nonbeing into being, thus opening the space of truth and building a world for man's dwelling on earth" (1999b, 43). The chiasmatic exchange of sound and sense, of words chosen in the right order, was a gateway toward truth and toward being, and in Heaney's thinking the same fit of word, feeling, and a grasping of the unsaid of language can be found.

Heaney, speaking of his own poem "The Diviner," notes how its genesis stems from a remark of Sir Philip Sidney in his *Apologie for Poetry*, that in Roman times a poet was called "*vates*," which means "Diviner." Heaney notes that the influence of the comment from

Sidney fused with visual memories of seeing someone divining for water near his own home in County Derry, and he goes on to comment that he is pleased that the poem "ends with a verb" and that he is glad that "'stirred' chimes with 'word,'" as this phonetic chiming has a semantic function as well, fusing the act with language (1980, 48). The connection with Agamben's ideas on the fusion of poetry and philosophy is clear here—there is a truth being told in the poem, and the fusion of sound and sense is central to the mode of telling.

I am aware that there are strong areas of contention, contestation, and indeed disagreement between all the thinkers mentioned here, both at intellectual and at methodological levels. Much of Adorno's work, for example, is devoted to a critique of Heidegger, while Derrida and Lacan enjoyed what can best be termed a frosty intellectual and personal relationship, and the work of Agamben might seem difficult to connect to the work of the other earlier thinkers. However, these issues are not germane to my argument, as I am not suggesting that these thinkers can be conflated into a homogenous group, nor am I seeing Heaney as a type of magic key that can unlock hitherto unrecognized correspondences between these thinkers. In this study, I am arguing that from what I see as his ongoing project of poetic thinking, it is possible to read Heaney within a rhizomatic constellation that includes these thinkers, all of whom value the aesthetic as a specialized mode of knowing. I can see lines of thinking connecting them all, though it is important to stress that these "lines, or lineaments, should not be confused with lineages of the arborescent type"; there is no hierarchical structure being set out here. The relationships of which I speak are rhizomatic and confined to the area of poetic knowledge and poetic thinking: the rhizome "operates by variation, expansion, conquest, capture, offshoots" (Deleuze and Guattari 1987, 21).

Far from seeing poetry as a decorative addition to language, each of them, in their different ways, sees poetry as a significant mode of inquiry into many aspects of our human being. Heaney, in looking at the descriptive and the hallucinatory, is attempting to signify aspects of the unconscious as a form of knowledge that can be accessed, albeit in an indirect form, through poetic discourse. In an interview with Dennis O'Driscoll, Heaney is asked the telling question "What has poetry taught you?" and he answers that it has taught him that "there's such a thing as truth and it can be told—slant" (Heaney and O'Driscoll 2008, 467). This term is borrowed from Emily Dickinson's poem "Tell the Truth but Tell It Slant" (1924, 506–7), and the fact that this term is borrowed from such an oblique poet as Dickinson is interesting in itself, as the many dashes and ellipses in her writing can be seen as opening a space for the unconscious dimension of her thinking. It is as if she knows there are aspects of her thought and feeling that cannot be written, but the dashes provide a space, a Derridean *non-lieu*, that allows that space to become a site of signification and a place of entry into the poem by the other.

In Heaney's thinking, access to truth needs to be oblique, as full understanding is very often beyond our capability, given that we are situated within language, thought, and culture and that a transcendent position is all but impossible to achieve. Thus, "slant" is the refracted manner in which aspects of feeling and emotions and the unconscious are accessed by the self, and poetry is the vehicle of this access. Heaney, like many of the thinkers mentioned above, suggests that knowledge and signification are transformational matrices of fluid and intersecting discourses and not readily fixed, foundational pillars that can be passed on, whole and intact, from generation to generation. One of the unifying factors in this thinking is that text is modified by context, which is, in turn, further modified by the altered text. For these thinkers, knowledge is relational: it is created through dialectical and differential processes and structures. Poetry, I would contend, with its intersecting and overlapping fields of syntactical and stanzaic structures, is a more accurate exemplar of this type of fluid structure than prose.

Heaney's *The Redress of Poetry* develops a visual image of this complicated truth of poetry in his diagrammatic structure called the quincunx. This term may have derived from Sir Thomas Browne's *The Garden of Cyrus* (2012, 10, 19, 22, 35), which traced the quincunx pattern in art, nature, and mysticism, or from James Joyce's short story in *Dubliners* titled "Grace," where the term described the seating patterns of five men at a church service (Joyce 1996, 172). In any case, it involves sketching a diagram of Irish literary identity in a way that transcends the simple Irish-English binary opposition. In a specifically Irish context, Heaney sets out the parameters as a five-point structure that would grant the plurality of what he terms an Irishness that "would not prejudice the rights of others' Britishness" (1995b, 198). This structure is a "diamond shape" of five towers, with each tower representing an aspect of Irish identity. These elements are a round tower of preinvasion Irishness and buildings associated with Edmund Spenser, W. B. Yeats, James Joyce, and Louis MacNeice (ibid., 198–99).

What is most interesting in this structure, an aspect of Heaney's work that has received surprisingly little attention, is that he is deconstructing the usual paradigm of Anglo-Irish relationships at the level of both the signifier and the signified. Even regarding how the problematic relationships between these countries are described, there has been an overwhelmingly binary logic at work: we speak of Anglo-Irish, of British-Irish, of English-Irish, of Irish-English relations. In political terms, Irish history has been dogged by a collateral binarity of focus: for the unionists, it is the connection with England that defines their position, while for nationalists, it is the sundering of this connection, best encapsulated in the monosyllabic slogan "Brits Out" coined by the Provisional Irish Republican Army (IRA), which is their main defining credo. In the quincunx, Heaney is offering a visual representation that traces a far more nuanced interaction of Britishness and Irishness, as he uses a central image of ethnic Irishness, surrounded by, and interacting with, the thought of Yeats, Joyce, MacNeice, and Spenser.

More significantly, it is not the towers per se that interest him, but rather their multiperspectival interaction with each other as processes from which different levels of meaning can be generated and through which different subrelationships can be enunciated. This connection is a rhizomatic one, as it allows for any and every one of the towers to draw lines of connection to the other towers and, by extension, to enact a deterritorialization of the different positions. He sees these towers as polysemic points of reference that validate different, but mutually informing, perceptions of Irishness in all of its complexity—a complexity that has all too often been simplified by various political and cultural agendas. In an intriguing analysis, Heaney talks about how each tower faces the other towers and looks at the resonances that accrue from this interaction. To look for analogues to this structure in the Anglophone, or Irish, canon would be in vain—but there are analogues to be found within the European tradition of thinking on the aesthetic, and we will look at two of them, the aforementioned connection with Heidegger's fourfold and a connection with the work of Gilles Deleuze and Félix Guattari.

Heidegger's conception of the "fourfold," that combination of earth, sky, the divine, and the human, can be seen as a parallel structure that grants the complexity and the polysemy of poetic thinking and poetic language (Heidegger 1971, 149). Like Heaney, Heidegger posits a nexus or constellation of different relationships that the aesthetic is able to access as a specific form of knowledge about the world. I would argue that these two figures, the quincunx and the fourfold, are further indexes of the connection between the aesthetic thinking of Heaney and Heidegger. Both thinkers stress the idea of connection and of complexity as they write about the experience of living in the world: "Will we dwell as those at home in nearness, so that we will belong primarily within the fourfold of sky and earth, mortals and divinities?" (ibid., 49). Like Heaney's quincunx, the stress here is not on the elements themselves as static entities or concepts; rather, the stress is on the interaction between them, as each one of the four "mirrors in its own way the presence of the others," and like the mutual reflections of the quincunx, the mirroring "binds into freedom is the play that betroths each of the four to each through the enfolding clasp of their mutual appropriation" (ibid., 177). This is really very close to the form of mutually reflective identity that Heaney traces in his quincunx, as it is the movement between the towers rather than the imagined materiality of the towers themselves that is significant for him.

For both Heaney and Heidegger, then, the stress on the spaces and movements between the different points suggests the very kind of relationship that Deleuze champions when he says that it is "not the terms or the elements, but what there is 'between,' the between, a set of relations which are not separable from each other. Every multiplicity grows from the middle, like the blade of grass or the rhizome" (Deleuze and Parnet 1977, vii), and in Heaney's fluid structure, literary, and by extrapolation political, relationships will be fluid and transformative as opposed to static and entrenched. Each movement will resonate with others, and a weblike structure of relationships will come into being, the process "shot through with lines of flight testifying to the presence within them of movements of deterritorialisation" (Deleuze and Guattari 1987, 55).

These resonances are polysemic and nuanced, as different perspectives engender different meanings from the same signifier. Thus, Heaney describes how, when Spenser's tower faces the round tower of the "mythic first Irish place," it sees "popery, barbarism and the Dark Ages" (1995b, 199). This description would seem to be part of that colonizer-colonized binarism whereby the colonizer sees the autochthonous culture as inferior and belated. However, Heaney goes on to argue that a different perspective will elicit a different meaning, as when Yeats's tower looks at the same image, it sees "a possible unity of being, an Irish nation retrieved and enabled by a repossession of its Gaelic heritage" (ibid., 199–200), while Joyce looks at this tower and sees an "archetypal symbol, the omphalos," or perhaps an ivory tower from which "the chaste maid of Irish Catholic provincialism must be liberated from the secular arms of Europe" (ibid., 200). Clearly, in Heaney's view, Irish identity is perspectivally dependent and observer dependent, a topic to which the discussion will return. Interestingly, Heaney's fifth tower is for the poet Louis MacNeice, Carrickfergus Castle, which symbolizes the Protestant heritage, which began with the landing of Prince William of Orange. For Heaney, the key here is that this tower, while symbolizing a British and unionist identity, no longer just looks back at mainland Britain but also looks "towards that visionary Ireland" whose name, to quote MacNeice, "keeps ringing like a bell / In an underwater belfry" (ibid.). Heaney sees MacNeice as connected to Spenser through his Britishness, to Yeats through his love of Connemara, and to Joyce because of his European sensibility, so there is that sense of connectedness and mirroring between the different versions of Irish identity. Heaney's undramatic style, "by writing his castle into the poetic annals, he has completed the figure" (ibid.), understates the originality of his conception. However, there is a key to the originality of this conception of a fluid and constellatory notion of a pluralistic, inclusive Irishness in the simile quoted from MacNeice's poem "Autumn Journal" (MacNeice and Dodds 1966, 131), which describes a bell ringing underwater, something that, again, is creative and imaginative as opposed to representational, though there are a number of English and Dutch folktales that describe a parallel phenomenon. A bell ringing underwater would be an activity from which the usual expectation, the sound of the pealing of the bell, would not be heard above water. So it can be seen to represent the symbolic of the activity of the unconscious, a very significant factor in any construction of identity, as such activity is always emotive and not fully accessible to rational discourse and analysis. The bell ringing in an underground belfry also has a resonance with the "dream truth" and with the "hallucinatory" of which he spoke when reading Bishop's poem. These unconscious and affective modes of expression allow for unvoiced aspects of the different interactions of Irishnesses to become overt, and thus to reconceptualize issues of identity that had long seemed carved in binary stone.

The strategies and epistemological critique that Heaney brings to readings of poetic texts are also relevant to his reading of political and ethical texts and structures. Given the effects of feelings, sensation, and the unconscious on the creation of meaning through language, a critique that looks at the denotative and connotative aspects of language, its conscious and unconscious dimensions, is important to any real understanding of the structures and strictures that frame our lives. Heaney is deeply involved in the inception of new modes of thinking and knowing about aesthetic, ethical, and political issues.

The interaction of these towers into a "field of force" (Heaney 1980, 56) mirrors what Heaney has always seen as the epistemological force of poetry, which is that it should be "a working model of inclusive consciousness. It should not simplify" (1995b, 8). Thus, in his thinking, the conscious and the unconscious can be seen to be at work in the spaces between the towers and in the interaction of those multiple perspectives in these spaces. Telling the truth slant, or seeing the world from a different perspective, as well as valuing that difference, is at the core of Heaney's aesthetic imperative, and he has invoked Osip Mandelstam to criticize "the purveyors of ready-made meaning" (ibid.1988, 91), as for him poetic truth constantly strives to reach beyond such ready-made meanings. The connection with Heidegger has already been adumbrated, and the quincunx has been seen to parallel the fourfold. In a more complicated frame of reference, Heidegger is making a parallel point by suggesting that it is through their "mutual appropriation" that each individual element becomes itself, so to speak: "This expropriative appropriating is the mirror-play of the fourfold" (1971, 177). It is the reflection and the interaction that are significant here, and these two terms, more than any others, are what connect Heaney and Heidegger as thinkers on the aesthetic. Both are involved in probing and understanding the "self-unfolding possibility of an originary-poetic-naming of be-ing" (Heidegger 1999, 26).

In this book, I will examine Heaney's prose in an effort to show how he "lets words speak" (Harries 2009, 116) in what could be termed a form of creative critique. His work has the ability to fuse the rational and the emotional and, hence, to enunciate a comprehensive level of knowledge about the topic under analysis. Just as Heidegger probes beyond the rational forms of discourse to locate areas of authentic being, so too does Heaney probe beyond the rational in order to locate the unconscious roots of different positions and paradigms. I will progress my argument through the following chapters, where I will trace how Heaney's poetic thinking sets out a form of knowledge wherein the haptic, the emotional, and the unconscious all find expression through its unusual and arational structures of signification and meaning. I use the term *arational* with a distinct purpose, as poetry is not "irrational" (though it does allow aspects of the irrational to be voiced), but neither is it purely rational; instead, it allows the rational and the irrational to interact, so that aspects of the irrational, the emotional, and the real, in Lacanian terms, are allowed to flow into the structure of knowledge that is enunciated in poetry. Through its imbrication of syntax, linguistic structure, associative structure of the signifier through rhyme, and image clustering, poetry allows "a glimmer of signification [to] spring forth at the surface of the real, and then causes the real to become illuminated with a flash projected from below" (Lacan 2006, 468). This dimension is core to Heaney's poetic thinking.

In chapter 1, "The Poet as Thinker—the Thinker as Poet," I will examine how poetry and thinking are closely aligned and how Heaney's work embodies this alignment. I will locate him as an aesthetic thinker and will examine comparisons with T. S. Eliot, who was also a poet and critic. Heaney's use of Greek terminology is seen as a point of connection with other thinkers such as Heidegger and Lacan, and by extension this Greek frame of reference connects Heaney with the origins of the European intellectual tradition. In *Crediting Poetry*, he makes connections between the *Iliad* and contemporary wars in Rwanda, and it is this syncretic imagination that makes his project so significant. His pervasive fusion of mind and body in his writing is also examined, as it is an ongoing trope in his essays. To achieve this dialectical fusion of conscious and unconscious, mind and body, he sets up a force field within his writing that has resemblances to Theodor Adorno's idea of a constellation of different ideas, and this connection will be further analyzed.

This chapter will also probe the connections between Lacan, Heidegger, and Heaney concerning their ideas on language, poetry, and thinking, and a detailed reading of the programmatic Heideggerian phrase "poetically man dwells" is followed by the connection of this phrase to the thought of Jacques Lacan. Connections between Lacan's arguments about language and the unconscious, and parallel arguments and explorations of the same issues in Heaney's own work, will be developed. Lacan's visual reading of Holbein's *The Ambassadors*, where he talks about the anamorphosis of the gaze, what Žižek terms "looking awry" (1991, 9), is shown to have strong analogies to Heaney's idea of telling the truth "slant," and further connections between all three writers will be developed through their suggestive use of Greek terminology, culture, and thought. Hence, the chapter offers a reading of Lacan's use of *agalma* and of Heaney's use of the *omphalos* and makes the point that both terms refer, in some degree, to the unconscious, a further point of connection between them. The chapter concludes by looking at connections between Heaney's views on poetry and thinking and some thoughts of Heidegger in his book *Poetry, Language, Thought* (1971), where he probes the connections between the two, going so far as to write a poem that discusses thinking as a way of demonstrating the close relationship between poetry and thinking concerning access to the body, the unconscious, and, I would add, the Lacanian real.

The second chapter, "Space: The Final Frontier," will look at issues of identity, colonization, and postcolonial anxieties that are addressed by Heaney and at how the binary terms that have signified the troubles in Northern Ireland, and indeed, much of Irish history, are unpacked in his work. He takes the terms *English-Irish*, *Protestant-Catholic*, *Unionist-Nationalist*, and *Loyalist-Republican* and deconstructs them by recontextualizing them in structures that are less binary and less binding on the imagination. He looks to Joyce as an exemplar for this process, and he explores and gradually outlines his own identification with British popular culture in magazines that he read as a child and as a young man. This plural perspective complicates the status of locating him firmly on the "Irish" side of the Irish-English binary opposition, but while deconstructing the certainties of colonizing hegemonic power, he is also unwilling to just step into the other side of the binary either. In a discussion that spans British comics and magazines, Joyce's influence on language, and Scottish poet Hugh MacDiarmid, this chapter teases out the complexities of how the English language not only is both constricting of identity as a colonizing force but can also be creative of broader concepts of identity through its protean ability to be used by different perspectives, each of which adds aspects of its own distinctness to it. This chapter will examine how the seeming certainties of canonical English are always haunted by aspects of the voice of the other and how, in their different ways, Heaney and Derrida trace this perception in their work. Both writers see identity—Irishness and Frenchness, respectively—as necessarily different from itself, and this split is brought about through language.

"The Epistemology of Poetry: Fields of Force," the third chapter, discusses notions of writing as a "field of force," which, in the case of Northern Ireland, can encompass the violence and the humanity of the conflict. Heaney's reading sets up a fluid structure that can also allow different oppositions to coexist, and this imperative will be traced through an examination of his essays "Englands of the Mind" in *Preoccupations* and "Through-Other Places, Through-Other Times: The Irish Poet and Britain" in *Finders Keepers*, as well as through his discussion of Wordsworth's "The Thorn" and the work of Sorley MacLean. The chapter will also look at the structural constellation that is suggested in his pamphlet *Among Schoolchildren.* A parallel example of this complexity and inclusivity is his etymological and cultural deconstruction of the name of his own home, "Mossbawn." Here, a textual unconscious is posited, with the overt conscious and rational signifiers being undercut and deconstructed by what Lyotard has termed the buried metanarrative of ideological structures of identity.

In chapter 4, "Poetics and Politics: Surviving Amphibiously," the political thread that can be traced through Heaney's work is analyzed, as he writes on the horizon of his contemporary experience of Northern Irish politics. In his early prose, a related series of questions is raised, wherein the dialectical relationship between poetry and politics is outlined in the personal essays, such as "Belfast" and "Feeling into Words," where his own relationship with politics is explored. However, the focus then moves beyond the personal in *The Government of the Tongue*, wherein eastern European writers such as Miroslav Holub, Zbigniew Herbert, and especially Osip

Mandelstam are studied with regard to how their poetry relates to the political. By broadening the context of Irish poetry, Heaney's analysis also transforms the texts themselves. I read his view of the relationship of poetry to politics as ethical, in that poetry allows for an alternative government, a government of language, a government of the tongue, that exists alongside actuality and holds up a possible alternative to that actuality and attempts to speak the truth to power. He makes the very valid point that poetry is a form of knowledge that can enunciate visceral emotions because it shares them as a starting point, as it is in "the rag-and-bone shop of the instincts" (Heaney 1980, 148) that poetry has its roots, and it then attempts to raise these roots to a higher power, while still granting their intensity, and it is his sense of poetry as something that can enunciate all that is "appetitive in the intelligence and prehensile in the affections" (Heaney 1995a, 11) that will be examined in this chapter.

Chapter 5, "The Place of Writing—the Writing of Place," analyzes the ambiguous relationship between place and writing. Heaney is well aware of the attenuating influence of the "appetites of gravity," as he describes them (1975, 43), which fuse a people to a place. I will concentrate here on what I see as his development of an alternative paradigm, which can exist between word and world. Rather than reinforcing essentialist equations between a culture and a place, poetry can transform those relationships, thereby achieving a political effect. Hence, the focus will be on the ability of literature to create, through language and imagery, another place "where the mind could take shelter from the actual conditions" (Heaney 1984a, 6). Indeed, one can trace this process of the deterritorialization of place from his very first essay in *Preoccupations* where he says: "Mossbawn, the first place, widened" (1980, 18). A parallel example in his prose is his essay on Kavanagh in *The Government of the Tongue*, entitled "The Placeless Heaven: Another Look at Kavanagh." Heaney's association with a chestnut tree, planted by his aunt at the time of his birth, was gradually replaced by an association with the "space where the tree had been or would have been," and he goes on to note that he saw this space as a kind of "luminous emptiness" (1988, 3). I would agree with Richard Rankin Russell in this context when he sees a connection between Heaney and Kavanagh in terms of their similar fusions of the "actual and the abstract" and in terms of their "supple linkage of inner and outer terrain" (2014, 107). The chapter outlines the effects of the idealization of place as well as the complex process of "two-mindedness" that he discusses in terms of Wordsworth's views of loyalty to England and France, in *Place and Displacement*, as well as Hugh O'Neill's sense of being both English and Irish, in *The Place of Writing*.

The sixth chapter, "Translations: The Voice of the Other," will discuss how Heaney grants both the effectiveness and the plurality of concepts of Irishness through his translations and through his writing on the nature of translation. This chapter will examine his philosophy of translation as an enhancement of the dialogue between self and other and will focus on his translations of *Sweeney Astray*, a translation of the Old Irish poem *Buile Shuibhne*; on his comments on translations of the poetry of eastern Europe, which has been such an influence on his work; as well as on his reading of Christopher Marlowe's "Hero and Leander." His own philosophy of translation has strong affinities with the thoughts of Paul Ricoeur, Giorgio Agamben, and Jacques Derrida, and some of them will be explored in the context of his three major translation projects. The first to be addressed is *Beowulf*, a translation that began officially in 1995 (but had been initially started in 1981) and was published in 1999, while the other two derive from the work of Greek writer Sophocles: *The Cure at Troy* (Heaney 1990) being based on *Philoctetes*, while *The Burial at Thebes* (Heaney 2004b) is based on *Antigone*.

In all three translations, as well as looking for some form of dialogue with the cultural context of these works, he is also using them as part of his attempt to "widen" Mossbawn, his own first place, and the placement of the word *bawn* in *Beowulf*, itself the foundation pillar of the canon of English poetry, is indicative of how translation becomes yet another component of his constellation of forces as he attempts to access the other and the Lacanian real. In the two Greek translations, *The Burial at Thebes* and *The Cure at Troy*, he is reinforcing the connection between Ireland and the European intellectual and philosophical traditions by allowing these ancient plays to become part of a dramatic constellation where they reflect, in unusual ways, upon the political and ethical issues of his contemporary Northern Irish preoccupations. Translation has a central place in European thought, as it allows culture to speak to culture, as well as allowing the past to speak to the present; indeed, it could be said that translation is what enables a sense of Europe as an intellectual and cultural entity. Heaney is very much part of this endeavor, as he places the conflict and violence of Northern Ireland within a Pan-European sociocultural context as a way of understanding it otherwise.

In the conclusion, I will bring together all of the threads that have been teased out throughout the book and will develop his reasons for changing the title of *Antigone*, a change that I see as synecdochic of his views on poetry and poetic language.

This book will demarcate Heaney's status as a cultural and aesthetic thinker who has contributed in a significant manner to our views on our own culture, and it will focus on the interweavings of aesthetics, ethics, and politics in a European setting. It will also argue that Heaney's work is part of a European tradition that attempts to heal what Giorgio Agamben has called a scission in cultural and philosophical thought. Agamben points out that this scission is between "poetry and philosophy, between the poetic word and the word of thought" (1993c, xvi). Despite the fact that it is merely an "implication" in Plato, it has become reified in the Western philosophical tradition. I will argue that Heaney is in accord with thinkers like Derrida, who feels that "philosophy and poetry cannot be separated" (2004a, 69); and with Heidegger, who opines that "the realm in which the dialogue between poetry and thinking goes on," needs to be probed "and explored in thought only slowly" (1971, 96); and with Agamben, who argues that "poetry is something one can do only through philosophy" (de la Durantaye 2009, 61). Poetry is seen as "a theorizing practice, a practice of thinking, and as a commitment to the thought that emerges in the subtle concreteness of segmented, saturated language"; it is, in Heaney's thinking, "an approach to knowing that dissolves into a variety of sensations or touches multiple scales of feeling" (DuPlessis 2006, 5). It is my contention that Heaney is very much a part of this discourse, and it is to this sense of thinking and poetry as coextensive that I now turn.

1

The Poet as Thinker —the Thinker as Poet

That this is only the second sustained study of Heaney's prose is surprising, but it is an issue that needs to be addressed at this stage. Generally, he is seen as a poet who gives occasional lectures, writes occasional pieces, and gives interviews; he is not generally seen as an aesthetic thinker, but this point is what I will be arguing, and I think some basics facts about Heaney's academic career will underline the relevance of my position. Seamus Heaney's intellectual career began not so much as a poet per se, but as someone who thinks, writes, and teaches about poetry and its cultural and social value. It is easily forgotten now, but Heaney earned an arts degree in Queen's University, where he studied from 1957 to 1961, obtaining a first-class honors degree in English language and literature, before going on to complete a diploma in teaching at Saint Joseph's College of Education in Belfast in 1961–62 and joining the staff of Saint Thomas's Secondary School in Ballymurphy in Belfast the same year. He had been offered a scholarship to Oxford, but declined in favor of pursuing a teaching career.

In 1963 he took up a lecturing position at Saint Joseph's College and remained there until taking up a post at Queen's University in 1966. In 1970–71 he took up a post as visiting lecturer at the University of California at Berkeley. After moving to Wicklow and becoming a full-time writer, he returned to teaching, as lecturer in English at Carysfort College of Education in Dublin, in 1975, and he taught there until 1981. He was given leave to take up the Beckman

Professorship in Berkeley in 1976. In 1979 he spent his first semester at Harvard, and from 1982 to 1985 he spent the spring semester there. In the summer of 1983, he taught a creative writing course at the College of Notre Dame in Belmont, near San Francisco. In 1984 he became a tenured academic at Harvard, taking up the post of Boylston Professor of Rhetoric and Oratory, and in 1987 he spent the full year there. In 1988 he delivered the first Richard Ellmann Memorial Lectures at Emory University, Atlanta, under the general title "The Place of Writing," and in 1989 he was elected Professor of Poetry in Oxford, and the lectures from that post were collected in *The Redress of Poetry*, in 1995.

In all of this work, which is based on teaching and thinking, as much as on the writing of poetry, there are also a number of individual pieces, lectures, essays, introductions to other books, and collections where Heaney writes about matters political, ethical, and aesthetic.

One of the most interesting aspects of Heaney's prose is that there is so much of it. Since the publication of *Preoccupations*, in 1980, a significant number of collections and important single essays and pamphlets have been published:

Preoccupations: Selected Prose, 1968–1978 (1980)
Among Schoolchildren (1983)
Place and Displacement: Recent Poetry of Northern Ireland (1983)
The Government of the Tongue: The 1986 T. S. Eliot Memorial Lectures and Other Critical Writings (1988)
The Place of Writing (1989)
Crediting Poetry (1995)
The Redress of Poetry: Oxford Lectures (1995)
Beowulf (introduction) (1999)
Finders Keepers (2002)
Thebes via Toomebridge: Retitling Antigone (2005)
"Mossbawn via Mantua: Ireland in/and Europe, Cross-currents and Exchanges" (2012)

When one looks at these publications in their totality, they encompass some one thousand pages of writing, and I think that in basic qualitative terms it is a significant output. Indeed, if Heaney were never to have written a line of poetry, one thousand pages, five collections of essays, and a substantial number of single-topic lectures and essays would amount to a significant academic output. Of course, he is and always will be best known as a poet, but as I will argue, poetry is a form of thinking, and as such it is important to see how he thinks and writes about poetry.

I realize that this view of Heaney as an aesthetic thinker and philosopher is perhaps unusual and that many would agree with Helen Vendler, who notes that "the relation of poetry to thought is an uneasy one" (2004, 2). Vendler here is talking about how poets think within poetry, and her aim is to uncover the type of thinking that is at work in lyric poetry, while at the same time stressing that "poetic thinking must not unbalance the poem in the direction of 'thought'" (ibid., 9). This chapter will interrogate this sense of overbalancing, as I hope to show that the relationship between poetry and thought, while uneasy, should be taken outside of the bounds of the lyric and should instead be seen as informing much that is new in thinking about the roles of ethics, politics, and aesthetics in our contemporary culture. Rather than seeing poetry as overbalanced by thought, I would contend that poetry is itself a form of thinking and that this conception of poetry is very much at the core of Heaney's own work.

With regard to critical thinking on poetry, Heaney has long been engaged with the work of T. S. Eliot, a poet who is also a critic, and, indeed, Heaney has been frequently compared to Eliot. Michael Cavanagh has noted, "Heaney is just as inclined as Eliot is to generalizing and theorizing" (2009, 6). Cavanagh puts it at its strongest when suggesting that "Eliot is the closest thing Heaney has to a literary father" (ibid., 74) and goes on to discuss this filiation in a full chapter. Certainly, there are connections between the two, and in an Anglophone context there can be little doubt that Eliot is very much a mentor figure, both practically, in that both writers are published by Faber, and theoretically, as they have both written at length about poetry and poetics and both been strongly influenced by Catholic and European thinking and culture. Eliot is certainly a seminal influence on Heaney concerning the relationship between poetry and thought. It is an influence that has developed over his career, and, indeed, one can detect an homage to Eliot in Heaney's *Electric Light* collection. He saw Eliot's *Collected Poems* as one of the "first 'grown up' books" he owned (Heaney 2002, 26), but rather than being an inspiration the book represented Heaney's sense of "distance" from the mystery of literature (ibid., 18). The early Heaney was stylistically and culturally far removed from Eliot, yet in *Electric Light* the polyglot allusiveness of *The Waste Land* hovers over Heaney's writing. Indeed, there is a sly homage to *The Waste Land* in "Vitruviana," where Eliot's lines from "The Fire Sermon," referring to how on "Margate Sands" he can "connect / Nothing with nothing" (1974, 74), find an allusive analogue in Heaney's "On Sandymount strand I can connect / Some bits and pieces" (2001, 53).

The title of this poem is equally allusive, referring to the style of Vitruvius, a Roman architect and writer of the first century BCE whose book *De Architectura* was later influential in the development of Renaissance architecture. Interestingly, that sense of association of which I spoke as being a central tenet of the unconscious is again prevalent here, as Heaney speaks of connecting "bits and pieces," an almost Frostian understatement that, through a form of litotes, stresses his own sense of the importance of the unconscious in the creation of meaning. Heaney has taken images from the literature of the European past and, by inserting them in his own work, transformed aspects of that work through this further language; it is as if he is using European literature as a form of cultural unconscious.

This European dimension of Heaney's work has become more pronounced in his later career. His series of translations from Greek drama speaks to an ongoing interest in the role of the classics and to his view of Ireland as very much a European country. *The Cure at Troy* (1990) and *The Burial at Thebes* (2004b) both demonstrate this desire to re-vision Ireland within the context of the European classical tradition; indeed, one could paraphrase Lacan and suggest that Heaney sees Europe as the unconscious "outside" (1977, 123) of Ireland and Irish culture and writing. Therefore, I would agree with Cavanagh about the importance of Eliot and think that Heaney has, specifically, taken from Eliot ideas about the epistemological status of poetry that are of value to him. However, much of Heaney's work on Eliot centers on the essays as opposed to the poetry, something that self-reflexively points to the centrality of the essay as genre in Heaney's own work. However, I would disagree when Cavanagh sees Heaney as locating himself, like Eliot, somewhere between literary journalism and the academy (ibid., 76).

I would disagree with the latter view, although it is a commonly held one. Although there are certainly connections with Eliot, and while Heaney has done a significant number of review pieces, I would contend that his writing is more aesthetic thinking than journalism. I would see Heaney's writing as being an example of what Heidegger has termed "thinking as poetizing." Heidegger was keen to stress connections between thinking and the poetic. He was anxious to critique the Platonic view that poetry was not of value in philosophical thinking as it was a distraction from rationality. For Heidegger, "thinking is primordial poetry, prior to all poesy, but also prior to the poetics of art, since art shapes its work within the realm of language." Heidegger, like Agamben, stresses poetry, or poetizing, as a special form of thinking that can encompass the body and the unconscious: "All poetizing, in this broader sense, and also in the narrower sense of the poetic, is in its ground a thinking," and he sees it as fully imbricated in what it means to be human: "The poetizing essence of thinking preserves the sway of the truth of Being" (1975a, 19).

In Heidegger's translation "The Anaximander Fragment," he talks about the necessary connection between poetry and thinking, noting that the piece can be understood only through a process of "thoughtful dialogue." He goes on to describe such dialogue in a singular manner: "Thinking is poetizing, and indeed more than one kind of poetizing," and he goes on to say that "thinking of Being is the original way of poetizing" (ibid.). It is no accident that Heidegger is writing about a Greek text here, as there is a strong intellectual tradition of locating philosophical and aesthetic thinking in a Greek context. As will be seen later, Heidegger sees translation as in many ways attenuating an original almost organic experience, but he nevertheless returns to Greek texts again and again, "not because they express ahistorically valid propositions," but, on the contrary, "because they are authentically historical: that is, they hold out the promise of a process of unconcealment that can occur if the present enters into dialogue with its past" (Wrathall 2002, 60). In other words, it is a form of thinking of the present through the past. Thus, this extract again demonstrates a core aspect of Heidegger's project, which involves setting out a homology between poetry and thinking. In this study, I am arguing for a new awareness of the value of what have traditionally been seen as "poetic" qualities in any form of thinking that attempts to achieve knowledge of the unconscious, or of the real, in the areas of politics, ethics, and aesthetics by using all the signifying and associative qualities of language.

In one of his earliest references to Eliot, Heaney is discussing the relationship between the individual text and its enabling context, and he agrees that the mature pleasure of poetry is to be aware of how an individual talent "has foraged in the tradition" (1980, 62). At this early stage, the relationship between text and context assumes significance in his view of poetry, gesturing toward his own future analyses of the political and literary traditions, as well as of the European cultural and intellectual context, within which his own work has developed. It is also significant, given the tenor of my argument, that in *Preoccupations*, Heaney approvingly cites Eliot's valuation of poetry as a form of discourse that can access the unconscious. He notes, in "The Fire i' the Flint," that Eliot's sense of the "auditory imagination" referred to the connection between the sense and the sound of the word that went beyond the ordinary range of language and united both the "primitive and civilized associations" that words have developed and speaks of "Eliot's dark embryo" (Heaney 1980, 81, 83), which again refers to the ability of poetry to access the unsaid, the other, the real of language. In this respect, Eliot is certainly an important figure of influence for Heaney, what Harold Bloom has termed a *tessera*.

For Bloom, the *tessera* describes the type of influence whereby the later poet provides what "his imagination tells him would complete the otherwise 'truncated' precursor poem and poet, a 'completion' that is as much misprision as a revisionary swerve" (1973, 66). He takes this term from Jacques Lacan's *Discours de Rome* (1953), where Lacan cites Mallarmé's remarks about how, as a coin passes from hand to hand, the motifs on each face of the coin are gradually worn away, thus becoming largely unnoticed. For Lacan, this metaphor suffices to remind us that "speech, even when almost completely worn out, retains its value as a *tessera*" (2006, 209). I would suggest that Eliot, and indeed Yeats, has just such a relationship with Heaney, as his own prose completes different aspects of each of these strong precursors. Therefore, Heaney's prose is related to Yeats's and Eliot's in the sense of being "a completing link" (Bloom 1973, 67). Hence, it is no accident that *Preoccupations* is prefaced with an epigraph from Yeats about the relationship between the aesthetic, the political, and the social (Heaney 1980, 7), and I would agree with Cavanagh when he sees this Yeatsian presence as exemplary as opposed to explanatory (2009, 7). Whereas Bloom's theory of influence refers to poetry, I think it is applicable to writing in prose as well, as every text is written within cultural and generic contexts, and the strength and philosophical breadth of the connection will become clear later.

Cavanagh has also cited the importance of Eliot's prose as an influence (ibid., 4), and he goes on to discuss the importance of other influences, as well as teasing out the relationship between Heaney and other writers. He traces the importance of significant essays in Heaney's career, citing Nadezhda Mandelstam's *Hope against Hope* and *Hope Abandoned*, Osip Mandelstam's "Conversation about Dante," Zbigniew Herbert's *Barbarian in the Garden*, Czesław Miłosz's *Native Realm*, Richard Ellmann's "W. B. Yeats's Second Puberty," and Daniel Corkery's *The Hidden Ireland*, as well as Yeats's own prose. Cavanagh goes on to add that "because prose matters to Heaney, it isn't surprising that most of the poets who have been important to him have written ambitious prose: Yeats, Miłosz, Mandelstam, Eliot, and Wordsworth." I would fully concur with Cavanagh concerning the importance of the prose, but I would progress the argument further: I would maintain that Heaney's work, as well as offering interesting and insightful readings of poetry, is a lot more than "ambitious prose"; rather, it is a type of poetizing philosophical discourse itself, one that parallels the writings of Eliot and Yeats. While both of these writers wrote about literature, they also wrote about their society and their culture, and about the role of writing and reading within this sociocultural context, and this context is the *tessera* that Heaney wishes to complete in his own work. As Cavanagh remarks, "Making sense of poetry is a professor's business," and he goes on to describe how Heaney has spent a lot of time in lectures and in essays "explaining everything, especially why some things can't be explained" (ibid., 5). Exploring these areas that cannot be explained is very much at the core of Heaney's own writing, and it is no accident that it is Eliot's perception of the auditory imagination that is important to him, as it describes the dark embryo that is at the unconscious core of thought and writing. For both writers, poetry has a special access to this level of human thought and experience, and this special access makes Heaney more of a poetic thinker than a teacher.

Harold Bloom, in his *The Anxiety of Influence*, records that Descartes, in his *Private Thoughts*, observed that while "it might seem strange that opinions of weight are found in the works of poets rather than philosophers," the reason is that poets write "through enthusiasm and imagination; there are in us seeds of knowledge, as of fire in a flint," and he goes on to develop this simile by explaining that, in terms of these seeds of knowledge, "philosophers extract them by way of reason, but poets strike them out by imagination, and then they shine more bright." Descartes is making the point that there is a lot more to "opinions of weight" than rational thought, and his very metaphor of weight, itself something that is experienced by the body as much as understood rationally, underscores this view. As

Bloom puts it, rational thought "took the fire from the flint" (1973, 40), which is, of course, the title of the chapter in *Preoccupations* in which Heaney talked about the influence of Eliot and about the motivated connection between poetry and the unconscious. Citing Eliot's dark embryo and Shakespeare's "ooze," he sees poetry's action as both "feminine" and "parthenogenetic"; it is a language that works through "echo and implication" and through a "net of associations" (1980, 83).

The terminology here is very specific—it refers to association and darkness and to an almost organic, prelinguistic connection between poetic origins and the unconscious. The centrality of the human body in any discussion of poetry is clear in this passage as well. It is this sense of poetry as a form of cultural thinking that connects Heaney with Eliot; for both writers, the spark that comes from the friction between the flints relates to the unconscious and somatic origins of significant levels of our thought and also to the sporadic and unforeseen ways in which glimmers from the unconscious come into the light of consciousness. So when Cavanagh writes about the paradox that, despite Heaney's affirmation that "writing comes out of lived experience," he is "just as inclined as Eliot is to generalizing and theorizing," he is, however ironically, drawing attention to the fact that the placement of Heaney's writing within the limit of literary criticism or journalism is to do an injustice to its breadth and scope and mode of operation.

It is precisely this fusion of "lived experience" and "generalizing and theorizing" that gives Heaney's thought such an original purchase on the texts and contexts that are the subject of his poetic thinking. The problematic aspects of such a fusion of the unconscious and the conscious, or the emotional and the rational, arise for Cavanagh because of the narrow critical context within which he is viewing the work of Heaney. Cavanagh sees him in a largely Anglophone critical context, wherein the line of demarcation between poetry and philosophy, or between feeling and rationality, or between the unconscious and the conscious, has been severely delimited. As noted in the introduction, the scission between "poetry and philosophy, between the poetic word and the word of thought" (Agamben 1993c, xvi), is a false one that is in need of rethinking, because in reality, "poetry is something one can do only through philosophy" (de la Durantaye 2009, 61). Heaney has always seen Ireland, and the matter of Ireland, within a European context. One has only to look at his placement of Northern Ireland within the historical and geographical contexts of a Nordic northern Europe in *North* to see how foundational such a paradigm is for him. This broad context provides him a space within which to develop his form of thinking about the aesthetic.

Heaney, like Maurice Blanchot, sees the space of literature as that which allows for a refiguration of the image through a certain sense of distance. For Blanchot, reading is born at the moment "when the work's distance from itself changes its sign" (1982, 201), and by placing the conflict in Northern Ireland at a greater temporal and spatial distance, such a creative space was generated that changed the "signs" of the normative binary readings of this conflict, be they colonial or postcolonial. Ann Smock has identified literature's space as the resurgence of the distance at which we must place anything we wish to understand or aim to grasp: "literature is this remove coming back to us, returning like an echo; and now it is no longer a handy gap, a familiar and useful nothing, but an unidentifiable something, the strange immediacy, foreign to presence and to any present, of remoteness itself" (ibid., 12).

This sense of seeing Ireland as part of a European tradition is one that is also a central argument of his essay writing, culminating in *Crediting Poetry*, where the image of tears and grief is paraphrased through the voice of the bard Demodocus singing of the "fall of Troy and of the slaughter that accompanied it," which causes Odysseus to weep. Homer, Heaney reminds us, says that his tears "were like the tears of a wife on a battlefield weeping for the death of a fallen husband." He goes on to note how Homer personalizes the pain and grief of loss by describing how, as the woman bends in grief over her husband, she feels "the spears, prodding her back and shoulders, and goes bound into slavery and grief" (1995a, 27). What is most interesting here is the effect of a story compared, in epic simile, to the pain and grief felt by a wife on seeing her husband's fallen and broken body. The effects of both the pain and the words of the poem are related, as they both draw tears from a human body. It is also a sense of the physical and somatic effects of language. As Derrida puts it, "The experience of language is, of course, vital" (Derrida and Birnbaum 2007, 34), and it is this vitality that is in question in Heaney's account of the spear prodding the woman's back and in the tears that this story engenders in Odysseus. One could almost see the *tessera* being completed here, as Heaney foregrounds the somatic aspect of poetry, especially its effect on the body, and the body's emotional reactions, even as he receives one of the ultimate accolades for the creation of poetry. The vitality of such language has long been at the core of the European literary tradition, a tradition that is imbricated in his writing from the opening paragraph of *Preoccupations* dealing with the word *omphalos*.

In what is, in effect, his first published paragraph in his prose books, he is describing the earliest memories of his own home place, Mossbawn. As his poetry indicates, concepts of home are seminal in his work and in his thought, and in this piece he offers a very individualistic description of that place. He focuses on the image of the pump, which is described as "a slender, iron idol, snouted, helmeted," and goes on to describe the sounds that he associates with that pump: set on a concrete plinth, marking the center of another world. "I would begin with the Greek word, *omphalos*, meaning the navel, and hence the stone that marked the centre of the world, and repeat it, *omphalos*, *omphalos*, *omphalos*, until its blunt and falling music becomes the music of somebody pumping water at the pump outside our back door" (1980, 17). This description is a seminal point in the Heaney aesthetic, and the connection he makes between Mossbawn and Greece has been well documented. Thus, Conor McCarthy sees how many of Heaney's poems are concerned with his "childhood home, his place of origin" (2008, 33), while Christopher T. Malone makes the point that critics have read his early poetry as attempting to achieve "solidarity with place, to assert a sense of home as centred—what Heaney evokes famously in the 'omphalos,'

'omphalos' sound of the water pump, a childhood memory recalled in *Preoccupations*" (2000, 1097).

What is interesting, however, is that Heaney does not overtly compare his home with the *omphalos*, the conical stone, located in the temple of Apollo at Delphi, which was a physical sign of centrality. At no stage are the two compared directly, either in metaphor or in simile. When the passage is reread, the comparison is being made between the *sound* of the word and the sound of water being pumped from the pump. It is a sonic, aural, associative connection that achieves its aim through that poetized use of language; through somatic similarity, syntactic similarity is created. A further aspect of this comparison is in the prosopopoeia of the pump: "a slender, iron idol, snouted, helmeted, dressed down with a sweeping handle, painted a dark green and set on a concrete plinth, marking the centre of another world." The repetitions of the word *centre* and the imagining of the pump as a helmeted Greek Hoplite are further factors in the adequation of the pump with the mythological stone. It is a different level of thinking than the logical norm, and it is one at which Heaney excels, as in this type of language, the sound, the shape, and the initial letters of words are all contributory factors in their meaning and signification.

This passage is a locus classicus of Heaney's poetic thinking. The structure and logic of the piece are clear: Heaney is setting up an equation between his own home place and ancient Greece. Metaphorically, this connection suggests that just as rural Greece was a location of European culture, so rural Derry is his location of culture, and there is a subtextual desire to locate the issues of Ireland within the broader cultural and political context of European culture and civilization: it is the initial step in "a movement of deterritorialisation" (Deleuze 1995, 30) that will become an abiding trope in Heaney's writing and thinking about place and identity. This process will allow for the deterritorialization of place and for the creation of the space of literature. However, it is important to note that these associations are not logically set out; what is at work here is a very special form of writing and thinking that uses the connections between sight, sound, and language, and this "seeing brings mortals to the path of thinking, poetizing, building" (Heidegger 1975b, 110).

What Heaney is building here is a very nuanced and sophisticated version of home, a version that bears out Blake Morrison's ideas about him as a sophisticated thinker who seems more straightforward than he actually is. To valorize a sense of place through a sonic and phonetic connection to the center of the Greek world is significant, especially as this paragraph is the beginning of his poetized thinking about identity, philosophy, ethics, and the aesthetic. By beginning his prose oeuvre with a Greek word, one that resonates with European and Hellenic culture as well as with the work of James Joyce, who also uses the term in *Ulysses*, Heaney is firmly locating that oeuvre within the European and Hellenic intellectual tradition. I refer, of course, to the *Telemachus* episode of *Ulysses*, wherein the Martello Tower is referred to as an *omphalos*: "God, Kinch, if you and I could only work together we might do something for the island. Hellenize it. . . . To ourselves . . . new paganism . . . *omphalos*" (1989, 5). Indeed, the Hellenizing leitmotif that is initiated in the opening sentence of *Preoccupations* would seem to have a lot in common with Joyce's project in which he, too, attempts to locate Irish culture within a broadly classical and European ambit. Heaney, like Lacan, views linguistic representation, which Freud termed *Vorstellung*, as "already organized according to the possibilities of the signifier as such. Already at the level of the unconscious there exists an organization that, as Freud says, is not necessarily that of contradiction or of grammar, but the laws of condensation and displacement, those that I call the laws of metaphor and metonymy" (Lacan 1992, 61). In this sense, Heaney's opening description of his South Derry home is contextualized within the intellectual tradition of Greco-Roman European thinking, and it would be an error to think that his interest in Europe, and in the writing of Homer, Virgil, and Dante, was something that developed later in his career: notions of home in Heaney's work have always been both *Heimlich* and *Unheimlich*.

In *Crediting Poetry*, the value of the European tradition and of the discourse of poetry is further enunciated by Heaney. Poetry, which is able to connect with the emotional, the haptic, and the somatic aspects of our humanity, has an ability to convey the pain of real emotion, an ability that is core to its strength as an almost constant aspect of human culture. Heaney overtly contrasts this level of somatic knowledge with contemporary satellite and broadband-based television technologies, which he seems to see as attenuated and not able to capture the full complexity of the emotional pain that is endured by others. Becoming "highly informed" in this shallow way leaves one "in danger of growing immune," and in contrast he feels that Homer's image of those spear shafts on the woman's back "has that documentary adequacy which answers all that we know about the intolerable" (1995a, 27). This passage demonstrates the value of the European cultural heritage to Heaney; it allows for the placement of pain and violence in a discourse that somatically understands how pain and grief affect us. At a phenomenological and somatic level, images of tears, of pain, of being poked by the shaft of a spear are all images that speak to our humanity—a humanity that is as common to the sailor on the wine-dark sea of *The Iliad* and *The Odyssey* as it is to the channel surfer referred to in the quotation. Television and computer screens, which are actively disembodied, connecting only with fingers on keyboards, or remote controls via a two-dimensional screen, allow for a surfing relationship and a superficial connection with others, whereas the stark, monosyllabic, alliterative clarity of "spear shafts" demarcates a different level of knowledge, a knowledge imbued with a sense of physical weight, a critical knowledge that is made stronger by a poetic knowledge. Here, Descartes's "opinions of weight" are voiced with respect to the actual weight of those shafts, as they poke and probe the human body; here is the Frostian sense of "this-worldness," what Heaney calls "the dead-on and the head-on-ness" that poetry is able to signify more fully than any other discourse.

Eliot worked at a philosophical level in his poetry and criticism and commented on social and political matters. He was certainly influenced by a sense of European and largely Catholic culture, pace his continuous references to Greek texts as well as his ongoing fascination with Dante. However, while he spoke of a European tradition, his actual intellectual focus was very much Anglo-American. Thus, while the placement of Heaney in the context of the work of Eliot is valid, as both men are poets and critics, it is clear that Heaney's texts operate within a far broader cultural context than do Eliot's, a context that is more philosophical, and Eurocentric, an example of which is to be found in Richard Kearney's book *States of Mind: Dialogues with Contemporary Thinkers on the European Mind*, published in 1995. In this book Kearney sets out his aim as interrogating ideas of what Europe means, of its "vision of itself and of its formative relationship to the wider world." The figures involved were chosen because they were public figures who were "unbound by partisan policy" and who "participate in the cultural realm of ideas and images, of education, academia, and the media, without constraints of party and propaganda" (1995b, 1, 2).

The book is divided into three sections. The first is entitled "Political Thinkers," with contributions from Julia Kristeva, Neal Ascherson, Charles Taylor, Paul Ricoeur, Edward Said, Noam Chomsky, and Vaclav Havel. The final section is called "Philosophical Thinkers" and has contributions from Jacques Derrida, Emmanuel Levinas, Herbert Marcuse, Paul Ricoeur, Stanislas Breton, Hans-Georg Gadamer, and Jean-François Lyotard. The second section is entitled "Literary Thinkers," and this section has contributions from Miroslav Holub, Jacques Darras, Umberto Eco, George Steiner, Marina Warner, George Luis Borges, Martha Nussbaum, and Seamus Heaney. This European milieu more aptly encapsulates the nature of Heaney's own writing than the nature of Cavanagh's more Anglophone one, and the generic context here locates Heaney's own work in this broader sphere of critical and cultural theory. It places him at the center of a nexus of European thinkers working on the core issues of philosophy, politics, and the aesthetic, and it foregrounds the interconnections that exist between each of these discourses through a particular awareness of the significance, perspective, and breadth of the poetic paradigm of language. Heaney's ongoing probing of the different aspects of poetic thinking connects him to this milieu even more.

Writing in *Preoccupations*, Heaney differentiates between what he terms *craft* and *technique* in poetry, and writing about the latter term he explains that technique, for him, as well as issues like meter and rhythm, involves "a definition of his own reality"; it also significantly involves the ability to "raid the inarticulate" and to bring the "the meaning of experience within the jurisdiction of form" (1980, 47). Heaney clearly sees poetry as a syncretic mode of expression where mind and body, form and function, the cognitive and the inarticulate, and the conscious and the unconscious are brought together in a form of knowledge that is different from and, I would submit, more comprehensive than many other forms of epistemological discourse. It is a way of defining reality that is often as much about feeling as about form. He is acutely aware of the somatic and unconscious dimensions of language and of the dimensions of language where we touch on aspects of communication that are normally repressed. It is no accident that he uses the terms *perception*, *voice*, *thought*, *touch*, and *texture* in this passage, as all of these words combine to create that model of inclusive consciousness of which he spoke earlier, and it is the complexity of thought, and this awareness of the interaction and interplay of these different aspects of language as we strive for knowledge and truth, that makes Heaney a significant presence in the European sociocultural public sphere.

It is also no accident that this passage occurs in a chapter entitled "Feeling into Words," as the primacy of the body and the unconscious, with regard to the feelings that need to be translated into words, reinforces once again Heaney's strong correlation between poetry and the body. In this use of the language of sensation, Heaney is very much at one with contemporary aesthetic thinking. Emmanuel Levinas has said, "If art consists in substituting an image for being, the aesthetic element, as its etymology indicates, is sensation. The whole of our world, with its elementary and intellectually elaborated givens, can touch us musically, can become an image" (1989, 134), while Derrida quotes Aristotle to stress the fundamental quality of touch, which "may well exist apart from the other senses," but without it, "no other sense would exist. As has been noted, all animals possess this sense, which is also the sense of nutrition" (2005a, 24).

Heaney, like Levinas and Derrida, is aware of the pervasiveness of language and of the need to fuse the rational with the somatic in order to achieve some form of real knowledge and truth. Heaney's working model of inclusive consciousness includes the unconscious dimension of language, a point on which he is very clear in all of his writing about the nature of poetry. In this sense, he is close to Heidegger's view of poetry as a vehicle that can unconceal things that were hitherto hidden; for Heidegger, poetry, or creative literature, is "nothing but the elementary emergence into words, the becoming-uncovered of existence as being-in-the-world" (1982a, 171–72). The senses of an inclusivity of truth and experience, and of uncovering what is in some way occluded, connect these two European thinkers at the level of the epistemological status of poetry as an aesthetic discourse.

The power of language to affect the senses, a point already noted in the image of the story of Troy producing tears in Odysseus, is foregrounded here, as the ear, the nervous system, and the unconscious are all seen as central to the effect of language. The dialectic of consciousness and the unconscious is central to Heaney's view of language. He recalls the influence of the "exotic" names on the wireless dial of the radio in his childhood home, the names of places that he hears on the BBC weather forecast, the "gorgeous and inane phraseology" of the Roman Catholic catechism that he would have learned at school, or the metaphorical descriptions of Mary in the Catholic ritual, all of which he remembers as part of the "enforced poetry in our household" (1980, 45).

He develops this idea by speaking about Wordsworth's poem "The Thorn," from *Lyrical Ballads*. Here, he is tracing the composition of the poem from comments made in a letter to Isabella Fenwick in 1843, where Wordsworth describes how a storm made the thorn an "impressive object," and he speaks about how a lot of the imaginative power of the poem focuses on the thorn bush and on how to make it permanently in language as impressive as it was to Wordsworth in the storm. He goes on to say that it is achieved because the thorn has become a field of force and that images and ideas from different parts of his conscious and unconscious mind were attracted to it by an "almost magnetic power" (ibid., 50, 51). Repeatedly, as we will discover, Heaney stresses the necessity of poetic thinking and writing as a way of understanding the dialectical relationship between consciousness and the unconscious and between the rational and the somatic. Generally, he is talking about language as it is used in poetry, and most often this discussion derives from a particular reading of a specific piece of poetry, but I would argue that his own writing is suffused with this awareness of the unconscious and somatic aspects of language, and, in this regard, his work rhizomatically connects with the writing of a number of intellectuals in the European public sphere, especially in the fields of Continental philosophy and literary and cultural theory. In his grafting of "poetry onto philosophy," he is mirroring Derrida, who sees such graftings as necessary uses of "certain ways of using homonyms, the undecidable, or the ruses of language," which he sees as having a "properly logical necessity" (Derrida and Birnbaum 2007, 31). Philosophy is no more able to avoid the unconscious and the somatic axis of language than is poetry able to avoid the syntactical and communicative aspects of language. The language we use in philosophy or in reasoned debate is the same as the language used in poetry or in the ordinary business of living: "There is no metalanguage that can be spoken" (Lacan 2006, 688).

For Lacan, and indeed for many of the writers in the European public sphere, language has become a central aspect of their epistemological and ontological projects. Interestingly, in underlining this point, he refers to the work of Martin Heidegger, and, equally interestingly, he misquotes him. In a volume entitled *My Teaching*, Lacan is talking about the centrality of language in contemporary philosophical thinking and remarks that for Heidegger, "in language man dwells." Lacan goes on to fully endorse this point and to explicate it further by noting the importance of this phrase, as even when extracted from Heidegger's text it speaks for itself: "It means that language was there before man, and that is obvious. Not only is man born into language in precisely the way he is born into the world; he is born through language" (2008, 27). Lacan, in this extract, is referring to a quotation from Heidegger's book *Poetry, Language, Thought*, where Heidegger is citing a late poem of Friedrich Hölderlin, in which occurs the already cited phrase "poetically man dwells," which becomes the subject of the final essay in the volume (1971, xiv). So Lacan's "quotation" from Heidegger is actually a misquotation: where Heidegger says, "*poetically* man dwells," Lacan has him saying "*in language* man dwells," and this discrepancy, I would contend, is a significant point. In this misquotation, we have a conflation by Lacan of "language" with "poetry" as the source of man's dwelling, and this point is pertinent to my argument, as for Lacan the language used to create poetry is of similar epistemological status as is the language used to write about poetry. In addition, for Lacan, the structure of language is such that it is related to the unconscious: "Most of you will have some idea of what I mean when I say—*the unconscious is structured like a language*" (1977, 20; emphasis in the original). I think this unconscious slip of the quotational pen is one of those Freudian parapraxes of which Lacan has often spoken, seeing them as "imaginary only inasmuch as the truth brings out its fictional structure in them" (2006, 376). Poetic language, for him, is crucial to thinking, as it is language at its most distilled level of operation.

This sense that truth is somehow fictional or almost accidental, and that it needs such strategies to reach the aspect of the unconscious that would make it fuller, is echoed by Heaney in his view that it can be told from only an oblique perspective. Heaney and Lacan agree there can be no overt access through language to any sense of full truth or knowledge; instead, it has to come by way of the connection between language and the unconscious, a connection that is far from direct or rationally driven. The relationship between language and the unconscious is a specific area in which Heaney has proved to be interested, both in his prose and in his poetry; indeed, he has stated that the initial stages of writing involve imitating, "consciously or unconsciously," sounds and images that flowed in from lived experience in the world (1980, 44). This idea of lived experience as part of any structure or system of knowledge has been at the core of a certain strand of European thinking on issues of epistemology. For Heidegger, existence necessitates acknowledging our creaturely existence, our "being in the world": "But *being in a world* belongs essentially to *Dasein*. Thus the understanding of being that belongs to *Dasein* just as originally implies the understanding of something like 'world' and the understanding of the being of beings accessible within the world" (1996, 14).

Similarly, for Lacan, access to the unconscious is necessary for any form of knowledge or truth: "When I express myself by saying that the unconscious is structured like a language, I am trying to restore the true function of everything that structures under the aegis of Freud, and that in itself allows us to see our first step. It is because language exists that truth exists, as everyone can come to see" (2008, 28–29). Lacan argues that truth and knowledge can be fully achieved only when there is some access to the unconscious, a process that is rhizomatically connected to Heaney's sense that truth can only be told "slant." One could make the further connection between Heaney's use of slant and Lacan's description of anamorphosis in Hans Holbein's picture *The Ambassadors*.

The Ambassadors (1533), Holbein's portrait of Jean de Dinteville and Georges de Selves, prominent figures at the court of Henry VIII, is among the most famous modern examples of anamorphic painting technique. On first examining this picture, one sees two Renaissance diplomats in all their finery, surrounded by the burgeoning technology of the scientific revolution, "symbolic of the sciences and arts as they were grouped at the time in the *trivium* and *quadrivium*" (Lacan 1977, 88), that drove the Renaissance *mentalitée* to explore, measure, and codify the world. At the bottom of the painting, at a forty-degree angle to the horizontal, is what looks like an oblong disc, placed at an angle, jarring somewhat with the scopic dimensions of the picture. It is only on close scrutiny that one sees it for what it is—a skull. In anamorphic painting, the artist constructs the image based on one or more eccentric points of view in order to embed an element or elements that are not discernible without the use of distorting mirrors, or unless viewed from a specific position. In light of this anamorphic skull, the positive and ameliorative Weltanschauung of the Renaissance is placed in juxtaposition to the mortality that bounds our existence. The existence of the skull is dependent on perspective, and in this sense it resembles the truth in Heaney's terms, as it can be seen only from a slanted perspective. This point is literally true in the case of the skull, as it is as one leaves the room and looks across at the picture that the skill assumes a three-dimensional perspective through anamorphosis. Lacan's point is that what we know, and what we see, is dependent on where we stand and from where we look. The "truth" of this picture can be fully known only by both looking straight at it to see the technology of the high Renaissance and also looking at it slant, so that the skull can be fully understood. Truth and knowledge arise from the interplay and interanimation in language, which is why Lacan prefers the term *language* to the term *poetry* in his transliteration of Heidegger's earlier quotation. He sees all language as working at this level, where different perspectives are needed for full speech, or knowledge, or truth to be found.

Thus, while a frontal gaze at *The Ambassadors* reveals much of the picture's truth, it is only when the gaze turns away from the full frontal perspective that the anamorphic glance allows the skull, which undercuts the rational vision of the picture, to emerge. It is only by looking at the picture at a slant that another dimension of the truth of the picture emerges. Slavoj Žižek uses this slant technique as a governing image in his exploration of Lacan through popular culture, calling it "looking awry" and pointing out that the object assumes clear and distinctive features only if we look at it "at an angle," that is, with an "interested" view, supported, permeated, and 'distorted' by desire" (1991, 9).

In both Heaney's poetry and his prose, this anamorphic perspective is fundamental to his style of writing, and it is part of what connects him to this European tradition of aesthetic thinking. Both types of knowledge, the conscious and the unconscious, are significant in his work. Speaking of a sense of place, Heaney notes that there are two ways in which a place is known and cherished, adding that while these ways may be complementary, they can also be antipathetic. He explains that one way is lived, while the other is learned, and both of them are likely to "co-exist in a conscious and unconscious tension" (1980, 131). In this respect, he parallels Lacan, who also sees the conscious and the unconscious as informing each other: "The capital Other, is already there in every opening, however fleeting it may be, of the unconscious" (1977, 130). Truth, for Lacan and Heaney, is reached only through such tension and oscillation. The ability to grant credence to the irrational, the aleatory, the emotional, and the unconscious as forms of knowledge connects these two thinkers, as does their sense of an interinanimation between different discourses that is creative of meaning, which makes Heaney's own writing very much a part of this Continental tradition of seeing literature as an important epistemic discourse.

In Heaney's work there is a parallel desire to connect with that other: "vowels ploughed into other. Opened ground" (1979, 33), and this "opened ground" is a metaphor for his search for deeper meanings in the normal activities of dwelling in his new home, Glanmore, in County Wicklow, to which he had moved in 1979. In many of these poems, he sees the earth, the world of nature, and memory of sensible things as the sources of his writing. In a telling comment explaining the source of his poem "Anything Can Happen," he notes that a poem always contains a "touch of the irrational." He continues that for both the reader and the writer, "it will possess a soothsaying force, as if it were an oracle delivered unexpectedly and irresistibly. It will arrive like a gift from the muse or, if you prefer, the unconscious" (2004a, 13).

This adequation of the unconscious with the Muse, one of the ancient Greek goddesses of inspiration, is significant and brings our discussion back to its origins in the *omphalos*, Mossbawn, because, in Heaney's view, poetry will always have a connection with the unconscious and the irrational. Moreover, for Lacan, this point is also where some forms of truth can be reached because if the unconscious is the discourse of the Other, then it has to be realized that "the unconscious, is not beyond the closure, it is *outside*" (1977, 131). Heaney sees the "opened ground" of Glanmore as an example of this "outside," and of much of his later poetry, as he will look outside of his own culture to probe the connections with the classical culture that serves as a foundation for contemporary European culture. In a sense, it will serve, in *The Cure at Troy* (1990) and in *The Burial at Thebes* (2004b), as a form of cultural unconscious. The same is true of the increasing level of classical references in his later books *The Haw Lantern* (1987), *Seeing Things* (1991), *The Spirit Level* (1996), *Electric Light* (2001), *District and Circle* (2006), and *Human Chain* (2010). Greek culture, as other, is a central plank in Heaney's epistemological project, and the same can be said of Heidegger and Derrida, not to mention Lacan, who also saw Greek language and myth as providing a form of access to the unconscious.

Lacan too has been drawn to Greek language and culture in his efforts to explain the unconscious. Lacan stood out among his "immediate contemporaries and colleagues in psychiatry as a philosopher who could read Greek and German fluently, and who put to good use his knowledge of the classics" (Rabaté 2003, 12) by allowing unusual terms to express aspects of the unconscious that would otherwise be difficult to signify and understand. His use of foreign, often Greek, terms stressed the presence of the unconscious in language, and its effect, but also underlined the difficulty of comprehending the unconscious. For example, he used the term *agalma*, which he sees as "that object which the subject believes that his desire tends toward" (1990, 87), while he used the term *aphanisis* to signify the lack, or absence, which he saw, following Ernest Jones, as causal of the castration complex (1991, 222). In his efforts to create an interpretive discourse that did full justice to all aspects of knowledge, Lacan stressed the need for an "apophantic" logic, a term again taken from the Greek (*apophanisis* means "revelation"), where Aristotle spoke of a "logic of affirmation and assertion."

Such apophantic discourse involves addressing "non-existence (of the sexual relationship, of the truth in its entirety and of the *jouissance* in its entirety)," but also involves acknowledging the haunting effect of the unconscious. This apophantic discourse is "sense and goes against meaning. It will never place itself on the side of universal quantifiers because it is always a particular saying" (Rabinovich 2003, 215).

In the context of this type of "saying," it is instructive to look at the original Greek usage of the term *agalma*. It arose in the context of Platonic discourse in *The Republic*, where Plato saw philosophy as a metaphysical activity that is separate from the senses. Indeed, one could see this text as the origin of the separation of poetry from thinking, as poetry has been seen as a distraction from the pursuit of truth through its rhetorical structures, its use of imagery to appeal and delight, and its address to the physical senses. In the myths in the *Phaedo* and *Phaedrus*, however, Plato suggests, "physical vision has a positive role to play in philosophic theorizing" (Nightingale 2004, 37). In *Phaedrus*, Socrates describes the process of the recollection of the Form of Beauty. The beautiful body on earth, shining with the radiance of true Beauty, is an "*agalma*" (Plato 1978, 573): "a sacred statue or object that embodies and represents the divine" (Nightingale 2004, 87). Jean-Pierre Vernant, in his discussion of *agalmata* and divine images, suggests that the purpose of such an image is to establish real contact with the "world beyond, to actualize it, to make it present, and thereby to participate intimately in the divine; yet at the same time, it must also emphasize what is inaccessible and mysterious in divinity, its alien quality, its otherness." For Vernant, the term's purpose was "to inscribe absence in presence, to insert the other, the elsewhere, into our familiar universe," and as such it reveals "the elsewhere in what is given to view" (1991, 153). Andrew Ford, in an interesting study of the origins of criticism in Greece, has made the connection between the *agalma* and the Muses (2002, 125), and he cites the work of Isocrates (436–338 BCE) who feels that a text "can 'embody' the inner, ethical qualities of its subject in its own unique way" (ibid., 238). Heaney has already spoken of poetry as a "moral and ethical force" (1988, 40), and he has addressed issues concerning the role of poetry and the "moral and ethical imperatives subsumed in it" (1989, 37).

Significantly, Lacan also sees the locus of the unconscious as ethical, as he makes the point that the "status of the unconscious, which, as I have shown, is so fragile on the ontic plane, is ethical" (1977, 33). To obtain a true sense of the ethical dimensions of knowledge, the unconscious must be involved in the mode of inquiry. The connection here between the Greek terms used by Lacan and Heaney as they each attempt to focus on the real of language, the other, and the unconscious is a further association in terms of intellectual inquiry and in terms of a return to the origins of European civilization as they each try to ground their work in that tradition.

Poetry has a particular ability to do so, given what Roman Jakobson calls its "poetic function," where the principle of equivalence is projected from "the axis of selection onto the axis of combination. Equivalence is promoted to the constitutive device of the sequence" (1971, 704). In this sense, the connections between words are no longer purely syntactically driven, but are also driven by associative, aleatory types of relationships at the level of phonetic association, relationships that are redolent of the unconscious. Poetry as a discourse, through sonic connections like rhyme, assonance, alliteration, and pararhyme, sets up different paradigms of connection between words at the level of sound, connections that can also liberate other meanings from these words. For Lacan, the "unconscious, which tells the truth about truth, is structured like a language" (2006, 737), and it is through the full range and power of language that aspects of the unconscious can be expressed and accessed. Thus, the structure of poetry that posits connections at the level of the signifier, the word, as well as at the rational level of the signified, the meaning, means that the different levels of connection can reinforce each other and complicate the meaning. I would suggest that these connections at the level of sight, sound, and rhyme are all signifiers of the unconscious charges that surround words and sentences. Meaning both coheres and inheres, and poetic language, through its associative and imagistic dimensions, is highly attuned to this aspect of signification.

I would further suggest that this very principle underlies Lacan's famous opaque style of speaking and writing, where puns, jokes, and mathemes are all used to supplement the rational discourse of the "symbolic order" and to access aspects of the real or the unconscious. Heaney's sustained references to Greek culture form part of a comparable agenda of attempting to use language to access the nonlinguistic and the nonrational, as we remember that it is through the sound of the word *omphalos* that the connection is made between Mossbawn and Delphi.

Clearly, for Lacan, Greek signifiers allowed him to address areas of language and signification that his vernacular was unable to represent. Possibly the alien nature of the alphabet is a way of gesturing toward the opacity of the unconscious, but also to the possibility of accessing some of the meanings of that unconscious. The juxtaposition of French and Greek performed this function for Lacan; for Heaney, the juxtaposition is one of familiar, grounded objects, contrasted with Greek and Roman cultural allusions, in a fluid structure that allows these allusions to act as the unconscious dimension of the familiar objects and thus to offer a different perspective on them. We have seen it in the conflation of the sound of water from the helmeted pump and the sound of "the Greek word *omphalos*," though the connection is also visually underwritten, as the top of these old cast-iron pumps had a similar shape to the helmets worn by Greek soldiers. Here the somatically familiar act of pumping water is made strange by its connection with the Greek word, and in a sense each of these discourses is reaching beyond the familiar language of a piece of academic writing.

One would not expect to find an outline of a domestic practice that predated the installation of running water in a literary essay, though it would be quite normal to find such a description in a poem, and, indeed, the pump does appear in a number of his poems as a polysemic image. In "The Early Purges," he speaks of the pump as the agent of death for the pups: "they were slung on the snout / Of the pump and the water pumped in" (1966, 23), while in "Rite of Spring," the pump is sexualized, freezing in winter, "the plunger froze up," and then, after straw is tied around it and set alight, "Her entrance was wet, and she came" (1969, 25). In "Sunlight" the pump is again personified as water "honeyed" in the "helmeted pump in the yard" (1975, 8), in "Changes" it is the "pump in the long grass" (1984b, 36), and in "A Drink of Water" he recalls an old woman who used to come to draw water from the pump, and the memory is recalled aurally through the pump's "whooping cough, the bucket's clatter / And slow diminuendo" that "announced her," and through the adequation between the woman's voice and the pump, as Heaney speaks of recalling her "grey apron," a white enamel bucket, and "treble / Creak of her voice like the pump's handle" (1979, 16). Therefore, the pump that begins *Preoccupations* is an established presence in the Heaney canon. The pump also has a symbolic function in linking his early home, Mossbawn, with his later *locus amoenus*, "the hedge-school of Glanmore" (ibid., 34). In "Glanmore Revisited," he recalls "Bare flags. Pump water. Winter-evening cold" (1991, 31), making the connection between the two places, a connection that is all the more overt in his poem from *The Haw Lantern* "Grotus and Coventina," a poem to which we will return in a later chapter.

Coventina is a Romano-Celtic goddess of water whose shrine, in Northumberland near Hadrian's Wall, Heaney had visited. He tells of how he saw some images "of this lovely little creature, recumbent on her elbow," while under the other elbow, "she had a pitcher that poured out a steady stream of water." He then tells of how in the museum he saw an altar dedicated to Coventina, "a little stunted brickbat of a thing, with the name 'Grotus' cut into it in very crude letters." The classical nature of this image is recontextualized when Heaney visited the shrine itself, which was in the "soggy, rushy corner of a field that could have been the corner of a field at home" (Heaney and O'Driscoll 2008, 294). This connection, which is redolent of the earlier constellation of the Mossbawn pump, and the term *omphalos* again animate his relationship with Glanmore, as the poem fuses Grotus and Coventina with their "difficulties with the water pump in Glanmore" (ibid., 295).

Once again, the pump is a metaphor for the unearthing of that which is hidden, and the image of language cutting into a rock is a further example of this apophantic discourse, as the classical and the local are fused into a fuller meaning, just as Glanmore, Mossbawn, and the classical world are fused in this poem. The shifting perspective required to encompass all of these connections requires a frequent amount of looking awry or slant, which is what Heaney's work sets out to achieve. One could see that it is the accretion of meaning here that is significant and also his sense that the poem is not a "matter of 'reference' but of *res*, of the things themselves" (ibid.). Here, in a nutshell, we have the conflation of the lived life and generalized theorizing that Cavanagh saw as mutually exclusive; in fact, they are mutually informing aspects in all of Heaney's work and lend to his thought that spark that can be found in the striking of flints together. As Tom Huhn argues, a thinking that is "tied too tightly to concepts" needs to be countered by "objects that elude, and thoughts that turn away from, the objectifications of thinking" (2004, 9), and Heidegger would agree, devoting a long discussion to issues of representation in *Poetry, Language, Thought*. One of his main points refers to representing and grasping what he calls "the thingness of the thing" (1971, 22).

This desire to incorporate the real, and the nonpresent of language, in language, has been part of Heaney's project ab initio, and the pump is very much an overdetermined symbol of this project, but it is also of broader significance. In reality, the pump is a device for bringing water from the depths to the surface, and as such it is a resonant symbol of what Heaney is setting out to achieve in his own work. The image of the *omphalos*, the stone that stood at the center of the world, being equated with the pump through the sound that the pumping makes, is achieved through the repeated saying of the word, the "blunt and falling music" of the sound of the Greek word. The connection is not logical but associative, and as such it is a paradigm of Heaney's valuing of the associative dimensions of language in his thinking. One could see the relationship between the actual pump and the pump as symbolic object as examples of Theodor Adorno's particular use of the term *dialectic*. For Adorno too, art involved a dynamic conflation, a dialectic, between different forces and constituent qualities. As he puts it, artworks are such "*in actu* because their tension does not terminate in pure identity with either extreme"; instead, these works become "force fields of their antagonisms" (1997, 176), and we will return to these force fields in chapters 4–6. Such a tension is not always easy or comfortable, but it is necessary for meaning.

Adorno sees this term as a "mode for exposing the logical powers of a concept, one that makes perspicuous its 'materiality'—its experience, object, practice, and history dependence" (Bernstein 2004, 43). A parallel process is to be found in Heaney's own use of the image of the pump and in his discussion of it in *Preoccupations*, where he speaks of remembering men sinking the shaft of the pump and digging down into the earth. He describes this very physical and real act as something that "centred and staked the imagination," making the pump a symbolic central point of his early notion of home (1980, 20). That this associative connection is set out at the beginning of his first book of essays is significant, as it connects the voice, the world of things, the sounds of lived experience, the unconscious, and Greek culture in a force field that is proleptic of the direction that Heaney's own work will take. For him, poetry, the poetic function, is a form of thinking, and his own thinking in these essays will encompass all aspects of experience in what will be an apophantic discourse. The presence of the pump suggests that in Heaney's thinking, as for Maurice Blanchot, "the language of thought is poetic language par excellence" (1982, 39), as he will incorporate the other of language, and the real that is almost impossible to signify in language, in his critical writing.

Like Lacan, Heaney uses Greek language and culture to symbolize the other that needs to be expressed in any writing that attempts to reach for knowledge or truth. The attempt to express what cannot be known rationally is at the core of the work of these two thinkers. For Lacan, in the unconscious there is "something definable, accessible, and objectifiable," and it is its "linguistic structure" that gives this status to the unconscious (1977, 21). In Heaney's writing, there is this same sense that there is something apophantic in language that can be traced back to Greek culture, where it was felt that when "a lyric poet gives voice, 'it is a god that speaks'" (1988, 93). Both writers see Greek culture as providing for the saying of the other, of the unconscious, of the unknown. In Heaney's thought, the aesthetic is also part of the mechanisms through which these forms of truth can be accessed, as it is a liberating discourse that can in some way circumvent the repression that drives desires, feelings, and somatic impulses underground; in this way it has parallels with drugs and alcohol, other modes through which the rational is enhanced by its hitherto repressed other and other modes through which the god, the Muse, the unconscious, can become overt.

While discussing a sonnet by his fellow Northern Irish poet Paul Muldoon, entitled "Symposium," Heaney connects the aesthetic with alcohol, noting that the title harks back to the original Greek meaning of the term, a gathering where "men met in order to drink and talk, and where in all likelihood they then proceeded to get well and truly, drunk and to talk nonsense" (2002, 377). This nonsense is very much the other of rational discourse and, as such, provides access to the somatic and haptic areas of knowledge that are repressed in rational discourse, and it is interesting that the term *agalma*, which we discussed earlier, first arose in Plato's *Symposium*. Heaney tells how one of the most important influences of Greek culture for him was what he terms a "clannish energy" that he associated with them, and he senses a "far greater closeness between the lived life and the official pomps in Greece than in Rome" (Heaney and O'Driscoll 2008, 294). The attempt to articulate the lived life, the energy, and the sensations that are associated with experience is central to Heaney's writing in both poetry and prose, and in doing so he is paralleling the critical pathway of Lacan, who has explained that the real, his term for that which is beyond expression, but behind experience, "is always and in every case in its place; it carries its place stuck to the sole of its shoe, there being nothing that can exile it from it" (2006, 17). This is very much in tune with Heaney's lived life and his sense of the "vitality . . . at ground level" in Greek culture, reminiscent of the sense of "this-worldness" that he found in Frost's writing. He finds this local dimension of the real, lived experience from Greek writing as important as what he terms "the big earth-moving machinery of the literature and the myths" (Heaney and O'Driscoll 2008, 294).

It is this sense of lived life and vitality that may provide that slanted perspective of looking awry that will allow for access to the unconscious and to the real, both of which are barred from normal language: what does not "come to light in the symbolic *appears in the real*" (Lacan 2006, 324; emphasis in the original), so it is necessary to access the real in whatever apophantic way we can. Poetry is one such mode of access, as the linguistic structure of the unconscious can be accessed at the level of rhyme and associative connections of the words, their form, and rhythm. As an artifact, the poem is very much a force field in which many different modes of language interact and intersect, and my argument is that Heaney sees poetry, and what Jakobson terms the poetic function, as outlined in the introduction, as part of a poetized form of thinking. It is part of an apophantic discourse that can access the nonlinguistic aspects of haptic and somatic meaning.

In this view, Heaney has a lot in common with Continental philosophy, which sees poetry as having an epistemological function in the discourse of human interaction. As Derrida has put it, "Poetry and thinking travel together, but their voyage is without truth; unguarded, it is totally exposed to the accident, to overturning. Like a hedgehog crossing the highway" (Malabou and Derrida 2004, 261), and Derrida has captured the particularist and situationist aspect of poetry that often eschews grand narratives in favor of a specific focus on an individual or singular event, with the ramifications of meaning left to be teased out by the reader. In much of his discussion of Continental philosophy, Derrida has stressed the adequation of the aesthetic and the rational. Writing about Kant, and about his book *The Conflict of the Faculties*, Derrida points to the essential role of poetry and of poetic discourse in Kant's thinking. Poetry, he suggests, is "at the centre of philosophy; the poem is a philosopheme" (2004a, 67–68), and he goes on to probe the poetic nature of a significant segment of Kantian thought. Similarly, writing in the context of an exploration of the work of Heidegger, Derrida has opined that thinking and poetry, "although radically different, are relatives and parallels, parallels that cut across and breach one another, that cut each other in a place that is also a kind of signature" (2007, 56). This signature is one that will be further analyzed in the coming chapters, as will the connection between poetry and philosophy, and it is to the work of Heidegger himself that this argument now turns, as, perhaps more than any other thinker in the tradition of Continental philosophy, it is Heidegger who has placed poetry as a necessary aspect of thought.

In an essay published in 1954, but written some seven years earlier, entitled "Aus der Erfahrung des Denkens," which translates as "The Thinker as Poet," Heidegger made this connection overt. The essay was published in a selection of essays on philosophy and aesthetics entitled *Poetry, Language, Thought*, a title that indicates the paratactic and associative thrust of Heidegger's thinking in this book. One of the core arguments of these essays is the homology that Heidegger sees as existing between poetry and thinking. In the introduction, Albert Hofstadter asks whether there is in the end any fundamental difference between the thinking poet and the poetic thinker, and he notes that at one level, a poet need not be a thinker, nor need a thinker be a poet; however, at a deeper level, to be a poet of the first rank, there is "a thinking that the poet must accomplish, and it is the same kind of thinking" that the "thinker of first rank must accomplish, a thinking which has all the purity and thickness and solidity of poetry, and whose saying is poetry" (Heidegger 1971, xi–xii). Throughout the book, Heidegger speaks about the connection between poetry and thought in a manner that is redolent of Heaney's own thinking. Accordingly, in speaking about reality and the "thing," Heidegger notes that feeling must be taken as part of the equation if we are to come to any complete assessment of reality.

What he calls "feeling" or "mood" is more "intelligently perceptive" and more "open to Being" than reason alone (ibid., 24–25).

Heidegger reminds us that the Greek language uses the same word "*techne* for craft and art"; however, he is clear that the word signifies neither art nor craft in the contemporary sense of those words. Rather, for Heidegger, the word *techne* denotes "a mode of knowing" and not a sense of making. He sees *techne* as "a bringing forth of beings" (ibid., 59). For Heidegger, thought must be accompanied by feeling, and language must express both if there is to be any real expression of the reality in which we live. Thought and feeling, very like Heaney's view of technique, are fused together, and for Heidegger, poetic language is the vehicle through which this fusion can be achieved, as it is a very specific but very real form of knowledge about the world. Citing the ideas of German poet Johann Gottfried Herder, in his *Ideas on the Philosophy of the History of Man*, Heidegger repeats Herder's idea that "a breath of our mouth becomes the portrait of the world, the type of our thoughts and feelings in the other's soul" (ibid., 136). Heidegger's philosophy is in many ways an attempt to make us see that "in poetic saying, language resumes its original function of allowing things to show themselves, allowing being to happen" (King 2009, 55). One immediately thinks of Heaney's comments on Grotus and Coventina about the thingness of the poem's genesis: "It wasn't a matter of 'reference' but of *res*, of the things themselves. Not so much elitism, therefore, as a res-ing of the stakes" (Heaney and O'Driscoll 2008, 295), and this "thingness" is as important as the symbolic and cultural capital that is attached to the classical figures themselves. The associative and punning logic of *res-ing* (raising) is an index of the apophantic aspect of language, which allows the associations of the signifier to have a relevance in the construction of a fuller type of meaning. The somatic and bodily act of saying the sounds is significant to Heaney, both in the sound of the word *omphalos* and in the vowels and consonants of the words *Grotus* and *Coventina*, and this saying is the other level of thinking with which Heaney's writing engages. The power of poetic thinking is to allow for the importance of the saying, of the texture, sound, and associations of the word, as well as the thoughts that they signify.

Heaney's version of thinking involves not just the idea of language but also the fact, the "thingness," of language in all of its somatic complexity. He points toward the sound of language, toward its connections with the unconscious and the emotional registers of our being. He is very close to the Heideggerian view that "speech is the audible expression and communication of human feelings. These feelings are accompanied by thoughts" (1971, 190). I have been arguing that Heaney's epistemological thrust has been to engage with all the resources of language in order to come to as full a range of thought as is possible, and I have been suggesting that he is best read not just in an Anglophone context but in a broader European one. In an Anglophone context, as we have seen, Cavanagh finds it very difficult to situate Heaney's fusion of generalization with lived experience; in a Continental philosophical tradition, however, it is clear that such a context readily exists: Heidegger sees language as that which "first brings man about, brings him into existence" (ibid., 192).

It is to one such area where reality and unreality are mutually intertwined that our discussion now turns, namely, the role of literature in expressing conservative or emancipatory ideas of sociopolitical identity. In the next chapters, Heaney's teasing out of such issues, whether he is talking about poetry or prose, is an example of the poet as thinker: "The writer is no longer his own creature, but stands arraigned before political tragedy, and bound to the collective fate of 'our predicament,' as he describes and testifies to it again in other essays such as 'Belfast' and 'Through-Other Places, Through-Other Times: The Irish Poet and Britain.' At moments of crisis like this, it is to Heaney the poet that Heaney the prose writer turns for a supporting witness" (O'Donoghue 2009, 125).

The next chapter will examine his thinking on the subject of the frontier, which is the limit point of one identity, be that literary, political, or ideological. For most, a frontier, or a border, is a point of closure and separation between selfhood and alterity, but in

Heaney's aesthetic thinking it becomes a point in a structure wherein different identities can interact and interinanimate each other with a view to the creation of more permeable structures of identity. Instead of being a restrictive place, it becomes a creative space in his poetized structures of thinking.

2

Space

The Final Frontier

In this chapter, I will offer readings of essays that demonstrate how Heaney expands the borders and the limits of texts and ideas and how, as an aesthetic thinker, he offers genuinely new perspectives and new ways of looking at paradigms of identity that have traditionally been seen as running on regular tramlines. He looks at the political context of different aspects of literature and also allows the cultural sphere to complicate the political binarism of British-Irish and colonizer-colonized. His engagement with the signifieds of postcolonial theory is framed by his very specific views on the role and force of literature as a genre, and of poetry in particular, in the constellation of discourses that form the public sphere. By so doing, Heaney creates new possibilities of meaning, which is precisely the task of the cultural thinker. I will argue that he both expands the frontiers of the discourse and expands the conceptual frontiers involved in the shaping of the discussion, and I will demonstrate that this mode of thinking coheres throughout his prose books. I will also look at Joyce as a strong precursor, at the cultural and linguistic politics of colonization and identity that form a context for Heaney's writing, and finally at his engagement with the literature of Scotland, which provides another perspective on Northern Ireland as a place and political and cultural entity.

The relationship between the aesthetic and the political has always been something of a vexed one. The use of literature for ideological purposes has a long history. That language is a structural factor in the politics of identity is very much a sine qua non in the realm of postcolonial studies. The discourse of the postcolonial paradigm is one that is fraught with such questions. In a Lacanian context, all subjectivity is defined with respect to what is called "the symbolic order," and this order is the structural matrix through which our grasp of the world is shaped and enunciated. For Lacan, the symbolic order is what actually constitutes our subjectivity: "Man speaks, then, but it is because the symbol has made him man" (2006, 229). The symbolic order is the matrix of language and culture, and it is the locus through which individual desire is expressed: "The moment in which the desire becomes human is also that in which the child is born into language" (ibid., 262). The social worlds of communication, intersubjective relations, knowledge of ideological conventions, and the acceptance of the law are all connected with the acquisition of language. Once a child enters into language, and accepts the rules and dictates of society, it is able to deal with others.

The symbolic, then, is made up of those laws and restrictions that control both desire and the rules of communication, which are then perpetuated through societal and cultural hegemonic modes. Lacan condenses this function in the term the *Name of the Father*, a cluster term for patriarchy and the existing system of laws, rules, and ideological expectations of the social structure into which one is born. Through recognition of the Name of the Father, one becomes a member of a society or culture: "It is in the *Name of the Father* that we must recognize the support of the symbolic function which, from the dawn of history, has identified his person with the figure of the law" (ibid., 230). The symbolic, through language, is "the pact which links . . . subjects together in one action. The human action *par excellence* is originally founded on the existence of the world of the symbol, namely on laws and contracts" (1991, 230; emphasis in the original). Language, then, is necessary for any political project, as it is the mode through which such a project is expressed, operationalized, and communicated to a people.

In the case of the history of empire, the consequence of imperial conquest is the gradual control of this symbolic order by the hegemonic imperial language—for example, Greek, Latin, Spanish, and, of course, English. In the case of Ireland, the gradual attenuation of the Irish language, both through imperial policy and through economic necessity, meant that in the mid-eighteenth century, this symbolic order underwent a paradigm shift from the Irish language to English. This shift was also true of the cultural code of the symbolic order, namely, literature. With regard to the Habermasian public sphere, the language of that sphere was now English, and the political binary opposition English-Irish, which has bedeviled Irish history, was now enacted in the idiom of language and culture.

Seamus Deane has asserted the importance of language in the colonial process—in ways it is the ultimate ideological state apparatus (ISA), as opposed to a repressive state apparatus (RSA) in an Althusserian sense, as it interpellates subjects to see the world in its own specific terms and gradually allows them to become enculturated into the culture of that language. Louis Althusser differentiated between the repressive state apparatus (the army, the law, the police) and the ideological state apparatus (religion, education, the family, the legal and political establishments, the communications media, and the arts) (2001, 143).

For Althusser, these ideological apparatuses are ways through which the state replicates itself in the future. Whereas RSAs function in the public realms, ISAs work in the private realm (though, as we will see, they also function in the public sphere of discourse and critique). Crucial to all of these apparatuses, and indeed to most of the RSAs, are different forms of language, and in an Irish context the area of language is a core signifier of identity and a core element in identitarian politics. There is a long history of linguistic colonization in Ireland, with the English language gradually supplanting the native Irish language. Of course, this form of linguistic colonization is not unique to Ireland. As Deane puts it, English is "not merely the language of a country or of an empire or of an invading culture; it is the language of a condition—modernity" (2003, 113). He means that the colonial and postcolonial encounter is rephrased in the encounter between modernity and tradition. To be countermodern is to be allied with the forces of tradition and backwardness, and in epistemological and political terms to be countermodern is to place the colonized culture in a classic double bind.

If the language of the colonizer is embraced, there will be a loss of differential indexes of identity and tradition and of the whole concept of "authenticity"; if the original language is recuperated, or revived, then the associated connotative implications are of an embracing of the past as opposed to the future, of tradition as opposed to modernity, and of ignorance as opposed to instrumental reason. Either way, the colonized is left disempowered, forever defining itself negatively in the symbolic order of the colonizer. Any real independence from the colonial symbolic order can be achieved only by espousing a nativist position, from which the colonized is seen as voluntarily embracing the more backward conditions of the colonized people, de facto retrospectively justifying the whole process of colonization, which was often glossed by terms like *protectorate*. In the context of culture, the same argument was made for the introduction of the more "civilized" and "sophisticated" literature of the colonizer. As Gauri Viswanathan has put it, the importance of English literature for this process could not be exaggerated, because "as the source of moral values for correct behaviour and action, it represented a convenient replacement for direct religious instruction" (1997, 93). She is in accord with the ideas of Franz Fanon, who made the point that the Negro of the Antilles will be "proportionately whiter—that is, he will come closer to being a real human being—in direct ratio to his mastery of the French language" (1968, 8). In other words, part of the success of colonization is to create a sociocultural Lacanian mirror phase where the colonial subject misrecognizes him- or herself in the image of the colonizer. Language, culture, and opinion formation all have the effect of embodying the ideological agenda of RSAs in the more easily assimilated modes of ISAs.

As an Althusserian ISA, literature, in this respect, is extremely effective, and it is one of the privileged signifiers of the linguistic mastery of which Fanon speaks. Literature, in a colonial paradigm, demonstrates the very specific semiotic and ideological force of written language—it is an example of "signs taken for wonders," as the literature of the colonizer, imbued with the ideological authority of the ISA, becomes "an insignia of colonial authority and a signifier of colonial desire and discipline" (Bhabha 1994, 102). Consequently, literature serves an attenuated Arnoldian function by providing a form of transcendental instruction that avoids any direct political charge, but creates an ideological symbolic order that must be embraced by the speaking colonial subject. In all postcolonial conditions, the issue of language is crucial, and Ireland, anomalous state as it may be (Lloyd 1993), is no exception. There is, for example, the vexed issue of whether Irishness is intrinsically bound up with the speaking of the Irish language. At the turn of the century, many of the Irish revivalists saw a clear connection between the Irish language and the essence of Irish nationalism and nation formation. However, if Irish writing can now be enunciated in the English language, this whole picture is transformed. Pádraig Pearse, one of the leaders of the 1916 Rising, and a strong Gaelic revivalist, made a revealing comment in this regard. Writing in *An Claidheamh Soluis* in 1899, Pearse commented about the work of William Butler Yeats as follows: "Against Mr Yeats personally, we have nothing to object. He is a mere English poet of the third or fourth rank and as such he is harmless. But when he attempts to run an 'Irish' Literary Theatre it is time for him to be crushed" (Ó Buachalla 1980, 9). The quotation marks around the word *Irish* speak volumes for the ideological imperative that underwrites Pearse's opinions. Like Fanon and Viswanathan, he sees the mode of signification as politically of the greatest importance, and clearly, for Pearse, culture is very much a second-level activity that must be at the service of politics and ideology. Pearse, like many others, saw Irishness as defined through the Irish language; the use of the adjective *Irish*, in connection with any mode of communication, whose language of enunciation was English, was an oxymoron, which could not be tolerated. If Yeats wrote in English, then ipso facto, he was an "English poet" in Pearse's terms. This linguistic choice explains the acerbic dismissal of Yeats as someone of little consequence, a dismissal that is undercut, however, by the telling final verb in the quotation because, if Yeats is of such little consequence, then why is there a necessity for him to be "crushed"? Possibly it is because given the importance of literature in the creation of a national symbolic order, a cultural frame of reference necessarily assumed ideological and political importance in the process of naturalizing and normalizing political and cultural agendas.

The key issue here is what we might term the epistemology of the proper adjective, in this case *Irish*. What is the epistemological mode, and, perhaps more important, the ideological mode, of this adjective? Is it a constative term, a descriptor of intrinsic qualities of Irishness that must be ticked off on a checklist before the adjective can legitimately be applied, or is it a performative term, changing function and mode owing to the altered contexts of its use? Heaney is aware that such a debate is not just a literary and aesthetic one; it has broad ramifications within the political sphere as well, because as he puts it in stanza thirty-one of *An Open Letter*: "Right names were the first foundation / For telling truth" (1983b, 13). If contemporary theory is to be believed, then all knowledge is binary and differential in function. According to Ferdinand de Saussure, "The linguistic sign unites, not a thing and a name, but a concept and a sound-image," and he goes on to add that "in language there are only differences" (1959, 66, 120). He means that any definition of the term *Irish* must be relationally contextualized in terms of its binary opposite, and in the context of Irish political, linguistic, and sociocultural history, that opposite is the term *English*. In contemporary theory, this binary is often written as "Irish/English," with the virgule serving as a border, a frontier, and a signifier of difference and connection between the two terms at a visual as well as an epistemological level. However, a lot of contemporary thinking sees this binarist view as necessary but not sufficient in tracing the nature of knowledge.

In an essay entitled "Cessation 1994," Heaney wrote of the effects of questioning the valance and permeability of conceptions of Irishness and Englishness. He recalls the "energy and confidence on the nationalist side," and a concomitant "developing liberalism—as well as the usual obstinacy and reaction—on the unionist side," and goes on to say that the "border was becoming more pervious than it had been." One of the more significant memories of the period that he describes is his own participation in an artistic initiative, and the name given to this enterprise is of particular significance in the context of our discussion. He recalls bringing a program of poems and songs to different places in unionist and nationalist Northern Ireland in May 1968, called "Room to Rhyme," and he goes on to add that he "thought about it again last Wednesday" (2002, 45). The Wednesday in question was April 6, 1994, the day on which the Provisional IRA announced their cease-fire. Heaney has written a lot about representations of the border and about the border as a site of liminality, or what Derrida might describe as *hauntology*, as spectral differences of identity haunt the place of synchronic presence, and of diachronic conflicting histories, and it will be worth examining some of his thinking on this issue, as he attempts to create a broader structure wherein this binarism can be dislodged from its strictures. Heaney's border will be less binary and less binding on constructions of identity.

In an essay entitled "Something to Write Home About," Heaney talks of one of his poems in *The Haw Lantern*, entitled "Terminus," which ruminates on the ideas of borders in an Irish context: both the political border between the Republic of Ireland and Northern Ireland and the more nuanced, localized borders of his own home place. He says that the Latin word *terminus* appears as *tearmann* in many Irish place-names, meaning the glebe land belonging to an abbey or a church and signifying land that was specially marked off for ecclesiastical use. From his early wanderings near his home in Mossbawn, Heaney speaks of knowing that the river Moyola was "a very definite *terminus*, a marker off of one place from another." On one side of this river lay the Protestant identity, those individuals who had come from Scotland to plant Ulster, the Orange Hall, the Protestant church, the estate on which lived the Chichester-Clarkes, one of whom would serve as prime minister of Northern Ireland from 1969 to 1971. On the other side was the parish of Bellaghy, or Ballyscullion, where his father's side of the family, the Heaneys and the Scullions, had lived for generations. The difference here was "palpable," as on this side of the river the dwellings were "thatched rather than slated," their kitchens had "open fires rather than polished stoves," and the houses "stood in the middle of the fields rather than in a terrace" (ibid., 49).

I would propose that the reason for Heaney's more fluid and porous attitude to the issue of borders can be located in this very local context, and perhaps also in the fact that the border was a river, itself fluid by its nature and touching both sides in its progression. In "Terminus" he speaks of the effects of this view of the border as complicating his perspective on political and cultural binaries: "Is it any wonder when I thought / I would have second thoughts?" He goes on to talk about seeing himself as a border figure: "I was the march drain and the march drain's banks / Suffering the limit of each claim" (1987, 4). Here, he is using the word *march* in a more inclusive context, as he explains: "The verb meant to meet at the boundary, to be bordered by, to be matched up to and yet marked off from"; as he puts it, "We were bound by that boundary as well as separated by it." Throughout this essay, Heaney speaks of borders as Janus-faced, citing the Japanese poet Bashó, who thinks it is important to keep the world of beauty in mind during our normal diurnal activities. Heaney sees Bashó as making the mind sound a bit like that Roman image of the god Terminus, "earthbound and present in the here and now, and yet open also to what Bashó calls the everlasting self, the boundlessness of inner as well as outer space" (2002, 51, 52, 53).

At the end of "Terminus," we see exactly this swerve, as Heaney moves on to discuss another border crossing that had macropolitical consequences: "Baronies, parishes met where I was born," and he goes on to imagine himself as the "last earl on horseback" who was still "parleying, in earshot of his peers" (1987, 5).

He is referring to the meeting of Hugh O'Neill and the Earl of Essex in September 1599. O'Neill was in rebellion against the forces of Queen Elizabeth, and Essex had been sent to Ireland with a large army in order to subdue him and bring an end to this rebellion. We would seem to be looking at a classical embodiment of the English-Irish binary opposition here, but like so much else, in Heaney's view of the world, the situation is more complicated than that simple explanation. Both men met in the middle of the river Glyde in County Louth, and their relationship was more complex than one of merely open enmity, as "O'Neill had been at the court of Elizabeth a generation earlier, and his patron in England at that time had been Essex's father, Walter Devereux, the first Earl" (2002, 55).

Heaney envisages this scene as one where each man is caught in a web of conflicting loyalties and contradictory allegiances, a field of force where the oppositional binarisms are complicated by a number of interacting and intersecting forces, and ironically both will suffer failure in their futures, with Essex being executed for treason in the same year and O'Neill losing the pivotal battle of Kinsale two years later in 1601. Heaney feels that the two men were at the "terminus in an extreme sense of that word," as in this situation owing to the "brutality of Power" there could be "no room for two truths." Against the binary brutality of this political and historical meeting, Heaney is willing to place the aesthetic as a counterweighting force that can create a condition "where the longed-for and the actual might be allowed to coincide; a condition where borders are there to be crossed rather than contested" (ibid., 56). In this sense, he would be in agreement with Derrida, who also sees borders as limits but not necessarily as barriers; they both see them as points of contacts that have to be traversed but not destroyed. For both men, borders mark a point of limit and contact between self and other, and there is a need to "cross the border but not to destroy the border" (Derrida 1997, 33). Derrida, like Heaney, argues that language and translation are crucial in this crossing of borders of all sorts, and he speaks of a "procession of one language into another" and the resulting movement of this procession "over the border of another language, into the language of the other" (1987, 77).

This movement between the language of self and other is at the center of his exploration of the encounter in "Terminus." Heaney sees that the pull of opposing forces felt by O'Neill, namely, a loyalty to Essex as a friend with whom he has shared a home and also an enmity toward him and the power that he represents, balanced by his loyalty to a sense of a Gaelic Ireland, is one that is mimetic of Heaney's own position. He is an Irish writer, writing in English, and coming from a province that was riven by the binary oppositions of English-Irish, Protestant-Catholic, Unionist-Nationalist, Loyalist-Republican. He would also be acutely aware of the political ramifications of his own cultural practice—that already cited connection between the RSA and the ISA—as English literature has always had a strong ideological component hidden within its aesthetic imperative.

The teaching of Shakespeare in India, for example, was predicated on the sociocultural dimension of Thomas Macaulay's "Minute on Education," published in 1835, which formed the basis for Lord Harding's policy, in 1844, of giving preference to English speakers for jobs in the government. Macaulay's aim was to create "a class of persons Indian in blood and colour, but English in taste, in opinion, in morals and in intellect" (Macaulay 1995, 430). Regarding this exfoliation of English culture throughout the British Empire, the teaching of the works of Shakespeare was of seminal importance; indeed, the proper name William Shakespeare functions as a transcendental signifier and as synecdoche for all things English and cultured. As Terence Hawkes has put it, "Shakespeare is a powerful ideological weapon" (1985, 43) that is a central feature of the discipline of "English" and by extension, a foundational plank in the imperial Weltanschauung. *The Tempest*, for example, with its routing of the bestial Caliban by an enlightened Prospero, can be seen as an allegory, and a justification, of the colonizing drive and as a locus classicus of the language of empire holding sway over its subjects. However, empires, by their nature, are transient, and even as the name of Shakespeare embodied, in synecdoche, the zenith of the British Empire, so it was through the use of this name that another colonial subject began to invert the language of empire into the empire of language. I refer to another strong precursor of Heaney's: James Joyce.

In the work of Joyce, the language of empire becomes suasively transformed into the empire of language, as the traditionally disempowering language of the other is deconstructed, *avant la lettre*, in a Derridean sense, in order to become a transformational discourse that reempowers the colonized subjects as they see themselves within a symbolic order that is transformed. In *Ulysses*, for example, in the "Cyclops" chapter, there is a picture of an ur-Celtic, archetypal Irish heroic figure. He is sitting in front of a "round tower," and he is described as "broadshouldered deepchested stronglimbed" and as "frankeyed redhaired freely freckled"; in other words, he is a classically Irish figure, from whose belt dangled a row of sea stones, on which were engraved, "with rude yet striking art," the tribal images of Irish "heroes and heroines of antiquity," enumerated as follows: "Cuchulin, Conn of hundred battles, Niall of the nine hostages, Brian of Kincora, the Ardri Malachi, Art MacMurragh, Shane O'Neill, Father John Murphy, Owen Roe, Patrick Sarsfield . . . Goliath, The Village Blacksmith, Captain Boycott, Dante Alighieri, Christopher Columbus, Saint Fursa, Saint Brendan, Charlemagne, Theobald Wolfe Tone, the Mother of the Macabees, the Last of the Mohicans . . . Napoleon Bonaparte, Cleopatra . . . Dark Rosaleen, Patrick W. Shakespeare" (1989, 244). This list of "*Irish*" heroes and heroines of antiquity is an example of a specific form of writing: a "catalog verse," wherein a list of entities is used to show progression, generation, or, in this case, commonality. The genre can be traced back to two of Western civilization's canonical works: the genealogical list in the book of Genesis and the list of Trojan War heroes in Homer's *Iliad*. In *Ulysses*, this catalog is placed in the "Cyclops" chapter, wherein Irish nationalism, in the persona of the monocular "citizen," and, by extension, the essentialist nationalist ideology of Irish identity, is being placed under critique. In this chapter, the opposition between colonizer and colonized in the particular binarism of Ireland-England is fused and blended into a new paradigm, one that is neither one nor the other and at the same time both one and the other, culminating in the fusion of a generically typical Irish first name, "Patrick," with the personified symbol of English literature and culture, "Shakespeare." Thus, the name "Patrick W. Shakespeare" is a strong precursor of Seamus Heaney's own problematization and complication of the age-old Irish-English binary opposition, one that is a type of poetic thinking that has valence in the world of identity politics.

To oversimplify, identity politics can be signified through the concept of the frontier, the outland of the self, which reaches into the concept of the other. At some stage, the frontier will be demarcated by a border, and on one side of this border will be "us," while on the other side will be "them." There has been a significant level of argument that sees literature as an ideological device that gradually turns "them" into lesser versions of "us," what Althusser, Fanon, and Hawkes have seen as an ideological process of enculturation into a hegemonic structure.

However, literature can also have another ideological function, for, as Bhabha notes, "colonial mimicry is the desire for a reformed, recognizable Other, as a *subject of difference that is almost the same, but not quite*" (1994, 86; emphasis in the original). For Bhabha, the whole conception of identity is far more complex than the colonial binarism of self and other would suggest. He sees literature as very much a liminal discourse, which problematizes these simplistic definitions of identity. For him, mimicry is like camouflage: it is not a "harmonisation of repression of difference," but rather "a form of resemblance, that differs from or defends presence by displaying it in part, metonymically" (ibid., 90). For Heaney, too, this sense of difference is central to the epistemology of the literary. Like the construct of Patrick W. Shakespeare, Heaney's own discussion of the role of literature in the construction of identity is equally nuanced and complex.

Writing in *Preoccupations*, Heaney speaks about the books, comics, and magazines that influenced his developing sense of self. He explains that his parents did not want too many English comics being brought into the house, under the grounds that they were "catch-penny," and also that they might be the thin end of the wedge that would lead to the "*Empire News*, *Thompson's Weekly*, *Tit-Bits* and the *News of the World*." He goes on to explain his gradual enculturation into the world of English comics, where he became familiar with all of those "ain'ts" and "cors" and "yoicks" and "blimeys" and became enthralled by the adventures of "Ginger Nutt" and "Smith of the Lower Fourth." He is aware it is a classic process of postcolonial ideology at work and describes the process as an example of "Cultural debilitations!" before explaining how it took "Joyce's *Portrait of the Artist as a Young Man*, and Kavanagh's *The Great Hunger*, to get over that surrender" (ibid., 22–23).

The mention of "surrender" and the exclamation of "Cultural debilitations!" would seem to underscore the ideological value of literature as a tool through which to enculturate the nascent subjectivity of the young reader into the mimicry of the colonizer. Indeed, the use of the exclamation mark, and the nongrammatical structure in "Cultural debilitations!" as a sentence, would seem to doubly reinforce this reading, as Heaney is an assiduous follower of the rules of language, and exclamation marks are quite rare in his writing. There are only thirteen instances of the exclamation mark in *Preoccupations*, and four of them are from direct quotations from other texts, so it is one of only nine others in his book.

Therefore, it would seem that Heaney is adhering to the classic postcolonial associations of literature as a hegemonic ideological tool. Thus, we would seem to be very much in the territory of Althusser's ISAs, as the colonial subject is interpellated into the culture of the colonizer through the works of, if not literature as high culture, then certainly works of literature as popular culture. Nevertheless, there is a difference here, and it is a difference firmly located in the somatic area of knowledge and in the world of lived experience. One of the characters already mentioned was "Ginger Nutt," but the description of this character is a chance for Heaney to insert his own language and to reverse those cultural debilitations of which he spoke. Nutt is "the boy who takes the 'bis-cake,' in south Derry parlance" (ibid., 22).

What is interesting here is the way in which poetry as thinking reverses the hegemonic impulse of popular culture. In this instance, the archetypal mischievous English schoolboy exasperates his authority figures at home and at school by going too far, hence justifying the colloquial expression "taking the biscuit"; this phrase is now appropriated into "south-Derry parlance," as the "biscuit" now becomes the "bis-cake." Here, Heaney is taking on the power of the English language and gradually making a claim for his own version of it through this very particularist appropriation of standard English; it is the power of language to enfranchise as well as to disenfranchise that is at stake here, and Heaney is setting up his own performative irruption of the symbolic laws and contracts of which Lacan speaks.

He is viewing language in a way that "does not limit the living being to its conscious and representative form" (Derrida 2005c, 157), and in this way is setting up different paradigms of connection between words at the level of sound, connections that can also liberate other meanings from these words. For Lacan, the "unconscious, which tells the truth about truth, is structured like a language" (2006, 737), and the truth about Heaney's poetic thinking is that, like Stephen Dedalus in *A Portrait of the Artist as a Young Man*, he "will not serve" (1993, 131) the dictates of the English language. One could see Heaney's "bis-cake/biscuit" opposition as paralleling Joyce's "tundish/funnel" opposition (ibid., 207–8) in the same book, as he carves out a space for his own perspective through the sound of the word as it is spoken in South Derry. The "bis-cake" serves the same poetized function for Heaney as "Patrick W. Shakespeare" does for Joyce: it is taking the English language and making a place for himself in it, just as he will do in his iconic translation of *Beowulf*, where he includes phrases from South Derry, like "so" and "bawn," which we will discuss in chapter 6.

One could see it as an example of Lacan's concept of the *agalma*, already cited in chapter 1, where in Greek culture the *agalma* represented the divine (Nightingale 2004, 87). However, we have already mentioned the connection between the *agalma* and the Muses (Ford 2002, 125) and also the sense that a text "can 'embody' the inner, ethical qualities of its subject in its own unique way" (ibid., 238). I would argue that the "bis-cake" is the first example of such an ethical force of language in Heaney's work, as he looks to the unconscious aspects of language, the sound of words as enunciated by specific people in a very specific part of Ireland, which can then be seen to have a "moral and ethical force" (Heaney 1988, 40). In this sense, he is also at one with Lacan who has also seen the unconscious as, at bottom, "ethical" (1977, 33). To obtain a true sense of the ethical dimensions of knowledge, the unconscious must be involved in the mode of inquiry. Heaney, as we have already seen in his comments on Ana Swir, suggests that poetic language, and poetic thinking, is a way of expressing the individual "subconscious and the collective subconscious" (1988, 107), and I would contend that it is the analysis and exploration of this epistemological aspect of poetry that are at the core of Heaney's project of aesthetic thinking.

Thus, Heaney forces the English language to accommodate his voice, as opposed to being rendered voiceless by the hegemonic imperial structures of that language. His is a sophisticated voice, ensuring that the repressed of colonization returns to telling effect in the literature of the colonizer in a new linguistic structure of meaning. He takes his involvement with the "tradition of the English lyric" as a given, but adopts a transformative perspective on this involvement by wanting to make the English lyric eat "stuff that it has never eaten before," and he is explicit in his descriptions of the nature of this "stuff," namely, "all the messy and, it would seem, incomprehensible obsessions in the North, and make it still an English lyric" (Cooke 1973). His feeling is that the lyric cannot be like an unchanging vessel, which is able to interact with different traditions and remain unchanged; rather, is it like the paint used to decorate such artifacts, taking on the colors and hues of the local pigmentation and becoming changed, but still recognizable. It is what Heaney calls an "act of comprehension and synthesis" (ibid.). This act of comprehension and synthesis refers overtly to the clash of the two traditions, but it also refers to notions of language and consciousness, as he wants to make the English lyric eat the messy obsessions of the North but still remain an English lyric. By accessing the sense of somatic knowledge that we see in his use of the word *eat*, he is looking for a synthesis of conscious and unconscious language as well, as it is only such a synthesis that will allow for full comprehension of the complexities of the situation. I would agree with Shane-Alcobia Murphy's view that "Heaney rids himself of his inferiority complex as regards his own language and accepts that he can be adept at his own dialect" (2006, 224).

I would contend that the example of such dialect here involves the South Derry pronunciation of *bis-cake* acting as a deconstructive lever, which will dislodge the ideological primness of the English lyric by forcing it to eat the "messy stuff" of instinct and feeling. I would further propose that this "messy stuff" symbolizes the unconscious and the inchoate that are at the core of poetic thinking. It allows the symbolization of those repressed and occluded aspects of life and culture without which knowledge can be anemic and lacking in any real sense of purchase. Heaney, in his "bis-cake" reference, is fusing poetic thought with philosophy in a manner that parallels the work of Agamben, who has noted that he "began by writing poems, but I don't believe I ever renounced that. On the contrary, it was as if I didn't really begin to write poems until philosophy entered my life" (de la Durantaye 2009, 61). It could be said that the "bis-cake/biscuit" couple is an example of what occurs when the ordinary is looked at from a different perspective, when, in other words, one looks awry or slant.

This looking awry is the first such instance in his work, and it is a trope that will be repeated right up to his emblematic choice of the first word of his translation of *Beowulf.* However, there is a strong tradition in his work of broadening the frontiers of language in order to relocate the Irish-English sociopolitical and linguistic binary in a more amenable context. In a manner redolent of Bloom's ideas of influence, Heaney looks for solutions to the problems of linguistic colonization in other precursors. Writing in the emblematically entitled "Tradition and an Individual Talent," about Scottish poet Hugh MacDiarmid, Heaney visits the return of the repressed in the case of one aspect of language. There is a strong influential connection between Eliot and Heaney, so the title of this essay is far from random or accidental. Intertextually referencing Eliot's "Tradition and the Individual Talent," Heaney pluralizes the discussion from "the" individual talent to "an" individual talent, thereby suggesting that such talents can be plural, and, by extension, so can their constituting traditions. Eliot, adducing what he termed the historical sense, set out a very contemporary idea of how art affects the audience by noting that each new work modified the perception of the existing ones in the minds of readers and that, essentially, it is the relationship between the tradition and the individual talent that ascribes to a position within that tradition: "The existing monuments form an ideal order among themselves, which is modified by the introduction of the new (the really new) work of art among them." Eliot here is speaking of a European and English high cultural canon, "the mind of Europe" (1920, 44, 46). He is writing about European mainstream culture from an aesthetic perspective, and the politics of the text are not really a feature of his discourse. The somatic, ideological, and situated condition of those individuals in whose minds the order of tradition is modified by this genuinely new text is not a matter of concern for him.

Given the Pan-European perspective, with its examples from Dante and Homer, it might seem odd that Heaney would refer to this essay in a consideration of Hugh MacDiarmid, who wrote in a very culture-specific, local discourse. I would suggest, however, that it is typical of Heaney's poetizing logic that he places a writer who is immersed in dialect, in the shadow of Eliot, and in comparison with Wordsworth in the opening lines of the essay in a form of litotes. Heaney is deliberately placing MacDiarmid in contradistinction to the canonical figures of Wordsworth and Eliot in order to open the frontiers of that canon and to pluralize Eliot's sense of tradition by examining the modality of expression used by MacDiarmid, a modality that is not part of a received Pan-European sense of tradition, but might, like the "bis-cake," transform the existing tradition.

Heaney sees the medium as very much part of the message. The conscious and unconscious dimensions of language are at the core of his own sense of aesthetic thinking, and so the specific dialect of MacDiarmid is reminiscent of the "bis-cake" and of the messy matter of Northern Ireland, which he wants the English lyric to ingest.

He sees MacDiarmid's project as a reactive one, noting that he wrote from an "enervating cultural situation" in which he saw any sense of a unique Scottish civilization as being etiolated by the influence of English language and culture. His use of "Lallans, his poetic Scots language" (Heaney 1980, 195), as exemplified above, would seem to place him in the role of a minor poet, as someone outside of any formal canonical tradition, but, interestingly, Heaney sees this choice of language as placing MacDiarmid in a broader cultural ambit. It is part of that synthesis of which he spoke earlier and of the sense of accessing aspects of the unconscious.

From Heaney's perspective, this synthesis points to a sense of an uncertainty about language in MacDiarmid's work, which is peculiar not just to MacDiarmid but also to others who write generally in English, but in a form of English that is at variance with "standard English utterance and attitudes." He goes on to add that it can be a problem of style for Americans, West Indians, Indians, Scots, and Irish (ibid., 196). As Heaney puts it, such self-consciousness is a necessary part of poetic thinking, as it is this self-consciousness that delves into a broader cultural unconscious that is referred to in the submerged Yeatsian quotation of "the foul rag and bone shop of the heart." This quotation comes from the late poem "The Circus Animals' Desertion" (1965, 357) and is a further node in the intertextual constellation within which the work of MacDiarmid is being discussed. His work is now being read slant, through the hauntological framework of Eliot, Joyce, and Yeats, probably the three most important figures in the literary modernist movement and writers who are seen as metonyms of a European high culture.

To read the idiosyncratic language of MacDiarmid in this light is to attempt to deconstruct the certainties that pervade Eliot's writings about the evolving of a singular European tradition. However, Heaney realizes that looking at it from the perspective of someone who is linguistically situated outside of this tradition, such certainties are far from ensured, and the function of poetic thinking is to render this uncertainty real in the world of ideas, a project that has strong affinities with the writings of Heidegger. As we have seen, for

Heidegger, all poetizing "is in its ground a thinking. The poetizing essence of thinking preserves the sway of the truth of Being" (1975a, 19). MacDiarmid's twisting of the English language so that it could take the shape and dialect of his home is part of a process whereby the literary refuses to be cowed by the political. Just as English power colonized Scotland as it did Ireland, so Scottish poetry will not change its voice to attune itself to an English linguistic discourse of colonization. No matter what cultural and educational ISAs are operative in a society, literature, and specifically poetry, is still able to enunciate emancipatory voices of counterhegemonic resistance; it can make the conception of a single literary tradition eat the stuff of the local and the actual, but the process does not stop there.

Instead, Heaney, through his perspective on Lallans and, specifically, through his reading of this dialect in the context of the high culture of modernism, inserts the same sort of wedge that he has done in his "bis-cake" reference and in his sense of making the English lyric eat the messy stuff of Northern Ireland, and he is also presaging what he will do in his highly significant translator's introduction to *Beowulf*. He is inserting the wedge of a lived sense of real-world home, as embodied by the dialect pronunciation of the spoken word in the language of the self, and of the colonized, into the hegemonic world language of the standard English of the colonizing other; instead of allowing himself to be culturally disenfranchised, he is instead becoming culturally creative and setting up his own views on how home can be enunciated in the language of the self that can, at the same time, become the language of the other. And in a manner that is specific to this discourse, poetry is capable of infiltrating and transforming the language of the other in order to make it eat the messy, local enunciations of the language of the self and not completely digest them, but instead alter itself to accommodate them. The nobility of poetry, says Wallace Stevens, "is a violence from within that protects us from a violence without. It is the imagination pressing back against the pressure of reality" (Heaney 1995b, 1), and this pressing can change the shape of that reality, which is precisely what Heaney is doing by inserting MacDiarmid into this very unusual version of a modernist canon. Just as MacDiarmid is "an" individual talent, which suggests that there can be many more such talents, so, by implication, there can be other versions of "tradition," and this notion is at the core of Heaney's own poetic thinking on the concept of the frontier. Thus, cultural debilitations become cultural invigorations, and ultimately cultural transformations as the unconscious pieties of home find some measure of expression in the language of the other—the *Unheimlich* invades the *Heimlich*.

It is no accident that in all of these frontier engagements, impressions of home and selfhood are foregrounded. Thus, *bis-cake* is the language of South Derry, the English lyric is being made to eat the "messy and it would seem, incomprehensible obsessions in the North" (Cooke 1973), while Lallans is based on the language of a specific part of Scotland. This kind of poetic thinking allows the voices of home to be heard in the language of power, and it disarticulates the hegemonic certainties of that language in the process. As already noted, this perspective is very much in tune with the Heideggerian idea that poetizing is thinking, because it takes into account the materiality and the differences inherent in language and in the performing of language and accords with his view that the "thinker of first rank must accomplish, a thinking which has all the purity and thickness and solidity of poetry" (1971, xi–xii). Heaney's analysis of MacDiarmid stresses the power of his dwelling in a specific dialect and notes the power of that dialect to press against the language of the normative center. Certainly, the changes to grammatology and orthography that are produced by a spoken dialect or accent thicken the language by grounding it in a locality, and for Heaney, as for Heidegger, this thickening has a strong philosophical charge concerning any serious thinking about poetry and its role as a constituting or emancipatory discourse.

However, it would be an error, and a gross oversimplification of Heaney's poetizing thought, to see these examples as synecdochic of a willed and easy act of linguistic repossession. In his essay "John Clare's Prog," in *The Redress of Poetry*, "one of his most important explorations and affirmations of the validity of local culture for contemporary poetry" (Russell 2014, 314), Heaney makes it clear that the hegemonic power of Standard English is not so easily cast to one side. Having explained the etymology of *prog* as "gain or profit in a bargain; booty," Heaney immediately seems to digress, as he writes about his own early poem "Follower," which appeared in *Death of a Naturalist*. He quotes the first line, "My father worked with a horse-plough," and goes on to note that while this line may seem "unremarkable," it was the result of some revision, as his original line was "My father *wrought* with a horse-plough." This verb was in common use in Heaney's South Derry vernacular; it denoted working with tools and connoted a sense of wholehearted commitment to the task. As Heaney observes, the word "implied solidarity with speakers of the South Derry vernacular and a readiness to stand one's linguistic ground" (1995b, 63); in short, it is a proleptic version of the "bis-cake," the messy stuff of the North, and the Lallans dialect of MacDiarmid. Heaney goes on to rhetorically wonder why he made that revision and to ask why he used the "more pallid and expected 'worked,'" and he provides the answer that it was because he "thought twice," and he notes that thinking twice about a local usage means that the writer has already been, to some degree, "displaced" from such a usage and has internalized some aspects of the "internal censor" of normative discourse: "You have been translated from the land of unselfconsciousness to the suburbs of the *mot juste*." Rankin Russell sees it as another example of Heaney's lifelong struggle to "balance the pull of his childhood regional culture and dialect with the equal allure of his adopted academic culture" (2014, 314). Heaney sees Joyce as one of the rare breed of writer who was as at home in his "hearth speech" as he was in his "acquired language," but notes that such Joycean "multivocal proficiency is as far beyond most writers as unbroken residence within the first idiom of a hermetically sealed, univocal home place" (1995b, 63–64).

The use of rational thought is interesting here, as it would seem to enact the very process of the Althusserian ISAs discussed earlier. To think within the cognitive and conscious norms of the voices of education and culture is to desire to be in league with, and commended by, that linguistic censor of which Heaney speaks and which Althusser sees as an ideological apparatus. This censor is both educational and cultural, for, as Althusser notes, culture "is the ordinary name for the Marxist concept of the *ideological*," while he sees education as the apparatus that has "replaced in its functions the previously dominant ideological State apparatus, the Church" (2001, 242, 154). The power of this censor is strong, but a deep or thickened version of language that is to be found in poetry will allow the frontiers of the "suburbs of the *mot juste*" to be extended and broadened so as to include the local pieties of home and the unconscious. The intersection and dialectical interaction of hearth speech and acquired language are at the core of Heaney's aesthetic thinking and of his epistemology of poetry. The skill of his writing can make it seem an easy process, but the prog, the gain or profit in this bargain between self-conscious and unself-conscious usage, is not easily achieved; however, it is worthwhile, and it definitely is at the core of Heaney's poetizing.

We have already noted Heidegger's approval of the notion that words voice the world and our connection to the other, and Heaney would agree with the power and transformative potential of the spoken word, especially with respect to the world-disclosing power of language. Indeed, in *Preoccupations*, Heaney quotes poems that foreground the importance of *breath* twenty times, using the word twenty-one times in total. His own use of the term underlines its importance for him. He is speaking of the work of Osip Mandelstam and notes that his early poems breathe in the air of the "whole European literary tradition" and exhale with "a tang of Russian" (1980, 218). Like Heidegger, breath is used as an interanimating force, which somehow fuses the human voice with language. The act of saying the language of the other in one's own voice conveys a power of personal ownership that can deconstruct the colonial hegemonic overtones of the English language. We have seen evidence of this need to inhabit the language of the colonizer on an individual basis, but now we turn to a more overt collective example of this process of redefining the frontiers of language. In this respect, there is also an echo of the thinking of Adorno in Heaney's view, as Adorno has spoken about a moment "of unself-consciousness" wherein the subject "submerges itself in language" and wherein language speaks "not as something alien to the subject, but as the subject's own voice" (Adorno and Tiedemann 1991, 1:44).

Heidegger also sees art as the discourse that reveals the truth, and truth, "as the clearing and concealing of what is, happens in being composed, as a poet composes a poem" (1971, 70). There are parallels with this view of the revelatory power of poetry in Heaney's eponymous essay in *The Redress of Poetry*, where he looks at the frontier between poetry as art and poetry as some form of political act with a force, or a sense of truth revelation, in the real world. Heaney, as ever, is patrolling the frontier of poetry, seeing it as being full of "self-delighting inventiveness," but at the same time as being part of a sociocultural context of "politically approved themes, post-colonial backlash and 'silence-breaking' writing of all kinds" (1995b, 5). He is keen to stress the integrity of both positions and uses the term *redress* as a syncretic vehicle through which to express this duality, a duality that parallels Heidegger's sense of art as the "letting happen of the advent of the truth of what is, is, as such, essentially poetry" (1971, 70). He stresses that care needs to be taken so that while using poetry as an "agent for proclaiming and correcting injustices," we do not in any way neglect the other frontier, which is "*poetry as poetry*" (1995b, 5, 6; emphasis in the original). Thus, the frontier between the aesthetic and the aesthetico-political teleology of poetry is one in constant need of patrolling and also one wherein the relationship between the tradition, or traditions, and the individual needs to be monitored. If, as Lyotard has suggested, the metanarratives of culture are now working at a societally unconscious level, then any individual writer needs to engage with the hegemonic metanarratives of colonization and language if he or she is to achieve some form of emancipation from them: "There is a mutual susceptibility between the formation of a new tradition and the self-fashioning of individual talent" (ibid., 6). Once again, we see the interaction of the individual with tradition, and, as ever with

Heaney, there is an interrogative dimension to this process, as the new writing will be part of a new form of tradition. The individual writer has the power to shape and change that tradition by looking to a new unconscious metanarrative, as embodied by *bis-cake*, the messy stuff of the North, and the Lallans dialect.

Nonetheless, in the cases of individual talents who are attempting to alter the traditions from which they are constituted, the situation becomes more fraught and the frontiers more difficult to define and demarcate. Even as writers and thinkers rebel against the hegemonic tradition, it has, in a way, already triumphed, because these writers "will have internalized the norms and forms of the tradition from which they wish to secede." To hark back to our earlier discussion of the postcolonial problematic, whether people write in Anglo-Irish, or Afro-English, or Lallans, writers of "nation languages" have always been "predisposed to accommodate themselves to the consciousness which subjugated them" (ibid., 6–7), and we saw this disposition in action in the change from *wrought* to *worked* in "Follower." However, poetizing thought will always resist such emblematic binaries and walled frontiers; such aesthetic thinking on these issues is far more fluid. For Heaney, the language of the self is always already haunted from within by the language of the other, and seemingly fixed frontiers turn out to be surprisingly fluid. It requires that anamorphic perspective that looks at language awry, or slant, to locate these occluded alterities.

I use the term *haunted* deliberately, as it refers to Derrida's concept of *hauntology*, which is first discussed in *Specters of Marx*, in answer to his question "*What* is a ghost?" (1994, 10), where ghostly hauntings are seen as traces of possible alternative meanings. Derrida's spectrality involves acknowledging the other that haunts the self; it involves acknowledging the possibility that the *h* in *hauntology* is a hovering presence over the certainties of ontology, and, above all, it is predicated on the future. Speaking both of the ghost in *Hamlet* and the ghost that haunts Marx's *Communist Manifesto* (where the first noun is *specter*), he makes the point that, at bottom, "the specter is the future, it is always to come, it presents itself only as that which could come or come back" (ibid., 39). I would maintain that there are strong similarities between the haunting of *biscuit* by *bis-cake*, the haunting of the canon by Lallans, and the haunting of the English lyric by the mess of the actual Irish experience and the hauntological perspective of Derrida. Both writers see the relationship between different manifestations of selfhood and alterity as porous and fluid and as always already shot through with aspects of each other, whether it is in the context of the relationship between hegemonic and resistant aspects of language or between the linguistic conscious and the linguistic unconscious. In Heaney's aesthetic thinking, the relationship between English as a language of oppression and English as a language of expression is a complex and fraught one, which is further complicated by the frontier between the written *biscuit* and the spoken *bis-cake.*

In the context of our discussions of local pronunciation as a way of asserting some form of ownership over a hegemonic language, it is interesting to note that phonetically, the term *hauntology* is similar to the pronunciation of the French word *ontologie*, which means that presence and absence are fused together in sound. This point is significant, as it allows for self and other to haunt each other in the area of language, and the frontiers here are indecipherable and impossible to demarcate. Just as the sound of the word *omphalos* and the sound of the water from the pump acted as an associative connection at the level of meaning in Heaney's writing, as did the punning *res-ing* of the stakes discussed earlier, so the same process can be seen at work for Derrida in the connection between the sounds of *hauntology* and *ontologie.* Both writers are using the connections of the signifier to create connections at the level of the signified, the level of meaning: the sound and the rhyme affect the signification, which is the core of poetized thinking. The same is true of Derrida's neologism *différance*, which puns on the double meaning of *differ* and *defer*, as well as on the fact that in French, the difference between *différence* and *différance* is only obvious in writing and not in speech. Derrida, speaking of this term, calls it, in language that has traces of Adorno's thinking, a "non-concept" in that it "cannot be defined in terms of oppositional predicates." Hence, as Derrida explained to Richard Kearney in an interview, it is "neither *this* nor *that*; but rather this *and* that (e.g. the act of differing and of deferring) without being reducible to a dialectical logic either" (1995b, 161).

For Derrida, the relationship between language and meaning will always be differential and never just the simplified signifier-signified conflation that is often assumed. In addition, the relationship between a colonized speaker of English and the traditional langue of English will be equally problematic. Derrida argues that there is "no subject who is agent, author, and master of *différance*, who eventually and empirically would be overtaken by *différance*" (Derrida and Weber 1995, 28), and I would feel that Heaney is of the same mind. For Derrida, "*différance* is literally neither a word nor a concept," and, in a parallel relationship with the *hauntology-ontologie* binary, which could only be discerned through writing, so "this graphic difference" (*a* instead of *e*), remains "purely graphic: it is read, or it is written, but it cannot be heard. It cannot be apprehended in speech" (Derrida 1982, 3).

I would contend that this nonconcept is a fitting term through which to explain Heaney's own sense of the linguistic complexity between the relationships of the English language as a vehicle of oppression or expression or both: for him it is both/and, not either/or; it is liberating and constricting at the same time. In the *bis-cake/biscuit* opposition, we can see the parallels with the oppositions, or frontiers, between *hauntology/ontologie* and *difference/différance*, as in both the difference between speech and writing is seen as being significant with respect to meaning. For Derrida, this view of language is radical and transformative, as it refers to an order that "resists the opposition, one of the founding oppositions of philosophy, between the sensible and the intelligible." This resistance is brought about by "a movement of *différance* (with an a) between two differences or two letters, a *différance* which belongs neither to the voice nor to writing in the usual sense," but is located "*between* speech and writing, and beyond the tranquil familiarity which links us to one and the other, occasionally reassuring us in our illusion that they are two" (ibid., 5). I would argue for the similarity of their respective positions because both men shared the perspective of speaking in the language of the colonizer. Just as Heaney felt the power of tradition, making him change *wrought* to *worked*, so too Derrida felt a related normative linguistic pressure. While living in the midst of an Arabic culture, Derrida was raised in a monolingual Francophone milieu. Hence, French was his only language. However, in the "culture of the French in Algeria and in the Jewish community of the French in Algeria," he points out that "France was not Algeria. . . . [T]he authority of the French language was elsewhere" (Derrida and Weber 1995, 120).

The similarities with Heaney's earlier points about being part of a culture, yet not part of it, are marked. Derrida's conceptions of *différance*, and his breaking down of seeming unities and totalities, has much in common with Heaney's view of poetry as the articulation of different forces within some form of structure that can reveal more aspects of the self to the self. In the interview just cited, Derrida says that, despite speaking French and being immersed in French literature and culture, "the Frenchman of France was an other" (ibid., 204). Much of his writing stresses this feeling of being at home, yet not at home, in French culture. In *The Other Heading*, he speaks of himself as someone "not quite European by birth," who now considers himself to be "a sort of over-acculturated, over-colonized European hybrid"; he sees his cultural identity as "not only European, it is not identical to itself" (1992, 7, 82–83). As we have seen, this sense of being both at home and ill at ease in a language is all too familiar to Heaney, who has spoken of retaining a sense of himself "as Irish in a province that insists it is British" and goes on to further underscore his sense of difference as he makes the point that while he speaks and writes in English, and publishes in London, he lives "off another hump as well" (1980, 35, 34).

For both writers, oppression and expression are the opposite sides of a frontier that is permeable and fluid. Heaney realizes that in any political movement toward liberation, it will be necessary to deny the "normative authority of the dominant language or literary tradition," and he traces this process in the career of Thomas MacDonagh, professor of English at the Royal University in Dublin, whose book *Literature in Ireland* was "published in 1916, the very year he was executed as one of the leaders of the Easter Rising." MacDonagh therefore was involved in armed insurrection against the British Empire and was executed for this act, and thus he embodies the resistance to colonization with which this chapter began, yet he was also an expert on the English lyric, "to the extent of having written a book on the metrics of Thomas Campion." The irony of someone who is expert on the cultural and linguistic inheritance of England taking up arms against the political entity that was England is not lost on Heaney, as the Irish relationship with the language and literature of England has always been complex, complicated, and highly nuanced. Heaney compares him to Joyce, who, despite his postcolonial creation of Patrick W. Shakespeare, was also fascinated by "the songs and airs of the Elizabethans" (1995b, 7).

Heaney uses both men as examples of the frontier that needs to be crossed and recrossed if transformation is to be achieved through language. Both MacDonagh and Joyce see no need to deny the power of language, even as they resist, in their very different ways, the sociopolitical hegemonic imperative of that language. Both men remind us that the integrity of the poetic word is not to be "impugned just because at any given moment it happens to be a refraction of some discredited cultural or political system" (ibid.). Of course, it is the thick language of poetry that allows for such investigations of the frontiers of writing, frontiers that traverse, but are never coterminous with, the frontiers of politics. For MacDonagh and Joyce, the English lyric still held an attraction, even as they fought against the political system that could be seen as sponsoring that poetic tradition.

Heaney feels that this frontier can be further deconstructed by looking at how the ideology attached to the signifier "English" can be unpacked by the voices and dialects that have come together to constitute "English." Rather than seeing it as a closed structure into which the micronarratives of local identity must be homogenized and attenuated, he sees it as a fluid structure whose frontiers can be permeated by those very voices, and in his reading of *The Penguin Book of English Pastoral Verse*, Heaney enacts this process of poetic emancipation in the face of the political and hegemonic. What is set out as *The Penguin Book of English Pastoral Verse*, with all the canonical, imperial, and culturally homogenous connotations that are implied by the proper adjective *English*, becomes something different when placed in a dialectical relationship with the classical antecedents to which Heaney alludes in his reading. Such external influences, in this case, far from attenuating the response to the lyrical impulse of the pastoral, instead thicken our reading of these works by complicating and interrogating how "English" this genre actually is. Heaney reads the poems in this book from a "slant" perspective in light of the different tradition that preceded them and from which they derive much of their formal structure. By looking at the connections between these poems in the book and the poems that preceded them, Heaney demonstrates the debt owed by the English language to Latin and French, to Latin and French in translation, to the classical pastoral convention and the English version of it, and, finally, to the texts that are present in the book and those enabling translations from the classics, which are absent.

This complex interrogation of the categories of text and context calls to mind a parallel interrogation in the work of Derrida who, in *Limited Inc.*, has noted that "nothing exists outside context" and that, consequently, the "outside penetrates and thus determines the inside" (1988, 152, 153). Derrida has made a related point in *Positions*, where he speaks of how each seemingly simple term is marked by the trace of other terms, so that the "presumed interiority of meaning" is "worked on by its own exteriority. It is always already carried outside itself" (Derrida, Bass, and Ronse 1981, 33). Heaney's project will correspondingly demonstrate a view of poetry that stresses the transformative and interpenetrative mode of action through which poetry achieves its ends of breaking down opposed binary positions. The title of Heaney's discussion, "In the Country of Convention," stresses this transformation, as it is the conventions that shape the genre, and he will look at the arbitrary nature of some of these conventions and will examine how changes in them will ultimately transform the genre itself.

Much of the poetry shares the conception of England as some form of "after-image of Augustan Rome" (Heaney 1980, 178), but by reading against the grain, or awry, Heaney offers a different perspective and a different tradition through which to view the poetry. He allows the classical context to imbricate his reading of the English texts in the book, and thus both present text and absent context permeate and interinanimate each other in a fuller exploration of the genre in the essay than is given in the book itself. Heaney's reading can be seen, in the terminology of Mikhail Bakhtin, as heteroglossic, in that different voices and different languages are allowed to confront each other and achieve some kind of "dynamic interaction, or dialogisation" (Bakhtin and Holquist 1981, 263). He pluralizes the title of the essay so that the "country of convention" of the title of the essay opens its borders to other countries, other languages, and other literary conventions and traditions.

Just as Heaney's reading of this book sees text and context interpenetrate each other, so, by implication, the genre of English pastoral has also set text and context in a dialectical relationship, a relationship that ultimately calls into question the frontiers of the English poetic canon as such. Heaney's reading of conventionality has become unconventional in its dislocation of the ground on which the epistemological premises of the book are based. In this reading, there is an obvious similarity with a reading by Derrida of Shelley's *The Triumph of Life*. Here, Derrida also questions the borderlines of a text, suggesting that a text is no longer "a finished corpus of writing, some content enclosed in a book or its margins, but a differential network, a fabric of traces referring endlessly to something other than itself, to other differential traces" (1987, 84). This teasing out of a fabric of traces is precisely the process of reading undertaken by Heaney in this essay; he takes the assumptions imposed by the title and format of the book and points to the attenuations of response that the selection criteria impose. The "Englishness" of the pastoral convention here is gradually deconstructed as its borders are teased open and are shown to contain a structure that is very dependent on other languages, other traditions, and other cultures—on cross-border traffic, in other words.

He questions whether the editors' "brisk dismissal" of the further possibilities of pastoral are well founded and goes on to suggest valid reasons for the inclusion of other writers—Edward Thomas, Hugh MacDiarmid, David Jones, A. E. Houseman—and also wonders about Louis MacNeice's eclogues, all of which he sees as enabling aspects of the genre (1980, 180). Finally, he further extends the limits of his critique by multiplying some "strokes and lines" that figure as political borders and asks whether such seminal works as Synge's *Aran Islands* (pastoral), Patrick Kavanagh's *The Great Hunger* (antipastoral), and John Montague's *The Rough Field* should not be included in the definition, before finishing the essay by wondering whether these works could and should be termed "frontier pastoral" (ibid.). Conceptually, this sense of a frontier has resonances with Derrida's idea of the fluid and permeable borderlines of a text: both thinkers stress the value of writing in breaking down rigid lines of demarcation and, instead, suggesting that writing in general, and poetry in particular, exerts a deconstructive leverage over such positions of fixity.

The concept of "frontier pastoral" functions here as both a borderline of the anthology and at the same time a point of possibility that will allow the "English" pastoral as genre to develop. In a further expansion of these limits, this development would necessitate an ongoing problematization of the epistemology of Englishness in the title, as now some form of "Irishness" would be included. Of course, as Heaney has already noted, the final poem in the anthology is Yeats's "Ancestral Houses" (ibid., 177), so there has already been a crossing of the "frontier pastoral." It becomes clear, then, that his reading of the conventions of the pastoral is quite unconventional in its implications and in its reading practice. I will argue that such transgressive and transgenerative crossings of frontiers are a central feature in Heaney's aesthetic thinking. Heaney's writing is very close to Derrida's in this regard, as he talks about borders in terms of permeability, noting that no context is "saturatable any more" and that "no border is guaranteed, inside or out" (Derrida 1987, 78). Heaney's probing of this border is another example of his sourcing of a place for the voice of his own identity, as well as attempting to expand the frontiers of what had hitherto been seen as a hegemonic.

Revisiting the idea of the English pastoral in a lecture for the Royal Irish Academy, in 2003, Heaney spoke of how the pastoral was a far more complex genre than it was given credit for by Barrell and Bull, the editors of this anthology, noting that they seem to see the pastoral as "at base, a false vision," positing a simplistic, unhistorical relationship between different landowning classes (Barrell and Bull 1974, 4). His own view, however, is that pastoral as genre (and he will write eclogues himself in *Electric Light*) is far more nuanced. For him, the literary is "one of the methods human beings have devised for getting at reality," and in a manner that recalls his idea of telling the truth slant, he adds that literature's diversions are not to be taken as "deceptions but as roads less travelled by where the country we thought we knew is seen again in a new and revealing light" (2003, 3). This poetizing view of pastoral, with its slant acknowledgment of Robert Frost as a seminal influence, sees the way in which it connects with a lived material experience of the land, and it also shows how relationships of ownership of place and land can always be seen in different lights, something that is significant in this discussion.

Such conceptions of hegemonic possession and ownership are at the core of another of Heaney's interventions into the role of poetry and politics in a postcolonial context. Poetry, which is created within a language of the other, can become a transforming discourse, which can in turn change the role and function of that other. As Maurice Blanchot observes, art embodies this transformative potential, as in the actual world things are "*transformed* into objects in order to be grasped, utilized" and more fully understood. However, in imaginary space, things are "*transformed* into that which cannot be grasped. Out of use, beyond wear, they are not in our possession but are the movement of dispossession which releases us both from them and from ourselves" (1982, 131; emphasis in the original). Blanchot, like Heaney, sees part of the function of art as the transformation of the given perception of reality. The function of imaginary space, a concept akin to Heaney's field of force, is the transformation of the actual and the creation of an alternative paradigm of truth and integration. It is in the context of such a transformation of the actual that Heaney's *An Open Letter* was written.

An Open Letter, published by Field Day, was written in response to the poet's inclusion in Blake Morrison and Andrew Motion's *The Penguin Book of Contemporary British Poetry* (1982), and begins by stating that his "anxious muse" has to refuse "the adjective." Here, it would seem, we have the victimized postcolonial striking for freedom from a constituted position of victimhood and enforced co-option. Having thus set out his stall, he seems to follow a binary oppositional course by beginning, stressing the Irish-British opposition, as "*Hibernia*" is where the "Gaels / Made a last stand" (1983b, 7). Here it would seem that Heaney is voicing the binary postcolonial perspective of a "simple history lesson" of colonizer and colonized, and in doing so he would be in good company. The perspective, which suggests that Ireland *is* part of the postcolonial paradigm, is shared by a number of contemporary texts, such as David Lloyd's *Anomalous States: Irish Writing and the Postcolonial Moment*. While the title points out the anomalous nature of the Irish situation, the subtitle underlines the essentially postcolonial nature of Ireland. Lloyd makes the point that he has become increasingly aware of the theoretical value of other postcolonial locations "in all their disjunctions and analogies with one another, to find ways in which to comprehend the apparent peculiarities of Irish cultural history," and he has found the "work of Indian 'subaltern' historians and the cultural struggles of American minorities" to be particularly relevant (1993, 2). For Lloyd, the similarities between the Irish experience and the experience of other colonies are clear. Given the historical framework adduced earlier in this discussion, it seems obvious that, to quote Homi Bhabha, the Irish question has "been reposed as a *postcolonial* problem" (1994, 229).

Similarly, Declan Kiberd, in his *Inventing Ireland*, speaks of the colonialist crime, in an Irish context, as the "violation of the traditional community" (1997, 292), a process that Ania Loomba sees as paradigmatic of the colonial enterprise in general. As she explains, the process of "forming a community" in a new land necessarily means the "unforming or re-forming of the communities that existed there already" (1998, 2). Edward Said also observes that Yeats, while almost completely assimilated into the canons of "modern English Literature" and "European high modernism," can nevertheless also be seen as belonging to the tradition of "the colonial world ruled by European imperialism" (1990, 69). Said's essay places Yeats as a postcolonial poet and hence, through synecdoche, places Ireland within the postcolonial ambit. Finally, in his introduction to *Nationalism, Colonialism, and Literature*, Seamus Deane makes the point that colonialism is a process of "radical dispossession" and that a colonized people are often left without a specific history and even, "as in Ireland and other cases, without a specific language" (1990, 10).

Clearly, Ireland provides an unusual case within the paradigm of postcolonial studies, in that it is deemed as being both postcolonial and nonpostcolonial at the same time. The reasons for this anomaly are interesting: Ireland does not fit the usual typology of a third world country being colonized by a first world one, nor does it fit into the European/non-European binarism, which is so often the sine qua non of colonization. At a further level, there is the fact that the Irish are white and thus racially similar to their colonizers, although there was a strong movement in parts of the Victorian British media to compare the Irish to various nonwhite races (L. Curtis 1968, 1971). These points, however, indicate a deeper problem at the level of the epistemological structure of the postcolonial paradigm, and this problem has been rehearsed in Abdul JanMohamed's seminal article, "The Economy of the Manichean Allegory: The Function of Racial Difference in Colonialist Literature."

JanMohamed's thesis is that colonial literature subverts "the traditional dialectic of self and Other" and sets up a fetishized "nondialectical fixed opposition between the self and the native"; the result is what is constantly reinforced here is the "homogeneity of his [*sic*] own group" (1995, 18, 19). The colonial perspective initiates and perpetuates this sense of an absolute homogeneity of races, hence the title of JanMohamed's article, referring to the third-century Persian cult representing God and Satan as locked in conflict and completely separate. Macaulay's idea of a separate class of Indians who would be English in all but racial composition, which we noted at the beginning of this chapter, would illustrate this point. Even as Macaulay attempts a form of interaction between the two, both races are strictly separated. JanMohamed's point is well taken: differences of race, language, religion, and culture were all used to reinforce the colonizer's sense of superiority to the colonized.

However, one could turn this argument around and make the equally valid point that much postcolonial writing takes this Manichaean allegory and merely inverts it, casting the colonizer as separate and other, while the colonized, locked in the role of victim, remains equally homogenous and disparate. Such an inverted Manichaean allegorical perspective is operative only when such differences are clear and simple. When areas of anomalous difference, or of more complex interactions between colonizer and colonized, appear, then such a perspective is found wanting. For example, this standpoint is true of the attitude of Ashcroft, Griffiths, and Tiffin when they speak of its being "difficult for colonized peoples outside Britain" to accept the Irish "identity as being postcolonial," given the "subsequent complicity" of the Irish in the "British imperial enterprise" (1989, 33).

In this example, binary oppositions between self and other have become reified and hypostasized into homogenous groupings with little room for interaction, let alone intersection. As Loomba perceptively notes, the question is now being asked of postcolonial theory as to whether, in "the process of exposing the ideological and historical functioning of such binaries, we are in danger of reproducing them" (1998, 104). I think, given the examples cited, that it is a real danger for the postcolonial paradigm. To allow oppositions to become reified is to attenuate the possibilities of influence, interaction, intersection, and, ultimately, transformation. It is also to predicate one's theoretical premises on the past as opposed to the future. If the colonizer-colonized opposition is seen as definitive within a culture, even though, as in Ireland, the initial acts of colonization occurred hundreds of years ago, then, ipso facto, developments in the fields of politics, society, and culture are limited by this reified definition of self and other. Issues of identity are ultimately settled by reference to this terminus a quo from which all such identificatory politics derives. Such a perspective narrows the theoretical scope of postcolonial discourse and oversimplifies complex issues of interaction and influence. This limited view is indeed a "simple history lesson" (Heaney 1983b, 7), and it is very much a danger for the postcolonial perspective. It is in this context that I would propose a reading of *An Open Letter* in the broader framework of his other work, as it will provide a more anamorphic reading of what seems, on the surface, to be that simple history lesson, but in fact is quite a complex recontextualization of the relationship between Ireland and Britain; it is a reading where the culture of Europe functions as a Lacanian extrinsic cultural unconscious that allows for a repositioning of the binary opposition between Irish and English identities and between colonized and colonizer.

I would contend that the final line in the stanza quoted above signals more than the end of the "simple history lesson"; it also signals the end of the politics and poetics of simplification in this text. In fact, the end of the simple history lesson is actually the beginning of a more complex exploration of the history of the relationship between Ireland and Britain, an exploration that we have already seen enacted in his teasing out of the "frontier pastoral," and we are back to Blanchot's idea of a transformative imaginary space and to Derrida's view of the work spilling over its border. I would maintain that Heaney's own thought is far more in keeping with these theorists than has been realized heretofore, and I will return to his essay "Something to Write Home About" to reinforce my argument. Here, Heaney speaks of a statue of Jupiter that was set on Capitol Hill in Rome, and he notes that the roof above the statue was "open to the sky," which to him suggests the idea that all boundaries are "necessary evils," though he is also aware of the human need for security that underlies the creation of boundaries in the first place. He feels that the aesthetic encapsulates this complex response to borders, boundaries, and frontiers, noting that a good poem "allows you to have your feet on the ground and your head in the air simultaneously" (2002, 48–49). It is clear that for Heaney, the duality of the sense of the border and boundary, this double capacity, is central to the genre of poetry, and we need to look more deeply at the openness of *An Open Letter.*

I would suggest that, far from being an act of simple resistance to the colonial power, the figural writing in the letter is much more nuanced, especially at the level of agency. He compares himself to three characters not known for their taking of militant stands: to Shauneen Keogh of Synge's *The Playboy of the Western World*, to the eponymous hero of Eliot's "The Love Song of J. Alfred Prufrock," and to the vacillating hero of Shakespeare's *Hamlet.* These comparisons render his letter as less of a return of the postcolonial repressed and more of an interrogation of ideas of subjectivity and identity, a position familiar from "Exposure," where he had defined himself as neither an "internee nor informer" but rather as an "inner-émigré" who has "grown thoughtful" (1975, 73). He is more than aware that his own credentials on the issue of nomenclature are far from pure. He reminds us that his "anxious muse" had been called British before and had "acquiesced" (1983b, 7). He is also aware that his own writerly and publishing context, as somebody who publishes texts in the *London Review of Books*, the *Listener*, and the *Times Literary Supplement*, and who is published by a British publishing house, Faber, would seem to place him almost naturally as a British writer. It is here that the poem offers a reading of postcolonial subjectivity that is truly transformative. Having spelled out the British context to his writerly subjectivity, a context that is positive in its influence on his work, and has clearly benefited his production of texts, Heaney goes on to enunciate another context within which he exists, one that also permeates and penetrates his subjectivity and his texts, noting that in his own political sphere no glass had ever been raised to "toast *The Queen*" (ibid., 9). Here, we see the further transformation of the "simple history lesson" into a far more complex weave of influence and intersection. His sense of Irishness does not preclude any connection with, or influence by, the British tradition; it does, however, preclude any subsumption by that tradition that attempts to suppress all other strands and strains. It is the relationship of the two contexts that will eventually transform both texts and subjectivities into a new openness of identity, an openness that is presaged in the title of the pamphlet. Ironically, during the queen's visit to Ireland in 2011, Heaney was placed at her table and the whole assembly did toast her, and I think this point underwrites the wisdom of his poetizing description of the ambiguities that are rife in the Irish-English relationship. On this issue, he has always had his feet on the ground and his head in the air.

If poetry is to be of value, Heaney has noted, it must avoid the "consensus and settlement of a meaning which the audience fastens on like a security blanket" (1988, 122). As I have pointed out elsewhere, the problems with such "consensus and settlement" are that the very complexity and ambiguity that are part of the force of poetry are denied and etiolated. If the security blanket of a consensual meaning is seen as something to be avoided, then perhaps the best way to proceed is "not by throwing off the blanket altogether" (O'Brien 2003, 29), but instead by examining more closely the weft and weave of the textile of the blanket in order to bring out the intersections, joints, and interfusions that create the blanket in question. This weave will disclose an ongoing movement that counteracts the essentialisms of the Manichaean allegory, and its postcolonial inverse, and instead will enact J. Hillis Miller's description of literature as composed of "crossings, displacements, and substitutions" (1987, 7).

Hence, the context of *An Open Letter* is more literary than political: the references are broad in the extreme with overt or covert gestures toward the writing of Shakespeare, Eliot, Synge, Yeats, Wilde, Larkin, Davie, Lawrence, Houghton, Jordan, Joyce, Milton, Holub, Foucault, Horace, Livy, and Middle English lyrics (this list is by no means exhaustive). The crossings and penetrations of such a broad range of writers, languages, and contexts form the intellectual and ethical perspective of Heaney's reading of the relationship of Englishness and Irishness. Perhaps the most important point of the poem is the stress on the singularity of the subjectivity that is enunciating its opinion and also how this subjectivity has been influenced by the complex interaction of these different cultural texts. *An Open Letter* is also focused on an individual; there is no group or protonationalist agenda here: "I'll stick to *I*. Forget the *we*" (1983b, 9; emphasis in the original). He goes on to cite the example of Horace, the Roman poet who fought at the battle of Philippi in November 42 BCE, which ended with the rout of Brutus's army and the suicides of both Brutus and Cassius. Heaney's reference to Horace who threw away his shield and became a "naked *I*" (ibid.) as "exemplary" speaks volumes for his sense of the role of the poet in such a political situation. The use of a classical allusion returns us to the influence of Europe, the classics, and the *omphalos*; it provides a broader context from which the Irish-English binary looks less imposing and can be seen as just one more element in a broader rhizomatic structure of European literature, culture, and politics.

The "naked *I*" is crossed and traversed by numerous contexts, and they are brought together in an aesthetic, as opposed to political, force field in his "new commonwealth of art" (ibid.). Heaney's perspective on the postcolonial is beyond the binary. Instead, it is broadened by his European context; it is aware, after Walter Benjamin, that the "documents of civilization have been written in blood and tears, blood and tears no less real for being very remote." It attempts to reach an understanding that points toward the truth of the interaction of self and other, a truth that can be created only by a "less binary and altogether less binding vocabulary" (Heaney 1995a, 19, 23). Such truth must, by its very nature, be intersubjective, and it is in search of such intersubjectivity that Heaney locates his views in *An Open Letter* in such a broad spatial and temporal commonwealth of art. Aesthetic thinking needs to be aware of both the hegemonic *biscuit* and the local *bis-cake* and to take both into account. A writer is initially a reader and, as such, is constituted by the hegemonic tradition that he or she reads; a thinker must interpret not just the text, but also this constitutive context. The field of force of *An Open Letter* is located in the same interpretive context as the adjudication between the first thought and the second thought of the genesis of "Follower," and the adjudication between the different voice rights of *worked* and *wrought*, and the aim of all three adjudications is the creation of a structure of language and thought that will allow both to interact and signify hauntologically in terms of self and other, conscious and unconscious. The crossing and recrossing of the frontier of writing, the ongoing transformation of Irish and English writing, and all the subtexts that combine in these broad structures will transform the nature of the English lyric by making it digest the intractable stuff of another tradition while still remaining an English lyric.

Of course, the hegemonic aspects of English as a language are deconstructed by this process, for the term *English lyric* is no longer prescriptive. It is no longer a set form into which the emergent writer must fit and work his or her language and thought; now it is a more fluid structure, whose frontiers are permeable and have been altered by the language and thought of the emergent writer and by the emergent linguistic tradition. The proper adjective is now as dependent on the expression of its subdialect as are these dialects on its overarching structure. Heaney cites the Yeatsian metaphor of the "Irish preference for a swift current," which he then contrasts with the English mind, "meditative, rich, deliberate," which "may remember the Thames valley" (1995b, 6). The confluence of these rivers will eventually merge in a sea where the frontiers have been washed away into a syncretic version of what is almost a world language of English, what he will later call in his translator's introduction to *Beowulf* "the Irish/English duality, the Celtic/Saxon antithesis were momentarily collapsed and in the resulting etymological eddy a gleam of recognition flashed through the synapses and I glimpsed an elsewhere of potential that seemed at the same time to be a somewhere being remembered" (1999, xxiv–xxv). Here, the frontiers of language and writing have become porous and are more guidelines than frontiers. Thus, his view of language, and linguistic history, is essentially a poetizing one, which sees poetry as the discourse where the different strands that cross the subject can be voiced and can be given the necessary weight that allows each strand to have a voice. In the next chapter, we will examine this idea more specifically as he looks to map out the different and permeable frontiers of language in a field of force.

3

The Epistemology of Poetry

Fields of Force

In the last chapter, we looked at representations of the frontier or border and at poetry both as an epistemological crossing of that border and also as a way of engaging with, and connecting, both sides of that border, whether these sides are self and other, Irish and English identities, or conscious thought and unconscious. This sense of poetry as a genre wherein the necessity of "either/or" choices can be replaced with the more encompassing "both/and" alternative further rhizomatically connects Heaney's thought with Derrida's, and with other contemporary European thinking, where meaning and signification are viewed as relational as opposed to foundational.

The notion of a field of force in which different ideological and political positions coexist, and mutually define each other, is at the core of this chapter. With regard to the border-crossing issue that was discussed in chapter 2, this chapter will provide a broader contextual framework wherein such border crossings become the epistemological norm. In political terms, such a fluid structure would allow for an alteration of the political binarisms that have bedeviled Northern Irish society and politics. Cultural and political ideas do not arise in a vacuum, and the sense of identity as fixed and foundational can be read in the context of the traditional scientific worldview, based on the laws of Euclidean geometry and Newtonian physics. This scientific perspective saw reality as material, as composed of atoms and as static; it saw the amount of energy in the universe as constant; and it saw the processes of the universe as being inexorably bound by cause and effect. However, James Clerk Maxwell's discovery of a "phenomenon which could not be accounted for in Newtonian terms, the electrical field of force" put a question mark over these assumptions. These ideas were developed by thinkers such as Albert Einstein, Louis de Broglie, Erwin Schrödinger, and Paul Dirac, who showed that beyond the apparently stable and harmonious world of classical physics, there lay a "meta-world" that was "not describable in Newtonian terms." This "meta-world" was radically different from the physical reality investigated by classical physics, "being composed of decentred, multi-dimensionally fluctuating energies rather than centred, regularly orbiting material particles." Moreover, "far from being linear or continuous with itself, that 'meta-world' was observed to involve leaps, jerks, gaps, irregularities and discontinuities" (Giles 1993, 14).

This type of meta-world is the source of the "field of force" as a concept, and it is a world composed of interactions between, and effects of, forces that seem to have little or no mass or matter in the conventional sense. Their force and impact can be felt, but they are almost invisible and not present in the orthodox sense. As such, it is an ideal paradigm for the uncertain forces, attachments, ideologies, and structures, especially those forces of the unconscious, that constitute identity. This paradigm has influenced a number of contemporary cultural thinkers, as the idea of a fluid mode of signification is one that sits well with structuralist and poststructuralist thinking, especially concerning its signification of aspects of reality that have hitherto remained inaccessible to language and understanding. John Protevi sees a lot of Derrida's thinking as based on a political physics similar to that outlined above, where "making sense," the creation of meaning, is achieved through the "forceful interaction of vectors in a field of force and signification. This general text of force and signification is the site of struggle for the 'democracy to come'" (2001, 13).

For Derrida, the kind of writing that Heaney sees as being able to access aspects of the real, what he calls "originary writing" (*archeécriture*), creates a "field of force that encompasses language, culture, and even our experience of 'reality' itself" (Bradley 2008, 54).

Heaney and Derrida share a view as to the power of a certain type of language—Heidegger's poetizing language—both to access aspects of reality that are seldom seen and, indeed, to create other facets of what we see as reality. The field of force is a way of explaining how entities, concepts, emotions, and sensations, which are impossible to pinpoint accurately, or to define concretely, can exert a force through which they can be encountered in some way. Such force fields are able to contain contradictory or contesting perspectives, something that is important when looking at a concept like identity, which becomes ever more complex the more we examine it. In this sense, Theodor Adorno's idea of the work of art as a "force field constituted by subject and object" (Adorno and Tiedemann 1991, 1:167) is a significant point of connection with Heaney's ideas as we outline them here. He saw every work of art as "force-field" and felt that they are "true only in so far as they transcend their material preconditions" (1981, 164). Adorno sees the finished artworks as "molded objects" that "become force fields of their antagonisms," and he also sees the aesthetic as a structure composed of a "dynamic configuration of its elements" (1997, 176, 301).

Adorno's negative dialectics can be seen as describing force fields composed of apparently contradictory statements, which "both reflect and resist the reality it tries critically to analyze." For Adorno, this structure allowed one to "hold opposing, even incompatible, positions simultaneously without worrying about their coherence" (Jay 1984, 266), though this structure in no way attenuated the complexity or the ethical difficulties of such a process. Rather, it was a manner of thinking through complexities by being aware that a different structure of thinking might be necessary. For Adorno, the complexity of some objects of thought meant that it was only by formulating new structures of thinking, structures where there might be seeming contradictions or antinomies, that thinking could fully engage with them. As we will see, Heaney's own structures of identity, the quincunxes, and the triangle embody such complex interactions and tensions, and they are set out precisely in order to signify the conflictual nature and complexity of such emotions. Another aspect of such forces is that often they "are experienced only in the results they render, and the products of forcefields are extended and qualified" (Boundas 2006, 4), and in this respect they signify the effect of the real, of which we have already spoken and which Heaney has mentioned himself.

On being asked by Dennis O'Driscoll about his venturing into the mythic territory of Northern Ireland, Heaney makes a point about the real effect of images on his writing. He notes how a line was crossed when he wrote "The Tollund Man" because when he wrote the first line of the poem, "Some day I will go to Aarhus" (1972, 47), he felt he was in a "new field of force" (Heaney and O'Driscoll 2008, 157).

This connection of feeling, inspiration, and the uncanny in the term *field of force* is at the core of Heaney's quite sustained use of the term. It allows him to convey the complexity of meaning and the sense in which some connections can take on a life of their own and suddenly offer a glimpse of the meta-world of the real. In order to come to an understanding of seemingly fixed and implacable signifiers of one form of identity or another, such a structure is necessary. For Fredric Jameson, this process is one of the core functions of the aesthetic, namely, the ability to reconstruct as a "field of force . . . the dynamics of sign systems of several distinct modes of production," which "can be registered and apprehended" (1981, 98), and Heaney would largely share this perspective. Speaking of a reading of the work of W. H. Auden, he notes that Stan Smith has seen Auden as both "afflicted and inspired" by the realization that he is a product of, as opposed to a producer of, "world-shaping discourses," and he contrasts Smith's deconstructionist reading with Geoffrey Grigson's, who had written about Auden concerning a specific sense of Englishness "until then unexpressed or not isolated in a single poem" (1988, 119), and there is a clear connection with his own sense of the uncanny that came from the image of the bog people.

Heaney's reading of Grigson is interesting, as he notes that while Grigson's readings of Auden may not be as analytical as Smith's, he nevertheless suggests that Grigson teases out the "cultural implications and attachments which inhabit any poem's field of force," and he goes on to say that this critical activity is significant in terms of both reading and writing poetry. The creation of such a fluid constellation, which comprises rational, emotional, and somatic aspects of experience, is paralleled by the act of reception, and understanding, of this structure. The structures of which Heaney is speaking encapsulate how a new rhythm gives a new life to our understanding of the world and of the seemingly diverse positions within it; it involves "a resuscitation not just of the ear but of the springs of being" (ibid., 120). It is precisely this kind of thinking that Heaney will bring to his discussion of identity in both an Irish and an English context.

The political extrapolations of this dialogue between icons of nationalism and unionism are discussed in detail in Heaney's essays, both in the context of contemporary politics in Northern Ireland and in the context of the relationship between Ireland and Britain, a topic that is explored in an examination of his essays "Englands of the Mind," in *Preoccupations*, and "Through-Other Places, Through-Other Times: The Irish Poet and Britain," in *Finders Keepers*. In the introduction, we looked at his structure of the quincunx and at his view that it could be a paradigm of new possibilities concerning the relationships between the different traditions and ideologies in a literary context. As was noted in the introduction, Heaney sketched this visual structure in *The Redress of Poetry*, where, in a specifically Irish context, he sets out the bounds in a five-point structure that would grant the plurality of what he terms an Irishness that "would not prejudice the rights of others' Britishness" (1995b, 198). This structure is a "diamond shape" of five towers, with the central one being the tower of prior Irelandness, the round tower of insular dwelling. The other four points are representative of Kilcolman Castle, Edmund Spenser's "tower of English conquest"; Yeats's Ballylee, where the "Norman tower" was a deliberate symbol of his attempt to "restore the spiritual values and magical world-view that Spenser's armies and language had destroyed"; Joyce's Martello Tower; and Carrickfergus Castle, associated with Louis MacNeice, where William of Orange once landed in Ireland (ibid., 199). Such a nuanced and inclusive structure, which has received very little commentary in the field of Heaney studies, is one that located Heaney as an aesthetic and ethical thinker of the first order. In a sociocultural context where the thinking on all sides has been binary in the extreme, he is willing to set out a new structure wherein fluency and change are central to his thinking.

The choice of the towers as the fixed points of his fluid matrix is a knowing nod to the centrality of this symbol in the Irish literary context; it is also a granting of the need to acknowledge the givens, the fixed aspects, of all identitarian ideologies that, while they might not be ethical or politically correct, are nevertheless potent and powerful, and it is the interaction of these towers, and the structure created by this interaction, the field of force, that symbolizes the value of poetry that has to be "a working model of inclusive consciousness." Telling the truth slant, looking awry, or seeing the world from a different perspective, as well as valuing that difference, is at the core of Heaney's aesthetic imperative, and he has invoked Osip Mandelstam to criticize the purveyors of ready-made meaning. He is attempting to set out a fluid and differential structure in literature that is attentive to the different sources and traditions of different parts of the Irish literary sphere, while at the same time looking to them not as fixed loci that are conservative in that they are the only points in the tradition but rather seeing them as nodal points in a force field that will be oriented toward the future. He goes on to graft these ideas into the political sphere; ready-made meanings have ossified political development in Ireland for centuries. Unionist and nationalist ideologies in Northern Ireland, and a political establishment rooted in the binary opposition of the Irish civil war in the Republic of Ireland, have all subscribed to such ready-made conceptions of meaning, and Heaney's innovative representation of the quincunx has interesting, and possibly far-reaching, ramifications for such developments.

Attention has already been drawn to the connections between this structure and Heidegger's notion of the fourfold. Like Heaney, Heidegger too saw that only through the interaction and the mirroring of each of the four elements could any of them fully become itself.

He sees the four elements—earth and sky, divinities and mortals—as having a discrete existence in themselves, but as also belonging to the fourfold. As he puts it in terms of the earth, it is "blossoming and fruiting, spreading out in rock and water, rising up into plant and animal," but even with this sense of specificity, "we are already thinking of the other three along with it, but we give no thought to the simple oneness of the four" (1971, 147). There is a parallel form of aesthetic thinking at work here, as each element is seen as reflected in the other, and the creative sense of identity and presencing is to be found in these reflections and refractions, which can be seen as constituting a force field. Heidegger sees the interaction and interanimation of the fourfold as being that which allows for the world to unveil itself: "The elements that are invoked are those of earth and world. In the strife that is initiated between them in the standing forth of the artwork is to be found the happening of truth" (Malpas 2006, 225). Just as Heaney sets out his towers to represent the complexity of issues of literary and political identity in a historically real Ireland, so Heidegger sets out the fourfold as a structure that is based on the real life, the *Dasein*, of human beings in the world: "Mortals dwell poetically on the earth and by so doing enter the fourfold. By dwelling, mortals preserve the four" (Tonner 2010, 175).

For Heaney, similarly, it is the interaction between these towers that is creative of meaning, the "lines of flight or of deterritorialisation" (Deleuze and Guattari 1987, 32), and it is interesting to note that the unusual term *quincunx*, already noted in the work of Sir Thomas Brown and James Joyce, also appears in the work of another thinker who was critical of conceptions of ready-made, or fixed, meaning and instead suggested a parallel epistemology of differential and relational meaning; I am referring to the father of structuralism and, one might add, of literary theory, Ferdinand de Saussure. In a manner that is proleptic of Heaney's view of meaning as created by the interactions of a field of force, Saussure is discussing the difference between synchronic and diachronic analysis of meaning. He points out that a synchronic analysis reports on a current state of affairs: it is "a simple expression of an existing arrangement, the synchronic law reports a state of affairs; it is like a law that states that trees in a certain orchard are arranged in the shape of a quincunx," and he goes on to note that such an arrangement is "not imperative." The association here between the shape of the trees and what Heaney has termed ready-made meaning is interrogative and fluid as opposed to fixed and located. For Saussure, synchrony is a relational structure that is always open to change, and he cites the example of the synchronic law that governed Latin accentuation, but stresses that this rule "did not resist the forces of alteration and gave way to a new law, the one of French" (1959, 92–93).

Heaney and Saussure use the term *quincunx* to describe a structure that is not common but is governed by relational and differential rules, all of which are not fixed and therefore are open to growth, development, and change. In his essay where the quincunx is first outlined, Heaney refers to lines from one of his own poems, wherein he makes this very point about the relationship between past, present, and future: "whatever is given / Can always be reimagined however four-square" (1991, 29). It is this very process of reimagining that Heaney's aesthetic thinking embodies. He has always tried to reimagine the conditions in which he found himself, and one could argue that this reimagining is precisely what poetry as a form of discourse can do, given its access to aspects of the Lacanian real: it is a way of letting down a "shaft into real life" (Heaney 1980, 41). Heaney will also attempt to apply these literary imaginings to the political, but it is useful to trace the idea of a field of force back to its origin in his own writing, which leads our discussion to an essay entitled "Feeling into Words," in *Preoccupations*.

In light of the argument being put forward in this book about how poetry is the discourse that is best able to access aspects of the unconscious and the real, the title of this essay is significant. *Feeling* as a term signifies the somatic and bodily aspects of knowledge; it suggests that our interaction with the world, on a corporeal level, can give rise to sensations, instincts, emotions, all of which work at an arational level and are, as a result, very difficult to explain in words. It is this arational level of signification, which poetry as a discourse, and much of the theory adduced in this book, attempts to access and explain. In this essay, Heaney begins with a personal example of how the unconscious can be verbalized using his own work. Writing of the work of Wordsworth, Heaney focuses on the fact that in *The Prelude*, Wordsworth talks about how the hiding places of his poetic power seem open, and he goes on to say that these lines resonate with him, as he sees poetry qua poetry as "divination, poetry as revelation of the self to the self, as restoration of the culture to itself"; in this reading, poems function as elements of continuity, but it is a specific and particularist form of continuity: the poem is like a shard in an archaeological dig, but its value is inherent in itself, as a singularity, and this value is not "diminished by the importance of the buried city." Heaney summarizes this position by stressing that poetry, as a form of knowledge, not only unearths these shards but also imbues them with life: he speaks of "poetry as a dig, a dig for finds that end up being plants" (ibid.).

I would contend that these words, significantly located at a very early stage of Heaney's writing on the subject of poetry, foreground the epistemological nature of poetry and of his aesthetic thinking. It is a discourse of revelation of aspects of the self to the self; it is a discourse that unearths that which is hidden; it focuses on the individual instance and looks to relate it to the overall structure—the shard relating to the city, which would then function as an *agalma*. It is also a discourse that animates such finds, turning them into something organic. I would suggest that it is a metaphorical discussion of the role of poetry in revealing hitherto repressed aspects of the unconscious to the self. Sigmund Freud, writing in *The Interpretation of Dreams*, has made the point that the theory of repression asserts that "these repressed wishes still exist" even though they are subject to "suppression [pressing down]" (Freud and Strachey 2010, 255). The finds act as *agalmata*, as they reveal aspects that have hitherto been occluded from view or from representation, and poetry is the discourse that facilitates this process of revelation.

Therefore, Wordsworth acts as a strong precursor for Heaney, although not quite in the sense of struggling with a previous influence, as envisaged by Harold Bloom in *The Anxiety of Influence* (1973, 5). Rather than wrestling intellectually with Wordsworth, Heaney takes him as a jumping-off point into a discussion of how poetry works to unearth aspects of a repressed individual or societal unconscious. Having looked at *The Prelude*, Heaney goes on to say that his own poem "Digging" was the first time that he thought his "feelings had got into words" and went on to rephrase it using the word *feel* instead (1980, 41). The focus on the somatic criteria of rhythm and noise underlines his probing of the connections between poetry and the body, and he goes on to look at how the relationship between language and the senses is enacted in poetry: how feeling gets into words. The initial use of *feel* is doubly relevant, as it is a linguistic defamiliarization that indicates how difficult it can be to signify these aspects of the real, and the word *feel* has also strong haptic and somatic associations, which are the areas of experience that are trying to be expressed in this apophantic discourse.

Having looked at Wordsworth as a general exemplar, he moves to the particular, going from the buried city to the shard, in his own terminology, to examine the poem "The Thorn." Heaney notes that for Wordsworth, the poem is occasioned by an actual thorn, seen after a storm on the Quantock Hills. Wordsworth had seen this particular thorn before, but it was the storm that brought it directly to his attention. In Heaney's reading, the storm provided the context that allowed for Wordsworth's "epiphany" (ibid., 50), and the meaning of the thorn was largely determined by the context of its envisioning after the storm and by Wordsworth's own perceptions and responses to this altered perspective on a familiar object. Consequently, what happens in the composition of "The Thorn" is a paradigm of the epistemological force of poetry, as the thorn, "in its new, wind-tossed aspect" (ibid., 52). This instance is the first time Heaney has used the term *field of force* in his prose, and we can immediately recall his own comments from *Preoccupations* on "The Tollund Man," cited at the beginning of this chapter, where the image of the Iron Age head had a comparable aura for him and was similarly uncanny (ibid., 57–59). It is significant in that it is referring to a structure wherein conscious and unconscious are fused in order to generate a new meaning.

Later, in the same essay, he sets out an initial transposition of the literary with the political and a trope to which he returned more systematically in his discussion of the quincunx. He is talking about the difficulty of being a Northern Irish writer who feels under pressure to respond to ongoing violence and makes the point that it is a pressure that he finds oppressive. The role of poetry, he asserts, is not to account for, or describe, or ideologically agitate in favor of, a particular political position. Instead, its role is to unearth the buried aspects of those ideologies, and this process occurs through both the sound and the meaning of words. His solution to this dilemma, the need for a writing that is a field of force between a humane reason and the religiously intense violence, has become one of the most quoted examples of his prose, and in this chapter we will examine it in connection with its relationship to the quincunx in particular and to his overall structure of poetry as a mode of knowledge in general. However, before addressing it, account needs to be taken of another occurrence of the term *field of force* that follows this one. Speaking about his second volume, *Door into the Dark*, Heaney sees this book as gesturing toward the idea of poetry as focusing on the "buried life of the feelings." He goes on to expand on this idea by explaining that for him, "words themselves are doors; Janus is to a certain extent their deity" (ibid., 52).

Thus, when he feels the pressure to respond to the demand for "war poets" (Morrison 1982, 55), as violence became overt on the streets of Belfast and Derry in the late 1960s and early 1970s, Heaney does not rush straight into descriptions of the violence or into "liberal lamentation" that people in Northern Ireland were killing each other because of different ideologies or because of "nomenclatures such as British or Irish"; nor does he attempt "celebrations or execrations of resistance or atrocity" (1980, 56). Instead, he looks for that epiphanic moment that we saw in "The Thorn," and he finds it in the image of the *Bog People* (Glob 1977), a book about Iron Age victims of ritual sacrifice. In these figures, he found "images and symbols adequate to our predicament," and he goes on to describe them using the metaphor of the field of force, which could encompass both the sense of a "humane reason" and the "religious intensity" of the ongoing violence (1980, 56, 57).

Of course, he realizes that his rather mythic idiom is removed from the political and media discourse that has arisen around the conflict and is far removed from the vocabulary of power sharing, talks, and economic interests. However, he argues that it is not remote at all from the racial and ideological prejudices of the paramilitaries who are enacting the shootings and bombings. This mythic idiom, and his sense of the value of the bog bodies as symbolic or repressed memory, makes them a form of the Lacanian *agalma*, as they embody aspects of subjectivity that cannot be directly expressed: as Heaney puts it, there is a religious intensity at work here, and religion, by definition, involves aspects of life and emotion that cannot be readily accessed.

I think we have seen, through the gradual development of his conception of the field of force, that it is precisely this interanimation between the politically correct, rational discourses of politics, media, and the public sphere and the innate, sectarian prejudices that have been repressed over a period of years that is important to his sense of poetry as a mode of knowing more about ourselves and our society. At this juncture, I would recall the connection between his ideas of a field of force and Adorno's, which were discussed in chapter 1. For Adorno, as for Heaney, the dynamic tension between different sources and forces is constitutive of both art and knowledge. He sees a work of art as "a force field even in the arrested moment of its objectivation. The work is at once the quintessence of relations of tension and the attempt to dissolve them." He also stresses the unconscious aspect of the aesthetic, as the created and built nature of the work of art is evidence of the tension that exists between the "formal aspect of language and its more inchoate aspects, as it names the element of 'form' in which form gains its substance by virtue of its relation to its other" (1997, 292). For both thinkers, the field of force, or constellation, operates to connect elements (historical, socioeconomic, cultural) that are not initially given as relational but that when "animated—constellated—into conjunction, create or reveal a signifying force field neither instrumental nor arbitrary" (Cunningham and Mapp 2006, 100).

In a manner that recalls Heaney's ideas of craft and technique, from chapter 1, Adorno also foregrounds the different aspects of language that must be brought together if any form of truth is to be achieved. As we saw, craft was related to the form and skill of the use of language, whereas technique involved deeper emotions and an attempt to give voice to feelings and sensations. Equally, for Adorno, art is a force field encompassing "ethical, metaphysical and logical, as well as aesthetic in the immediately recognizable sense of that term" (Wilson 2007, 44), and his views on language can be extrapolated further. Adorno argues that language contains two axes, "an expressive axis oriented toward the object (language is to express the thing itself, *name* it) and a communicative axis. The two axes are construed as linguistic analogues of the intuitive and logical moments of the concept respectively" (Bernstein 2004, 42). This perspective is close to Heaney's binary of craft and technique, and further connections become clear when Adorno's axes are explored in more detail, as they set in motion an ongoing dialectic between "'expression,' or that which adheres to the particularity of the object," and the need to communicate "through concepts that, ultimately, must sacrifice such particularity. Experience emerges from the 'force field' constituted through these two moments of language" (Gandesha 2004, 106).

I would contend that these "two moments of language," and their existence in a field of force, are the way in which a fuller knowledge can be accessed. The "force field" that connects the emotional, the rational, the conscious, the unconscious, the somatic, and the cerebral is a structure that pervades Heaney's writing, as he sees it as a constituent of poetized thinking. In a book that offers genuine insights into Heaney's poetry, Neil Corcoran speaks of detecting a "tendency to over-schematic or even specious binary thinking" (1998, 230) in Heaney's work. I would agree that they are there, but would take the point further; I think it has become clear that he focuses on given binaries of thought in order to dislodge and relocate them in a more fluid structure, wherein their own adversarial potency will become lessened through being part of this broader, and more plural, structure.

In his pamphlet *Among Schoolchildren*, for example, Heaney spoke about a great-aunt, Catherine Bradley, and about an example of her school needlework, from 1843. It included the following verse, embroidered on her "sampler": "Ireland as she ought to be / Great glorious and free." The embroidery beneath this verse was of a shamrock, the traditional symbol of Ireland, but "squeezed to the right of the verse" were the words *God Save the Queen* (1983a, 6). Here, the prevalence of binarisms in Heaney's thought is embodied on a piece of Ulster linen. Heaney looks at these two emblems of Irish and English iconography on the material and poses the question as to how these binary signifiers should be interpreted. Should we see the sampler as favoring the Irish icons of identity, stressing how Ireland "ought" to be, inclining to the idea of being free of British influence, as signified by the shamrock? Alternatively, should we interpret it in the opposite manner, as embracing such influence as part of the union between Great Britain and Ireland, as signified by the rubric "God Save the Queen"? In both instances, the sense of the gravitational pull exerted by a specific form of identity is clear: Ireland is both rightfully Irish and hence wrongly called British, or vice versa. Issues of identity, of both Ulsterness and Irishness, are very much under examination in Heaney's discussion of this sampler.

Throughout this pamphlet, and in *Place and Displacement*, the pamphlet that he wrote about Wordsworth, Heaney stresses the bifurcation of ideologies and identities that has marked his growth and his developing ideas on identity. From learning about Jane Austen, Tennyson, and Lawrence, and from attending sherry parties at the house of a professor in Queens University who hailed from Oxford, to acting with the Bellaghy Dramatic Society and playing a United Irishman and Robert Emmett, we see someone who was being influenced by both the Irish and the English aspects of Ulster culture. In many cases, such binarisms were expressed in the antagonistic tones of self and other, or of us and them, and as Heaney puts it the exposure to aspects of both cultures brought about an uncertainty with respect to cultural and ideological identification, as is clear in the indecisive avatars that he cites in *An Open Letter.*

The physical oscillation between weekly exposure to "the elegances of Oscar Wilde and the profundities of Shakespeare" (ibid., 7) and the weekend, with its religious devotions in the chapel and acting as *fear a' tigh* (master of ceremonies) at the Gaelic Athletic Association *ceilidhs* (dances), has its psychical and identificatory effect encapsulated in a number of posed questions: "Was I two persons or one? Was I extending myself or breaking myself apart? Was I being led out or led away? Was I failing to live up to the aspiring literary intellectual effort when I was at home, was I betraying the culture of the parish when I was at the university" (ibid., 8). The preconditions that set up this questioning are defined through spatial and temporal oscillations. Temporally, he spent the weekdays of term at Queen's University in Belfast, studying English literature and becoming enculturated into the middle-class, literary, cultured ethos that was connoted by "sherry parties on the Malone Road." At "weekends and during the holidays," he was immersed in Catholic, rural, Gaelic, nationalist social, and cultural practices in County Derry (ibid., 7). Spatially, he oscillated between city and country, Belfast and Bellaghy, the academy and the parish. This physical movement, constituted in time and space, serves as a paradigm for the psychical and cognitive motion of what one might term Heaney's epistemology of poetry. It informs statements that see the poet as being "displaced from a confidence in a single position by his disposition to be affected by all positions, negatively rather than positively capable" (Heaney 1984a, 8). While he feels fractured by this movement, he is nevertheless crossing and recrossing borders and boundaries, and if his physical journeys could be mapped, they would embody the very grid-like structure that is often used to show a force field.

If we look at this sense of movement between places, it allows us to reconfigure the interaction between the two different mottoes on Catherine Bradley's sampler. Heaney talks about how, in the embroidery on that piece of Ulster linen, "two value systems which now explode daily, are lodged like dormant munitions on one piece of, no doubt, Ulster linen" (1983a, 6). Interestingly, what connects the two is the fact that they are each part of the sampler and the fact that they each occupy an aspect of the reader's consciousness—they are another field of force whose meaning is achieved through interaction as opposed to actual presence, through what Adorno would term a dialectic of expression and communication. It is through the dialectical interaction of the two positions that the signifier "Ulster" achieves its fullest meaning, as the mind shuttled between the notion of an Irish and a British Ulster. I use the term *shuttle* deliberately, as it is a metaphor used by Derrida to describe a process that he calls "negotiation," but is very similar to Heaney's expression of the interaction of craft and technique in the field of force that is poetry. By the end of *Among Schoolchildren*, "Catherine Bradley's sampler, with its ambivalent if not duplicitous texts, still hangs in the balance, and more precariously than ever. It has great allegorical force as a representation of divisions within the country" (ibid., 13).

It is the idea of balance that is important here, as Heaney will negotiate between the different ideological signifiers of differential identity that appear on the linen sampler. For Derrida, the term *negotiate* connotes the shuttle, *la navette*, and the sense of movement "to-and-fro between two positions, two places, and two choices. One must always go from one to the other, and for me negotiation is the impossibility of establishing oneself anywhere" (Derrida and Rottenberg 2002, 12). The movement of the shuttle, as it creates the piece of material, is a metonym of Heaney's concept of the field of force, and the interaction of these two images is creative of that sense of plural and fluid identity of which we have been speaking. Heaney has elsewhere expressed his sense of the value of negotiation between the different traditions in Northern Ireland. In an interview with Mike Murphy, Heaney talks of the "otherness" of farmers like Jim Gilmore or the Garvins or the Evanses. He knew they were Protestants, and were different, but there "was ease in terms of human negotiation," and his ongoing interaction with his Protestant neighbors gave him "a benign sense of the possibility of such negotiations, partly because of humour, which in one sense was an effacing of the difference and in another sense an evasion of it" (Murphy 2000, 83). He has always been aware of the need for the back-and-forth negotiation of which Derrida has spoken, and the connection between the two indexes of identity on the sampler is not necessarily antagonistic. Just as the movement of the shuttle creates the textile, so the movement between different positions, ideologies, and modes of knowledge creates the text.

It is this field of force that creates meaning through its interactions. "Ulster" is both the Irish and the British symbol, and their interaction in a specific location; this ambiguity is paralleled by literary Irishness, in the quincunx, where identity is defined and signified by interaction and connection between the different towers of different aspects of Irishness. Each enunciation of identity is a sample, a sampler, which draws from all the different constituents of identity, but in one specific and narrow manner. One reading of the sampler can locate it as a statement of Irishness, with "God Save the Queen" tacked on as a supplement, while another can read it as espousing a British identity, where Ireland is "great glorious and free," but only in the context of being part of the union with Britain. It is the connection between these different readings that is significant—the piece can mean both at the same time, but in a reading that is a negotiation, in the Derridean sense, of identity. Rather than seeing the ambivalence and duplicitousness of the two images on the sampler as negatives, Heaney takes that extra step and, by locating them both in a field of force, is able to grant the authenticity of each, while also attesting to the permeability of both. As he puts it, "We go beyond our normal cognitive bounds and sense a new element where we are not alien but liberated, more alive to ourselves, more drawn out, more educated" (1983a, 16), and the drawing out here is part of that force field that is aware of the nuances and complexities of identity. The meaning of the root of education, the Latin *educare*, is "to lead out," and Heaney's aesthetic thinking attempts to do just that—to lead out beyond normal cognitive bounds. The way to achieve it is not to see either of the terms as self-sustaining, but rather to inscribe them into a differential structure, a structure that is compared by Lacan to "links by which a necklace firmly hooks onto a link of another necklace made of links" (2006, 418).

In the same essay, Heaney outlines a related set of seemingly differential signifiers of identity, which again can be reconceptualized within a field of force that is proleptic of the quincunx. He tells of finding a word, *lachtar*, in Dineen's *Irish Dictionary*, and the origin of the word was cited as the dialect of the Irish language spoken in his own county, Derry. The word means "a flock of chickens," and it "had survived in our district as a common and, as far as I had known until then, an English word," but he now realizes that this word was "like a capillary stretching back to a time when Irish was the lingua franca of the whole place." Heaney speaks of his original reaction—a sense of postcolonial regret at being robbed of part of his heritage, but goes on to work through this binarist epistemological politics and reach a further shore, where the "concept of identity was "enlarging and releasing" and would eventually help him to relate his "literary education with the heritage of the home ground" (1983a, 9). We are again in the force field of biscuit and "bis-cake," of the English lyric and the messy stuff of the actual, and of modernism and Lallans: in all of them, there is that negotiation and creation of a fluid meaning from static samples of identity. The use of *capillary* is also interesting, as it is suggestive of an unconscious and somatic aspect of language, which is drawing on submerged sources of energy. It is a word, and a thought process, to which he will return in his translation of *Beowulf*.

In his own probing of a poetized form of thinking on identity, memories of his personal past similarly act as metaphorical capillaries. He recalls a Christmas morning when he and his Protestant neighbor Tommy Evans compared their toys. Heaney remembers a sharp pang of jealousy as he saw "a brightly painted wooden battleship, all reds and whites and many blues," obviously symbolic of the power of Britannia over the waves, though the ideological baggage was less important to the young Heaney than the way in which the ship negotiated the "calm waters of the rain-butt at the gable." All

Heaney had in comparison was "a kaleidoscope, a little prism of brilliance and illusion, a lightship rather than a battleship," and on attempting to make it emulate the other ship, he managed to ruin it, as the water made it soggy, and "its insides had been robbed of their brilliant inner space, its marvellous and unpredictable visions were gone." This passage may seem like a brief rehearsal of a childhood experience of disappointment, or lament, or loss, but in fact it is another example of his poetizing thinking at work. Taking the failed comparative boat as an enabling metaphor, he creates yet another field of force: "The world of rain-butts and battleships may be the *milieu* in which we have our early existence, but the chances for our existence should not be reduced to that. The kaleidoscope of our inner freedom of choice and vision should not be submerged in the element of slogan and prescription" (1983a, 14–15). The kaleidoscope, with its changing pattern of colors, is a visual example of the field of force, as colors, shapes, and images are constantly changing and developing. It is the interplay of the colors and shapes in the kaleidoscope that is significant, and it is this interplay that he values when he brings this essay to its climax by quoting from the Yeatsian poem that gives the essay its name, "Among School Children" (Yeats 1965, 217–19).

In this poem, a template is set out that he will use to create the structure that will allow the earlier binarisms of *lachtar* as both an Irish and an English word, of the Irish and English symbols on the sampler, and of the boat and the kaleidoscope to be fused together in a liberating aesthetic structure. The great synthesizing suasive surge of the poem's final stanza, with its syncretic image of the chestnut tree and the dancing body, is an analogue of how poetry can access aspects of the real: "O body swayed to music, O brightening glance, / How can we know the dancer from the dance?" (ibid., 219). Heaney correctly calls this image one of "the high watermarks of poetry," and the reasons he gives for this ascription are telling indeed in the context of this discussion. He sees the stanza as having "all the energy and physical presence of a green breaking wave," as it is "deep and on the move," has a "thrilling self-propelling force," is "solid and mysterious at once," and, crucially, is "gone just as it reveals its full crest of power, never fully apprehended but alluring with its suggestions" (1983a, 16). Here we see the dynamics of his field of force at work in this metaphor, as the structure is fluid and mobile, and the meaning is to be found in the movement between presence and absence, between the crest and the trough, between statement and suggestion. What attracts Heaney to the Yeatsian stanza is the expression of the indefinable real in the sap that unites the leaf, the blossom, and the bole of the chestnut tree and in the interaction between the langue and parole of the dance and the dancer.

It is the relationship between all the elements that is unearthed by poetic language, and here, Heaney would suggest, is where the true signification of the real is to be found. One could see a strong associative connection between Heaney's epistemology of poetry, and its capillary dimension, and the rhizomatic paradigm of knowledge as set out by Deleuze and Guattari. They take this metaphor from botany, where a rhizome is a spreading underground stem that can appear almost anywhere at a distance from the parent plant and become a separate entity. Regarding knowledge systems, they see the rhizome as reducible "neither to the One nor the multiple," in a manner analogous to the relationship between the "leaf, the blossom and the bole" and the dancer and the dance. Like these resonant images, the rhizome "is composed not of units but of dimensions, or rather directions in motion" (Deleuze and Guattari 1987, 23), and any attempt to locate identity in fixed pillars of signification, without regard to such motions, is doomed to simplify and attenuate the complexity of meaning that is to be found in any and all statements of identity.

While the term *lachtar* may have seemed English, it was in fact Irish in origin, and it is the interchange between each language and tradition that causes meaning to be created. The field of force of identity is a necessary kaleidoscope, as the reflections and patterns, reminiscent of Heidegger's "mirroring," are constantly changing. Heaney's rhizomatic perspective on identity in the quincunx attempts to map the fluidity of his sense of literary identity onto the political sphere, and he has made coherent use of this fluidity of identity in his discussion of English identity, just as much as he discussed Irish identity in the quincunx. The idea of the shuttle flitting back and forth as it creates the text or textile that he implied in the quincunx is also used in his discussion of perceptions of Englishness, in his significantly titled "Englands of the Mind," in *Preoccupations*; thus, both indexes of identity on the sampler, and in *An Open Letter*, are thoroughly investigated.

In this exploration of Englishness in the work of Ted Hughes, Geoffrey Hill, and Philip Larkin, Heaney is stressing the plurality and the fluidity of conceptions of Englishness, just as he did, and continues to do, with similar ideas of Irishness. One could see this perspective as rhizomatic in that "one of the most important characteristics of the rhizome is that it always has multiple entryways" (ibid., 14), and in this essay he examines and probes some of the multiple paths of entry into notions of Englishness. As Heaney puts it, all three poets complicate identity, positing connections between a "here and now" and "there and then" England, and all three are "hoarders and shorers" of a specific sense of what it means to be English. Each of them treats England "as a region" (1980, 150). As is often the case with Heaney, underneath the seeming simplicity of this definition lurks a paradox, as it is impossible to posit a singular "real England," while at the same time to treat their own specific regions of England as synecdoches of the whole nation. In his timely and thought-provoking book entitled *Seamus Heaney's Regions*, Richard Rankin Russell has made a strong case for a regional perspective on Heaney's work, seeing the "region" as a way of engaging with while at the same time transcending the national and international politics of Northern Ireland. Thus, he sees Hughes as an important figure for Heaney as they are both poets who "loved the tradition of English literature" while at the same time feeling "deep affinities with the margins of that tradition" (2014, 128). Here, both the part and the whole stand in dialectical mutual definition.

It is the interaction between past and present, sameness and difference, and part and whole that signifies the plural rhizomatic identity that is of interest to Heaney, who, as we have seen consistently in this discussion, prioritizes the fluidity of signifiers of identity and the many different perspectives that constitute these structures of identity. Like Derrida, he suggests that individual elements of identity—flags, mottoes, languages—are each only aspects of the full picture. In addition, like Derrida, he looks to the absent context that helps to make up each text: "No element can function as a sign without referring to another element which itself is not simply present." For Heaney, specific aspects of Irishness or Englishness have value only when they are interwoven with others, so that they mutually inform each other, as the *navette* is constantly oscillating from one to the other. This process is like the meaning of the dance in Yeats's poem, where the movement can be exemplified only by the dancer, who is only a dancer as long as he or she enacts and performs the movement—the langue is explained by the parole, but the parole can come into being only because of the langue, so that each mutually informs, and transforms, the other. This interweaving, this textile, "is the *text* produced only in the transformation of another text. Nothing, neither among the elements nor within the system is anywhere ever simply present or absent" (Derrida, Brault, and Naas 1981, 26).

Identity, be it Irishness or Englishness, is a text, and the association with the term *textile* is overdetermined in the context of the sampler, as a textile is produced by the interweaving and shuttling of different threads, just as a text is produced by a parallel process of shuttling between selected elements, even though the imperatives of politics and ideology attempt to reify such structures and make them seem permanent. In his reading of the three versions of Englands of the mind in this essay, Heaney unpicks the elements that are combined in the respective constellations or fields of force. He discusses Eliot's concept of the auditory imagination, which referred to the preconscious elements of sound and rhythm. Through its intense focus on the full range of language, poetry is the discourse that allows one to examine, analyze, and come to some understanding of the manner in which such structures are created. It foregrounds the real aspect of words and their somatic effect that delights the mind and body and thinks of the relationship between the word as "pure vocable, as articulate noise, and the word as etymological occurrence" (Heaney 1980, 150).

The idea of words as possessing an energy and a force that is not purely related to their rational signification is another example of how poetry as epistemological discourse has access to aspects of the unconscious and the real that are not to be found elsewhere. Heaney is very aware of these rhizomatic and plural dimensions of words, and he strives to understand their role in the creations of literary, and by extension political, structures of identity. Thus, he will analyze Ted Hughes's reliance on the Anglo-Saxon and Norse elements of the English language and, in careful readings of some of the earlier poems, parse the way in which this heritage is carefully referenced, so that the England then and the England now, the Englands of the past and present, are in a dialectical process of mutually informing each other in his work. Heaney later asks who else but Hughes would call a collection *Wodwo* and makes the thought-provoking point that the Middle English poem *Gawain and the Green Knight*, with its "beautiful alliterating and illuminated form," is closer in spirit to Hughes's own poetry than Hughes's poetry is to the poetry of his English contemporaries (ibid., 156). Interestingly, the poem "Wodwo" is founded on water and has connections with Heaney's own very fluid and permeable ideas about identity.

Heaney sees Hughes as attempting to give voice through his poetry to the preconscious or unconscious aspects of life, to the Lacanian real, and to the bodily sensations and emotions that are usually untapped by language. He sees the core symbol of Hughes's work as "founded on rock" (ibid., 158). For Hughes, this rock is symbolic of his very deep relationship with his own England of the mind. In light of our earlier comparisons between Heaney's thinking and the poetizing of Heidegger, it is significant that he uses a loose translation of the Heideggerian term *Dasein* to describe Hughes's very grounded and somatic England of the mind. This combination of rock and a sense of beingthereness would seem to be a very strong set of signifiers of English identity, but it is more significant, to Heaney's idea of a fluid structure of identity, that it is not seen as the most grounded sense of Englishness, of an ur-Englishness. Instead, it is just one sense of Englishness among others, and it is in their interaction that Heaney attempts to set out the force field of English identity.

Heaney goes on to show that while Geoffrey Hill also adverts to the Anglo-Saxon aspects of language, his main influence is how it has been changed and softened by medieval Latin and European influences, and Heaney goes on to characterize this sensibility as "Anglo-Romanesque." In contrast with Hughes's focus on the ground and the rocks of England, Hill is more concerned with the buildings that are created on these rocks. To extend the metaphor further, Heaney sees Hill's work as being set against the "tympanum and chancel-arch" and influenced by Latin (ibid., 151, 160). Again, we are looking at a structure composed of choices, accretions, additions, and selections: Englishness is no more a given or a transcendental signified than is Irishness.

Thus, in "Hymn XXIV" of the *Mercian Hymns*, the poem focuses on a "carved pediment" or a tympanum, which is the engraved area between the "lintel of a door and the arch above it—which exhibits a set of scenes" (ibid., 160–61). In this ekphrastic account of the scene, which denotes condensed versions of the Garden of Eden and the Harrowing of Hell, Heaney observes that a few carvings are able to call upon the whole body of Christian doctrine. In Heaney's reading, Hughes looked at the rock as rock, as part of the land and as symbolic of an unconscious physical resonance of that land. Hill, on the other hand, looks at the rock as signifier, something that is connected through writing with a church history that is not originally English at all. For him, the rock is a baseline from which something more elevated can be constructed, and it is the structure of the carving that resonates for Hill, as he associates the carving with the carver, "a master-mason" (ibid., 161). Just as Hughes fuses the land, the present English language, and the dialect and structures of Old and Middle English, so Hill is fascinated by the structural imperative of the mason, especially in the lines from "Hymn XXIV": "intent to pester upon tympanum" (ibid., 159). Heaney explains that *tympanum* also has the sonic signification of *drum* and that the word *pester* derives from the original Latin root *pastorium* and means to "hobble a horse." This etymological exploration of the words, and their association, connecting present and past through translation and through linguistic capillaries, becomes his reading method, as he notes that "interlacing and entanglement of motifs" (ibid., 161), is also a way of describing one aspect of Hill's writing style. Here the visual and the verbal become entangled and interlaced in a field of interpretative force.

Hill's structural integration of Englishness with the Latinate texts and imagery of the Middle Ages is another England of the mind—one that has resonances of the Anglo-Saxon world of Hughes, but one that is also very different from it. There is no single, or singular, Englishness from which each poet draws; rather, they each create their own version of Englishness through poetic language. The self-reflexive aspect of Hill's work, as he is talking about the nature of writing and signification, is made stronger when we take into account Derrida's point that in "that long ago era when writing was unknown, most of the words used to designate a poetic composition were borrowed from the art of the weaver, the builder, etc." (Derrida and Attridge 1992, 166). Each of these Englands of the mind is created through poetic writing, and the mason as writer is an important aspect of this structural landscape.

This brings our discussion of Heaney's reading of these three poets, and their conceptions of Englishness, to the work of Philip Larkin, who uses a version of the English language that is influenced by the Norman Conquest and by the work of Chaucer and Spenser. As Heaney puts it, there is a gap in Larkin between the perceiver and the thing perceived: it is the language of "a real man in a real place." Larkin's is a voice that is self-aware of the contemporaneity of his Englishness. His work is a turn of English identity that is a stage beyond both the Anglo-Saxon and the Middle Ages; he is that part of the development of the poetic form that stems from a time when the public sphere was gradually becoming secular and plays began to displace the sacrament of the Mass "as a form of communal telling and knowing." His England of the mind is one that looks at seaside postcards and trains and the postwar disappointments that pervaded England in the 1950s. His is a modern voice, not one that plumbs the historical and mythic depths. He is the "not untrue, not unkind voice of post-war England" (Heaney 1980, 164, 165, 167).

As Heaney notes, while Larkin's England and his sense of what it means to be English are not as deep as Hughes's, or as solemn as Hill's, they are nevertheless "dearly beloved" (ibid., 167). The England of Larkin is one of customs and institutions, so once again it is a field of force within which different versions of England, rural and urban, past and present, prior Englishness and accreted Englishness, are brought into a fluid interconnection that creates new meanings. The same is true of social class, as Larkin is able to bring different societal groupings and idiolects into his England of the mind.

Heaney is acutely aware of the buildedness of the England that Larkin creates, calling him a coiner of compounds. His constellation of Englishness is more synchronic than diachronic. Whereas Hughes and Hill both, in their different ways, look back to history and philology, Larkin looks across his own culture of the present, taking in different modes of speaking, different social classes, and different versions of modernity. It is this interlacing and construction that Heaney finds in Larkin—his England is populated less by rock than by words and accents and aspects of culture that in ways different from, but parallel to, the physical essence of life enunciated by Hughes have been submerged and largely unaccessed by English literature to date.

His England takes in the different versions of the English language, some of which have not been registered in English "literature" before. In Larkin's work, the lyrical and the demotic are interconnected in a very distinct rhythmical structure, iambic tetrameter, which echoes a long line of literary forebears: "They fuck you up, your mum and dad. / They may not mean to but they do" (Larkin and Thwaite 2003, 89). For Larkin, this image is his fern and ivy or the unearthing of the mason's skill: here is his particular addition to the structure of an England of the mind—the use of demotic language and the transformation of such language by its placement within the structure and syntax of poetry, itself almost a synecdoche of high culture and literature, when taken as a qualitative descriptor. The Englands of the mind, which each creates, are signified by their specific use of language and imagery.

When we examine that language, we find that their three separate voices are guaranteed by three separate foundations that, when combined, "represent almost the total resources of the English language itself" (Heaney 1980, 151). Therefore, both Hughes and Hill make use of rock and stone as symbols and metaphors in their poetry, but both do so in very different ways. Whereas Hughes is grounded to the rocks of England, and to an Anglo-Saxon sense of Englishness that is grounded in rock, Hill is different: Hughes probes the rock, whereas Hill builds on it linguistically. There is a buildedness to his work, and the interrelation with Hughes is interesting in that while Hughes attempts to access the unconscious physicality of the earth and rock of England, Hill is building on that rock, incorporating Latinate accretions and creating a superstructure on top of the substructure of Anglo-Saxon that Hughes has mined.

Indeed, one could see this essay as suggesting a triangular structure through which to trace these different notions of England that parallels the quincunx, with its different versions of Ireland, with Hughes, Hill, and Larkin mutually informing and interinanimating each other's view of English language and identity. Each is influenced by the other, resulting in a field of force that creates the Englands of the mind that are mutually sustaining yet mutually separate at the same time. To reinterpret this triangle in the terminology of the quincunx, the Anglo-Saxon tower of Hughes is a short squat tower, built of rock and full of the scop's twang of consonant, kenning, and what Heaney has termed the "fern and ivied world of nature." Hill's tower is made of Romanesque arches and vaults; it takes the Anglo-Saxon world and adds to it the dialects and linguistic input of Latin and the Franco-European influences of Middle Age Catholicism, as well as the embroidery and complicated ironwork of the time. Larkin's tower, to continue the metaphor, is more self-aware, more modern, and more situated in an England that is no longer imperial and is now trying to find its way anew in a contemporary world. Each enunciates a separate foundation, and when they are combined in different ways, they create a force field, a constellation, that can be called "Englands of the mind." As Heaney has written elsewhere about Larkin, his work is sensitive to the "dialectic" between "the death-mask of nihilism and the fixed smile of a pre-booked place in paradise" (1995b, 153), and all identity is composed of such transient and ephemeral structures, which ideology attempts to reify and ossify; as we have seen, this process of reification and ossification is true in the case of both Ireland and England. Englishness, like Irishness, is a transient and fluid constellation of different ideas as opposed to a position of fixity. This triangle, like the quincunx, is a far more accurate account of how identity works as well as an emancipatory paradigm for how it could work in contemporary society and culture.

In *The Government of the Tongue*, he uses another spatial image to embody this idea of a field of force. Commenting on Osip Mandelstam's ideas on the purity of poetry, he notes Mandelstam's metaphor that equates poetry with the making of "Brussels lace," an activity that involves "real work" but whose "major components, those supporting the design, are air, perforations and truancy" (1988, 87). Here we see another use of the textile metaphor that Derrida coined, but one that is also appropriate to the sampler with its different identifications, as it is the spaces between the elements as much as the elements themselves that are able to signify the real in Heaney's thinking. The same is true for the spaces between the towers of the quincunx and the spaces between the different "Englands" of Hughes, Hill, and Larkin. In this sense, writing is not so much about signifying what is already there, but about "surveying, mapping realms that are yet to come" (Deleuze and Guattari 1987, 85). Heaney argues that identity is always dialectical and often pluridialectical in the sense that the interaction is not just binary but ternary in the case of the "Englands of the Mind" and quincuncial in the context of Irish identity. In both of these structures, the voices speaking, and those listening, are plural, and this factor is significant in Heaney's thinking.

Derrida has made the point, in *Of Spirit*, that the origin of language is responsibility (1989, 132), in the sense that to speak, necessarily, is to speak to someone else, to assume the responsibility of addressing some other person. In a binary opposition, something is defined in contrast to the other side of the binary and, as such, can be placed in an ethical context by taking note of the differences and connections that exist between self and other. With respect to speaking, the self is seen as addressing the other and is in turn addressed by that other. This intersubjectivity is precisely what Heaney terms the sense of "needing to accommodate two opposing versions of truthfulness simultaneously" (1984a, 4), and indeed is the very condition that has been emblematically rendered in Catherine Bradley's embroidery sampler, where "two value systems, which now explode daily, are lodged like dormant munitions" on one piece of Ulster linen (1983a, 6). Heaney's perspective is analogous to Blanchot's, who sees that in imaginary space, "things are *transformed* into that which cannot be grasped" and that this transformation "releases us both from them and from ourselves" (1982, 131). Blanchot, like Heaney, sees part of the function of art as the transformation of the given perceptions of reality. The function of imaginary space, a concept akin to Heaney's field of force, is the transformation of the actual and the creation of an alternative paradigm of truth and integration, and through looking at reality awry, that reality is transformed.

Thus, regarding the quincunx, to see these figures at different corners of the diamond of towers, with a further tower at the center, as a static structure, is to miss the point about Heaney's conception of the field of force. It is in the dynamic interaction between these towers that this quincunx becomes an adequate emblem of the complex structure that his poetized thinking brings to bear on Irishness. It is through the interaction of these figures, their mirrored reflections and refractions, just as it was in the interaction of text and context in Catherine Bradley's sampler, that the complexity of the poetic structure is revealed. Meaning, as was the case in Derrida's *navette*, is created in the movement and the changes in perspective between the different towers, and the effect of these forces can be seen in the new versions of Irishness that come into being, just as is the case in the creation of the different Englands of the mind of Hughes, Hill, and Larkin and in that subliminal sense of Englishness that could be seen in Auden. In Blanchot's sense, the meaning comes in the imaginary space created by literature, where the binarisms of self and other are merged in a constellation, and it is with a consideration of this sense of self and other, often in Irish studies a shorthand for Irish and English, that this part of the discussion will close.

The interaction between self and other is the core of his essay from *Finders Keepers* "Through-Other Places, Through-Other Times." In this essay, we see a further deconstruction of language, as he takes a signifier that is ideologically shot through with the residue of colonization and conflict and replaces it with a cognate term that opens the horizon of expectations of the signifier in question along with its attendant signifieds. Comparing a recent book, *The British Isles: A History of Four Nations*, by Hugh Kearney (1989), with his own coeditorship of *The School Bag* with Ted Hughes, Heaney notes that both books apply similar editorial guidelines. These guidelines were motivated by a conviction that is expressed at the beginning of the paragraph where the two books are compared: "I have a dread of pious words like diversity but I believe in what they stand for," and he goes on to add that both Hughes and himself were determined that their editorship of this anthology would "insist on the diverse and deep traditions that operate through and sustain for good the poetry written in Ireland, England, Scotland and in Wales." It is with this version of diversity in mind that Heaney approvingly cites Richard Kearney's view that it is only by adopting what he calls "a Britannic approach" that any possible sense can be made of the histories of England, Ireland, Scotland, Wales, Cornwall, or the Isle of Man. Taking this approach, and pondering its ideological aspects, Heaney suggests that here, while there is an awareness that the word *British* can function like "a political reminder, a mnemonic for past invasions and coercions," there is also a different signification possible, as the word *Britannic* can be used as this cognate, but different, signifier, which "works more like a cultural wake-up call and gestures not only towards the cultural past but also towards an imaginable future" (2002, 378–79).

At this point, we move from "Englands of the mind" to "Britains of the mind," and the political implications of this field of force will be discussed in the next chapter. For now, it is sufficient to note that such a perspective enunciates Heaney's idea of the through-other as significant in terms of identity. Identity is always shot through with aspects of the other, as we have seen, and this point has been consistently argued by Derrida, who notes that political or cultural identity "is not the self-identity of a thing" but rather involves a difference within identity. Derrida suggests that "the identity of a culture is a way of being different from itself; a culture is different from itself; language is different from itself; the person is different from itself." Once this more plural version of identity is taken into account, it becomes clear that "fighting for your own identity is not exclusive of another identity, is open to another identity" (Derrida and Caputo 1997, 13). These ideas coalesce with Heaney's own views on identity as permeable, shifting, and fluid. Both writers are affected by their own heritages, with Heaney seeing himself as Irish in a state that sees itself as British, while at the same time being an important figure in literature written in English, though with a strongly Irish element. Similarly, Derrida was a French Algerian Jew, born in "El Biar, Algeria, near Algiers. Both his parents came from old Algerian Jewish families." So while he is French, it is not in the same way as a "Frenchman of Paris." Years later, Derrida summed up his sense that, "as a child in Algeria, he was an outsider to French literature and culture" (Mikics 2009, 13, 21).

Both Derrida and Heaney are culturally amphibious figures whose experiential grasp of plural and hybrid identities is central to their own worldview. Thus, Derrida can call himself someone who, while "not quite European by birth," nevertheless considers himself "to be a sort of over-acculturated, over-colonized European hybrid" (1992, 7–8), whereas Heaney speaks of how, while he teaches English literature and publishes in London, he reminds us, as we noted in the previous chapter, he lives off another hump as well. Each man is shot through with the through-other, with a field of force where the different indexes of identity are whirling and in constant flux and motion. Their attitude is beyond the binary of self and other; rather, it is about a new constellation caused by the interpenetration and imbrication of self and other. It is a syncretic perspective, one that, for Heaney, offers the possibility of arriving at "a final place which is not the absence of activity but is, on the contrary, the continuous realisation of all the activities of which we are capable" (1983a, 16).

This continuous realization of a plurality of perspectives is something that he admires in the work of poet W. R. Rodgers, who originally used the term *through-otherness* in a poem called "Armagh." Rodgers had an experience of plural identities that echoed those plural identities of Heaney and Derrida. He worked as a BBC producer in London, but before that time he had been "the Presbyterian minister in the rural parish of Loughgall" in County Armagh. In a reading of some of his work, Heaney also traces connections with the Scottish inheritance. He goes on to repeat the triangulation we spoke of earlier in his readings of Hughes, Hill, and Larkin by speaking about the identity of Rodgers in a parallel triangulation: he speaks of the triangulation of Rodgers's understanding of himself between London, Loughgall, and the Lowlands and goes on to suggest a parallel with the "triple heritage" of the Irish, English, and Scottish traditions. For him, these traditions are not "other" but "through-other": "There is through-otherness about Armagh," which is captured by new dead "garrulous kings / Who at last can agree" (2002, 364, 366).

The irony here is that for Rodgers, the different identities, captured in synecdoche by the garrulous kings, occur only in death, whereas this essay suggests that it is possible to achieve a type of through-otherness in life through art and possibly, as we will see in the next chapter, through politics. The sense of a "mix-up" suggests an irrational and possibly unconscious aspect of this concept, which ties in with our earlier discussion of poetry as accessing the real of language and experience. It is as if Heaney is suggesting that the complexities of identity need to be addressed by a structure that is adequate to the rational, irrational, and atavistic dimensions of a series of permeations between selfhood and alterity. Of course, he is only too aware that the movement from self and other to "through-other" is not a smooth one, nor is it one that he has personally found easy. There is a strong resistance to giving up the pillars of one's identity, especially when those pillars are seen as under threat from other ideological strands of identity.

Heaney's own *An Open Letter*, as we have seen, bridles at his being called a British poet, and he makes the point that it is because of the coercion that he, along with "the rest of the minority," felt as he made his "Jacobite way under the Williamite arches every July," a process that sharpened his sense of otherness "rather than encouraging any notions of through-otherness" (ibid., 368). However, rather than espousing this more postcolonial position, Heaney has attempted to interrogate it and move beyond it through his use of the field-of-force structure that allows for multiple versions of Irishness to interact, for multiple versions of Englishness to interact, and then, ultimately, for versions of Irishness and Englishness to interact in a way that is through-other. Heaney has set out a number of examples of this through-otherness, and interestingly all of his examples move from a purely literary resonance to a more politicized one, as part of his stated aim in creating the quincunx was "to bring the frontiers of the country into alignment with the frontiers of writing" (1995b, 199).

Thus, when Heaney speaks of the work of Sorley MacLean, who wrote in Scots Gaelic, in the context of his work being available to an Irish readership through translation, itself a very significant vehicle of the through-other, he notes that it was the publication of a dual-language edition, including the poet's own English versions, that "helped to canonize MacLean in the new through-otherness of English and other nation languages." Heaney sees this through-otherness as helping to disturb the "tidy assumptions" of those individuals from Northern Ireland and the Republic of Ireland, respectively.

Given that MacLean is a native speaker, the assumptions would be that he would be both Catholic and anti-British. In fact, MacLean was a "Gaelic-speaking Free Presbyterian" who was also "a passionate Socialist whose heroes included James Connolly," and who had fought as "a British soldier in the Western Desert" (Heaney 2002, 379–80). The different and syncretic reaction of the different parameters of identity in the person and work of MacLean makes Heaney's point for him: once there is that sense of flow, then all previous solid and stolid expectations and assumptions are open to serious and radical revision.

Heaney goes on to cite similar cases where stereotypes can be confounded by the through-other, notably Donegal Gaeltacht–dwelling and Irish-speaking poet Cathal O'Searcaigh, whose "exploration of his homosexuality in 'the first official language' wrong foots many of the old expectations." Once again, it is through the cross-pollination of elements of the field of force that changes can be brought about in language and attitudes. He goes on to posit a similar value in the translations by Paul Muldoon of the poems of Nuala Ní Dhomhnaill from Irish into English. Rather than seeing the two languages in competition, these translations offer a new sense of connectedness between them; the translations create another field of force where meaning, rather than being entombed in either language, is now created in the movement of thought between the two languages, in what Blanchot would term the space of literature. It is an example of how "what was problematic has become productive, even arguably reproductive" (ibid., 380). We will see another example of this productivity in Heaney's reading of Thomas Kinsella's translations of Irish poems in *An Duanaire*.

This productivity and reproductivity of the through-other are at the core of his sense of the value of the field of force, and they are also central to his view of the epistemological structure of poetry. He sees it as a genre where there is a space for the unconscious, for the somatic, and for the real. Through its enunciation of these areas, it allows for that shattering of assumptions of which he spoke, and it allows for the transformation of such assumptions into more fluid, more democratic, and more pluralist paradigms of identity, a point he overtly stresses when he speaks of his inclusion of Ulster Protestant poet Louis MacNeice in his quincunx: "The admission of MacNeice in this way within the symbolic ordering of Ireland also admits a hope for the evolution of a political order, one tolerant of difference and capable of metamorphoses within all the multivalent possibilities of Irishness, Britishness, Europeanness, planetariness, creatureliness, whatever" (1995b, 200). It is to these multivalent possibilities of Irishness that our discussion now turns, as, having outlined plural and complex sense of Irishness, Heaney goes on to show how they need to be addressed in both the aesthetic and the political spheres.

4

Poetics and Politics

Surviving Amphibiously

It has become a truism to say that politics and poetry should not be conflated. This suspicion of the role of poetry in the public sphere has existed as far back as Plato, but became something of an orthodoxy in the period that saw the rise of fascism in Europe. Fascism in Germany, Italy, and Spain merged the divisions between the rational and the emotional and between the constative and the performative, as the public sphere became a dramatic space where the concept of the people, the *Volk*, was embodied and dramatized through massive sociocultural performative theater. Walter Benjamin was one of the first critics to see the inherent dangers in this conflation of the poetic with the politic. All of the areas we have discussed thus far, which analyzed how poetic language and thinking are able to access aspects of selfhood that are not available to the normal paradigms of language, come into play in this fusion of the aesthetic and the politic. In this chapter, I will outline the critical consensus on this topic and then demonstrate that Heaney's own reading of the connection between the poetic and the politic is original, in an Irish context, and also bears comparison with the work of theorists as diverse as Murray Krieger, Ernesto Laclau, and Chantal Mouffe.

The term used for this conflation is *aesthetic ideology*, and it has been defined by Terry Eagleton as involving

> a phenomenalist reduction of the linguistic to the sensually empirical, a confusing of mind and world, sign and thing, cognition and

> percept, which is consecrated in the Hegelian symbol and resisted by Kant's rigorous demarcation of aesthetic judgement from the cognitive, ethical and political realms. Such aesthetic ideology, by repressing the contingent, aporetic relation which holds between the spheres of language and the real, naturalizes or phenomenalizes the former, and is thus in danger of converting the accidents of meaning to organic natural process in the characteristic manner of ideological thought. (1990, 10)

This process of converting the aporetic accidents of meaning into organic narrative constructs is precisely what is at stake in the conflation of poetry and politics. This ideology is a constituent factor in any nationalistic discourse. Benjamin was one of the first to see that appealing, as it did, to ideas of organic connection between a people and a place, aesthetic ideology was not a supplement to fascist epistemology, but rather was integral to it and to all advanced versions of nationalism. Benjamin thus credits fascism with "a full-blown aesthetic ideology (as opposed to a ragbag of half-baked aesthetic mannerisms), thereby inviting us to take fascist aesthetics extremely seriously" (de Graef, De Geest, and Vanfraussen 2008, 74).

The full-blown nature of such aesthetic ideology can be traced back to misreadings of Kant and Hegel, both of whom found the aesthetic to be problematic in terms of their different systematic attempts to outline the nature of ontology and epistemology. For Kant, aesthetic judgment is free from concepts: "the judgement of taste is not based on concepts; for if it were, it would be open to dispute (decision by means of proofs)." However, the other proposition of the Kantian antinomy is that the judgment of taste must be based on concepts; otherwise, "there could be no room even for contention in the matter, or for the claim to the necessary agreement of others." Accordingly, such judgmental criteria are "synthetic a priori," and they allow for a possible reconciliation between different faculties: "One who feels pleasure in simple reflection on the form of an object, without having any concept in mind, rightly lays claim to the agreement of everyone, although this judgement is empirical and a singular judgement. For the ground of this pleasure is found in the universal, though subjective, condition of reflective judgements, namely the final harmony of an object . . . with the mutual relation of the faculties of cognition (imagination and understanding), which are requisite for every empirical cognition" (1928, 198, 145, 32). On reading this view of the aesthetic as a mediation between the "empirical" and the "universal," the one and the many, and the subject and the object, it is easy to see how Kant could be misread through the lens of aesthetic ideology, and there is a similar case to be made regarding Hegel's *Aesthetics*, which saw the symbol as the mediating force between subject and object.

For Hegel, the aesthetic allows for the "Idea as Ideal" to sanction a "completely unified mediation and interpenetration" of "universality" and "concrete particularity." Hegel sees such unified interpenetration as an "ideal presentation" that occurs when "the universality of the powers is pervaded by the particularity of the individual and, in this unification, becomes a subjectivity and individuality which is fully unified in itself and self-related" (1975a, 236, 241). As is clear, perceptions of the aesthetic facilitate a fusion between different orders, and Hegel is keen to explore this paradox. For him, what is ultimately real is the coalescence of the self-knowing spirit with the actual world in which we live, and this sense of synthesis is sanctioned in part by the aesthetic, which brings about the "Idea": "The Idea existent in sensible form is the Ideal, i.e. beauty, which itself is truth implicit" (Mure 1965, 85). This description of the Idea "accords with Hegel's account of it in his works on logic, in which he describes it as the absolute unity of the concept and objectivity" (James 2009, 31).

In his discussion of painting as an aesthetic mode, Hegel again emphasizes the synthesizing function of the aesthetic:

> So the principle of subjectivity is on the one hand the basis of particularization and, nevertheless, on the other hand, the principle of mediation and synthesis, so that painting now unites in one and the same work of art what hitherto devolved on two different arts;

> the *external* environment which architecture treated artistically, and the shape which sculpture worked out as an embodiment of the *spirit*. Painting places its figures in nature or an architectural environment which is external to them and which it has invented in the same sense as it has invented the figures; and by the heart and soul of its treatment it can make this external background at the same time a reflection of what is subjective, and no less can it set the background in relation and harmony with the spirit of the figures that are moving against it. (1975b, 798)

The fusion of the external with the spirit through aesthetic understanding and representation is at the core of Hegel's absolute idealism, a mode of thought that is a development of the Kantian transcendental idealism of which we have already spoken. For Kant, there was a "thing in itself," a *Ding an sich*, which could not be fully apprehended by consciousness; for Hegel, however, and for Fichte and Schelling, the idea of the "thing in itself" is something of a contradiction in terms, because a thing must be an object of our consciousness if it is to be an object at all.

Nonetheless, just as the concept without its objectivity is not genuinely a concept, so too the Idea is not genuinely Idea without, and outside of, its actuality: "Therefore the Idea must go forth into actuality, and it acquires actuality only through the actual subjectivity which inherently corresponds with the Concept and through subjectivity's ideal being for itself" (Hegel 1975a, 144). Such partial readings of idealist epistemologies are the philosophical groundwork for aesthetic ideological political positions. Ideas of fusion and unity, and an organicist sense that the aesthetic, and aesthetically charged discourse, has power to sublate differences into a new and organic whole, are the result of such misreadings or partial readings. Christopher Norris brings out the hidden agenda of such high romantic (and postromantic) writers, who see in the power of language the ability to "transcend the opposition between sensuous and intellectual modes of apprehension" (1988, 116). Benjamin too, saw the dangers of such a process, and he summed them up with great prescience:

"*All efforts to aestheticize politics culminate in one point. That one point is war.* War, and only war, makes it possible to set a goal for mass movements on the grandest scale while preserving traditional property relations. That is how the situation presents itself in political terms" (2008, 41; emphasis in the original). Consequently, there is a strong trend of European thinking that points to the clear and present dangers of fusing poetry and politics, as that way, it seems, fascism lies. One of the strongest critiques of aesthetic ideology was provided by Paul de Man, whose final collection of essays was, in fact, entitled *Aesthetic Ideology* (de Man and Warminski 1996). His deconstructive readings probed the interstices of such organicist and aesthetic thinking. The aesthetic is seen by de Man as a central factor in any kind of organicist approach to politics and culture. As a suasive discourse, which reconciles contraries and brings about a fusion of different entities, the aesthetic can be seen as a powerful political force. In this collection, he traced this quasi-politicized sense of the aesthetic to readings, or rather misreadings, as he sees them, of the work of Kant and Hegel, and it is his essays on these two central philosophers that constitute the core of this collection.

Three of the essays deal with Kant: "Phenomenality and Materiality in Kant," "Kant's Materialism," and "Kant and Schiller," while two deal with Hegel, "Sign and Symbol in Hegel's Aesthetics" and de Man's "Reply to Raymond Geuss" on the subject of the latter's reading of Hegel. De Man sees aesthetic ideology as stemming from misreadings of both thinkers, misreadings that deny what he calls the "materiality of language" or "inscription." By this term he means the rhetorical and uncontrolled aspect of language that offers resistance, through tropes, ambiguities, and metaphorical deviations, to aesthetic and systematic tantalizations. Many of these late essays, and writings in *Allegories of Reading* (de Man 1979) and *The Resistance to Theory* (de Man 1986), are devoted to teasing out, through close readings that focus on the epistemological influence of rhetorical tropes, the aporias and antinomies inherent in seemingly monadic totalities, receptions, and systems. Most of these readings, especially in the romantic and postromantic tradition, are valorized by the aesthetic ideology that is the subject of this book, and ultimately this quasi-organicist ideology can be traced back to Kant and Hegel.

As we have seen, philosophers place a huge onus on the category of the aesthetic in their respective philosophies. In his introduction to de Man's *Aesthetic Ideology*, Andrzej Warminski explains how the category of the aesthetic is central in Kant "as a principle of articulation between theoretical and practical reason" and in Hegel as "the moment of transition between objective spirit and absolute spirit" (de Man and Warminski 1996, 3, 4). Both Kant and Hegel place the aesthetic at a nodal point in their attempts to bring together subject and object, mind and matter, and the nominal and the phenomenal. As de Man notes, for Kant, "the investment in the aesthetic is therefore considerable, since the possibility of philosophy itself, as the articulation of a transcendental with a metaphysical discourse, depends on it" (ibid., 73). He goes on to read both philosophers with a focus on how language, especially the rhetorical use of language, problematizes the aesthetic desire for fusion. The idea of the Kantian sublime posits a move beyond the possible fusion of concepts and intuitions, beyond real-world knowledge that can be grounded in practical reason. However, since the sublime is an aesthetic category, it must then involve some sense of phenomenal cognition. It can gesture "beyond" the antinomies of sensuous experience, but it can be articulated only through a language that, in its materiality, refuses, because it is unable, to transgress beyond subscribed limits. As de Man puts it, albeit in a slightly different context, "It depends on a linguistic structure that is not itself accessible to the powers of transcendental philosophy": "How can faculties, themselves a heuristic hypothesis devoid of any reality—for only people who have read too much eighteenth century psychology or philosophy might end up believing that they have an imagination or a reason the same way they have blue eyes or a big nose—how can faculties be said to act, or even to act freely, as if they were conscious and complete human beings?" (ibid., 79, 87). By focusing on the epistemological value of the tropes of language, de Man deconstructs (to use correctly a much-abused critical term) the seeming aesthetic totalities that have generally been read into Kantian philosophy, especially by Schiller and Kleist and the whole romantic tradition.

This example of his methodology gives some flavor of the work in general. He subjects the Hegelian categories of "sign" and "symbol" to a similar reading, demonstrating how "symbol," the privileged trope in Hegel's *Aesthetics*, is generally seen as the "mediation between the mind and the physical world of which art manifestly partakes" (ibid., 91). Here again, the category of the aesthetic is used to fuse the subject with its object, and here again a deconstructive reading of the argument through which Hegel reaches this conclusion brings out the aporetic nature of this argument. Focusing on Hegel's statement that art is "a thing of the past" (ibid., 94), he goes on to argue that it is because Hegel places impossible demands on art, and these demands are frustrated by the materiality of language, which refuses the totalization of the symbol and makes his philosophy "an allegory of the disjunction between philosophy and history . . . literature and aesthetics . . . literary experience and literary theory" (ibid., 104).

This epistemological critique comes to its high point toward the conclusion of his "Kant and Schiller" essay, when, talking about the role of the aesthetic in politics and in education, he goes on to cite a quotation wherein the role of the aesthetic as an expression of feeling is compared to the aesthetic in politics, where the people function as the raw material to the politician just as clay is a raw material for the sculptor: "The people are for him what the stone is to the sculptor. Leader and masses are as little of a problem to each other as colour is a problem for the painter. Politics are the plastic arts of the state as painting is the plastic art of colour. Therefore politics without the people or against the people are nonsense. To transform a mass into a people and a people into a state—that has always been the deepest sense of a genuine political task" (ibid., 155). The author of this passage is Joseph Goebbels, the Nazi minister for propaganda, and this image, to my mind, brings de Man's critique of aesthetic ideology to its logical conclusion. The aestheticization of politics, and the use of cultural politics for political purposes, allows for monstrous activities that become situated outside the realm of epistemology and instead lurk within the ambit of aesthetic judgment. What happens to the people who happen to be the wrong color, in any sense of this term, for this particular artist is obvious and is the nub of de Man's ongoing critique, which brings us full circle with regard to his writings during the Second World War, because in December 1987 it became known that a Belgian researcher, Ortwin de Graef, had discovered reviews of books, concerts, and conferences written by Paul de Man in the years 1940–42. Except for a few articles in *Les Cahiers du Libre Examen*, a journal associated with the University of Brussels, and a few more in a Flemish-language journal, *Het Vlaamsche Land*, some 170 were written for the important Belgian newspaper *Le Soir*. During the period that de Man published in *Le Soir* and *Het Vlaamsche Land*, they were under some Nazi censorship (Hartman 1989, 13–14). Some of these articles were anti-Semitic and were seen as supporting Nazi cultural politics in Europe at that time.

Irony aside, the example of someone who has written with such clinical precision about the dangers of aesthetic ideology being seen to have himself succumbed to its very siren song makes a number of points. First, it shows that the line between organicist constructions and theoretical deconstructions is a thin one, and, second, it shows that literature is protean, as it can be both creative of, and deconstructive of, organicist aesthetics. In my opinion, there can be little doubt that de Man, having experienced the seductive power of Nazi ideology, spent a lot of his subsequent academic career attempting to come to an understanding of how it happened and subsequently deconstructing the premises that constituted this ideological position. However, most important for the purposes of this chapter, it shows that the relationship between the poetic and the politic is both complex and intricate. If one were to attempt to represent this relationship diagrammatically, the image of a line or a binary opposition would not suffice: one would need a more nuanced and fluid construction; one would need something like a field of force, like a quincunx, and it is here that the work of Heaney with respect to its connections between poetry and politics becomes a significant factor.

Heaney was writing at a time when politics was a huge contextual factor in the poetry of Northern Ireland. The fact that in the United Kingdom, seen for so long as a bastion of freedom and democratic accountability, there was a region that treated Catholics in a manner that seemed to be less than fair, to put it in its kindest terms, caused great interest in the media, who were demanding to hear the voices of the minority. Blake Morrison described it as searching for "the war poets" (1982, 55), and there was a surge of interest in poetry, probably because, as we have been discussing in earlier chapters, poetry allows the saying of things that can otherwise not be articulated through the normal discourse of the public sphere. However, the specter of aesthetic ideology loomed over the efforts of poets writing about a conflict within which they were culturally, ethnically, politically, and religiously immersed. Any poets writing about the topic left him- or herself open to such criticism.

The opening paragraph of Edna Longley's essay "Poetry and Politics in Northern Ireland," in *Poetry in the Wars*, extends the scope of such criticism, incorporating, as it does, the views of Conor Cruise O'Brien on this relationship between the poetic and the politic. The essay begins:

> Poetry and politics, like church and state, should be separated. And for the same reasons: mysteries distort the rational processes which ideally prevail in social relations; while ideologies confiscate the poet's special passport to *terra incognita*. Its literary streak, indeed, helps to make Irish Nationalism more a theology than an ideology. Conor Cruise O'Brien calls "the area where literature and politics overlap" an "unhealthy intersection"; because, "suffused with romanticism," it breeds bad politics—Fascism and Nationalism. But it also breeds bad literature, particularly, bad poetry, which in a vicious circle breeds—or inbreeds—bad politics. (1986, 185)

Such suspicions of the dangers of mixing politics and aesthetics were widespread, with many commentators "positing the possibility of completely severing the aesthetic from the political" (Whalen 2007, 10).

Indeed, Heaney's own volume of poems entitled *North*, published in 1975 when violence was rife in Northern Ireland, has come under fire from precisely this perspective, with a number of critics suggesting that he had succumbed to versions of aesthetic ideology by becoming the *vox loci*, or the voice of the tribe, for whom the territory of Northern Ireland was deemed sacred. In a poem called "Kinship" (1975, 40–45), Heaney wrote from the perspective of an autochthonous, nativist persona who is the voice of the colonized, the disempowered, and the dispossessed of both myth and history. In this sense, he is voicing what we have termed the aesthetically ideological. Conceptions of a territory that is sacred to a people are usually defined through the aesthetic, a point made at some length by de Man: "for it is as a political force that the aesthetic still concerns us as one of the most powerful ideological drives to act upon the reality of history" (1984, 264).

In "Kinship," Heaney traces a journey in memory back to his childhood when he helped his grandfather to cut turf and then proceeds to a mythic identification with those native peoples whom the colonizing powers seek to civilize whether they want to be civilized or not. Roman historian Tacitus stands in synecdoche for the voice of colonial and imperial rationality, looking down from metaphorical ramparts at the speaker of the poem below, who addresses him by name. The apostrophe asks that Tacitus should "observe" how the speaker makes his grove on "an old crannog / piled by the fearful dead," and Tacitus is also the addressee for the long following section where "our mother ground" is described as being "sour" with the blood of those persons sacrificed. In a horrifying but strong image, Heaney speaks of these victims as lying "gargling / in her sacred heart," while the legions look on from the ramparts. Tacitus is then rhetorically asked to come back to this "island of the ocean" and to report how "we slaughter / for the common good." It is the pronouns here ("report us . . . we slaughter . . . our love and terror") that would appear to locate the poem as a signifier of aesthetic ideology, where land and language seem to cohere to present that organicist conception of the *Volk*, under whose auspices it is deemed correct to slaughter those individuals who are not of the *Volk* (Heaney 1975, 45). Another poem in the same volume, "Punishment" (ibid., 37–38), sees him write about the practice in Catholic, nationalist areas of taking young women who had been having relationships with British soldiers, tying them to railings, and covering their hair in tar. In this poem, he compares these actions to the killing of an Iron Age young woman, the Windeby girl, discovered by archaeologist P. V. Glob (Glob 1977), for adultery by her tribe and again, using a personal pronoun, locates the speaker of the poem in the ideology of the tribe as he addresses the Iron Age Windeby girl and conflates her with contemporary young Northern Irish women, her "betraying sisters," who have been "cauled in tar" by nationalists who resent their relationships with British soldiers. He criticizes his own dualistic attitude of both "civilised outrage" and also an understanding of the "exact / and tribal, intimate revenge" (1975, 38). These poems have seen Heaney face some stringent criticism for this voicing of a political and ideological understanding and seeming tacit support for these violent actions.

Different critics have isolated these points and have extrapolated from this a prorepublican, pronationalist, and proviolence stance. Ciarán Carson has called the Heaney of these poems "a laureate of violence—a mythmaker, and anthropologist of ritual killing," and he sees the conflation between contemporary and Iron Age actions as suggesting that "there never were and never will be any political consequences of such acts" (1975, 183, 184). Blake Morrison makes the point that it is almost as if he were having these poems "written for him" by his nationalist, Catholic psyche and that his perspective grants an "historical respectability" to the "sectarian killing" (1982, 67, 68). David Lloyd makes the point that in these poems, "Irish ground, linked as the associations are through Kathleen Ni Houlihan, the motherland, together produce the forms in which the aestheticization of Irish politics is masked," and he goes on to criticize what he sees as Heaney's identitarian aesthetic that "gives sanction to the 'tribalist' interpretation of the Anglo-Irish conflict" (1993, 17, 4).

I have argued at length elsewhere on this topic and have pointed out what I see as overt simplifications in these critiques that fail to do full justice to the complexity of Heaney's positions, as well as not fully coming to terms with the nature of the epistemology of poetry, which attempts to access aspects of the real that cannot be fully grasped by normative discourse (O'Brien 2002, 2003). In the criticism of these poems, it would seem that the dangers of aesthetic ideology have been made overt once again. By fusing poetry and politics, Heaney, it would seem, is guilty of replaying uncritically "the Romantic schema of a return to origins which restores continuity through fuller self-possession, and accordingly rehearses the compensations conducted by Irish Romantic nationalism" (Lloyd 1993, 20).

However, this reading is very much to oversimplify Heaney's intersections of poetry and politics. To conflate the "I" of the poem with the "I" of the poet is to confuse the discourses of poetry and politics, as well as being a complete misunderstanding of the created and imaginative projection that is the speaking subject of such poetry. As was made clear in the previous chapter, his conceptions of literary identity are plural and polysemic, looking at movement across, and through, a series of positions. Indeed, his use of the aesthetic within the political discourse functions as a type of critical fission, as opposed to an organicist fusion, as he uses the aesthetic, and poetry in particular, as a way of complicating and pluralizing political identities and ideologies. I would contend that his imbrication of the two creates both good poetry and good politics, to contradict Edna Longley. Heaney is all too aware of the dangers and the problems of conflating the language of poetry and the language of public discourse, and this long excursus into aesthetic ideology was undertaken in order to demonstrate the very high stakes involved here, as the criticism of his position in *North* has demonstrated. David Carroll, writing about the aesthetic, has made the telling point that the politicization of art and the aestheticization of politics make the same mistake in "applying to one field the specific models, procedures, and ends of the other, and thus deriving or determining one field from the other." In his view, it results in the relative specificity of each field being "lost in the process" (2000, 123). Heaney is aware of the differences and thus is in no danger of falling prey to aesthetic ideology, despite the claims of some critics.

The imperative to write about the political situation came from his early experiences of such a fractured political sphere in Northern Ireland. Writing in *Preoccupations*, Heaney speaks about the influence of Philip Hobsbaum on himself and on other young Northern Irish poets, and he notes how Hobsbaum was urgent in advising that the sociopolitical conditions in Northern Ireland at that time should "disrupt the decorums of literature" (1980, 29). Therefore, from an early stage in his thinking, Heaney has been looking at how the poetic and politic could be brought into mutually enhancing contact. The voicing of how a "lyric I" created by Heaney can empathize with his tribe in shaving the "heads of the notorious," or can understand the "exact and tribal intimate revenge" enacted by a community on those individuals who are seen to consort with a political or tribal other, is a necessary part of the fluid structure that will be his construction of political identity—it is one more tower in the structure. We noted this point in the previous chapter, as he hoped to map his literary identity of the quincunx onto the political sphere, his aim being "to bring the frontiers of the country into alignment with the frontiers of writing" (1995b, 199). It is no accident that he puts writing first. Writing, poetry, the discourse of the real, is the one medium that can cast new light on the political. Like Kant and Hegel, Heaney sees the aesthetic as of great significance; however, he is not merely looking for organicist conflation or simple answers. Instead, he is looking to create a complicated response.

It is futile to attempt to discuss a campaign of violence and counterviolence in which nearly four thousand people were killed without admitting to emotional attachments, racial prejudices, and senses of communal anger and fear, which is what Heaney does in his poetry and in his deliberations about the role of poetry in discussing and understanding the actuality of politics. To see those lyric "I's" as a linear and complete representation of the opinions, ideologies, and emotions of "Seamus Heaney," the human being, is to be both reductive and naive regarding the complexity of the conscious and unconscious representation of subjectivity that is at the core of literature as a discourse. Above all, literature is fictive in its epistemology, no matter what genre is being used. In fact, these poems, and it is important to note that it is only in poetry that Heaney voices this sense of ideological and almost tribal identification, allow him to voice one aspect of the complex field of force that is constitutive of identity in a broad sense. This understanding of tribal, ethnic, and religious violence is a necessary part of the field of force; it is not the only part, nor for him is it the dominant part, but it is there, and it needs to be acknowledged if any real sense of an understanding of the motivations of people involved is ever to be reached.

Heaney is far too nuanced a thinker to just espouse aesthetic ideology without complex reflection, and again we remember his injunction about literature, namely, that it should not simplify, and from his earliest thoughts about poetry and politics it is important to keep in mind the complexity of his response. To speak in ordinary discourse is to repress feelings that are present, and poetry as genre allows for the expression, and the return, of this repressed. However, to see the negative impact of poetry on politics and vice versa is to see only one aspect of this debate, and while I have rehearsed the dangers of the conflation, I will now look at the obverse side of the discussion, as there is a school of thought that sees the aesthetic as a benign, and indeed critical, discourse that can engage with, and influence, the political sphere for the better.

Heaney lived in Belfast at the beginning of the Troubles, and issues of identity and political allegiance were played out not in journal articles and academic discussions but on the streets. Here, politics was very much something experienced in the lived life, the real, of Heaney and his family. Heaney speaks of living on the "wrong side" of the Lisburn Road, near a loyalist area called the Village, and of frequenting a fish-and-chip shop, which was on the outer edge of a loyalist area. He tells of being recognized by a young English girl, working behind the counter, from an arts television show on which he had appeared the previous evening and being addressed as follows: "Aren't you the Irish poet?," and he goes to add that before he could answer, the owner interjected, "Not at all, dear. He's like the rest of us a British subject living in Ulster!" Heaney ends that anecdote with the following, telling, sentence: "And Irish and all as I was I'm afraid I hesitated to contradict her" (2002, 367). This reticence is completely understandable in light of bombs, barricades, and ongoing violence. Speaking about the same time and the same area, Heaney recalls how journeys to the cigarette machine or the chip shop were punctuated by being questioned at barricades by Protestant vigilante figures. This reticence is hardly the stuff of a tribal nationalist who has hitched his wagon to the republican star. Instead, it is part of a complicated reaction by a poet to his political context.

In this context, politics became, almost by contextual default, the business of poetry. Heaney, as ever, reacts thoughtfully to the pulls of race, repression, tribalism, and the civil rights movement. In *Preoccupations*, he sets out his thought process in a series of binaries, saying that he is "fatigued by a continuous adjudication between agony and injustice," and he goes on to describe this process not in rational terms, but in a more physical metaphor, seeing himself as being "swung at one moment by the long tail of race and resentment, at another by the more acceptable feelings of pity and terror" (1980, 30). The term *adjudicate* is important here, as it signifies a process of weighing alternatives and of attempting to plot a reasoned course between acceptable and unacceptable reactions, while also granting the intensity of feelings and emotions. As we have already rehearsed, poetry as thinking is the ideal vehicle for this process. In the last chapter, we cited Heaney's view on the need to relate a field of force wherein he could accommodate the violence and the humanity of life in Northern Ireland. Here we will look at this field of force, which is primarily aesthetic, as he strives to respond to the political violence by finding and voicing those befitting emblems of adversity. It is my contention that this creation of emblems is a necessary part of his force field, and this intrusion of the poetic into the politic is one that, contra Cruise O'Brien and Longley, and contra the previous debates about aesthetic ideology, can be a positive and emancipatory force, and I would look to two perhaps unlikely sources as evidence: American critic of poetry Murray Krieger and post-Marxist theorists Ernesto Laclau and Chantal Mouffe, whose work, I will argue, allows for the achievement of a greater understanding of Heaney's poetics and politics and of his view that the former can be a positive force in the discourse of the latter.

Krieger is quite direct about his own views on the value of the aesthetic, suggesting that "the aesthetic can have its revenge upon ideology by revealing a power to complicate that is also a power to undermine" (Krieger and Krieger 1991, 258), and this view is surprisingly *ad idem* with de Man's views on theory, where he sees the force of a theoretical reading as upsetting "rooted ideologies by revealing the mechanics of their workings" (1986, 11). Given their similar preoccupation with romantic theorists, their rhizomatic agreement is less surprising than it might at first seem. While romanticism has been, as de Man observed, the source of much organicist thinking, Krieger, through the assertion of a different perspective, one that sees organicism as just one aspect of the discourse, proposes to show that, "built into the mystical dialectic of organicism, with its magical imposition of unity, is a negative thrust that would explode it." Keeping in mind the binary structure of knowledge, and the differential aspects of cognition, he makes the point that the call to unity that is expressed in much writing on the aesthetic "occurs only in the company of its opposite, the call for a *variety* that gives to any attempted unity a dynamics that threatens its stability" (1989, 40–41). Rather than being in need of demystification, the literary text instructs us in the art—and, far in advance of deconstruction, performs the work—of undoing unities and opening up apparent closures: "Totalization is that which the discourse of ideology imposes, and it is that from which, potentially, the counter ideological discourse of the literary text can liberate us" (1994, 73). For Krieger, the aesthetic is a core discourse through which to look awry at structures of reality and thus to change our perspective on that reality.

Krieger associates the thought of Friedrich Schlegel with "restlessness" and with a "continual need for movement," which keeps "the post-Kantian version of organic form from settling into the confinement that the more simple notion of closure propounded by those who would reject organicism would impose upon it" (1989, 41), and this reading is one that is very much in keeping with Heaney's own desire for a field of force wherein movement between different aspects of a structure of identity, whether it be the quincunx, the triangle of Englishness, or the complications of Irish identity, is a central factor in the creation of meaning. For de Man, it is theory that unlocks the closed door of organicist aesthetic ideology, as it points out the impossibility of language actually sanctioning such fusion, despite the desire of readers of Kant and Hegel to see it happen. Krieger, more like Heaney, sees the literary as the genre wherein this critique is situated. David Carroll sees Krieger's work as significant because it demonstrates how the question of literature is "radically different from the question of either history or politics," and he goes on to stress that "it is precisely this difference or distance from history and politics that gives literature its critical force and provides it with ways of resisting, complicating, and recasting accepted notions of history and politics" (2000, 121).

Richard Kearney makes a parallel point, noting that every cultural narrative is in some way "a reinterpretation of its own history," an attempt to retell a story of the past as it "relates to the present, an act of 'understanding otherwise' the motivating sub-world of symbols which informs our consciousness of the world" (1988, 10). Heaney's quincunx is a way of "understanding otherwise" the complexities of Irish literary identity; his silence in the chip shop is a way of trying to avoid either side of that binary and to understand otherwise the even greater complexities of political identity before actually voicing them. For all of these writers and thinkers, there is a motivated connection between poetry and politics, but it is not necessarily a negative one. In fact, one could see all "poetry as political in one way or another, since even the choice to eschew explicit political involvement or references constitutes a form of political action (or perhaps more precisely inaction)" (Dasenbrock 2003, 51).

I would further maintain that poetry, or poetic thinking, is a seminal constituent of a politics that espouses an emancipatory and egalitarian mode of political thinking. I have been arguing that poetry as a mode of knowledge has the ability to access parts of language that are not accessible to normative discourse and also that Heaney's poetic thinking has pluralized and complicated ideas of literary identity, as we saw in the last chapter. In this chapter, I am proposing that the transposition of that literary pluralization onto politics is a central achievement of Heaney's writing. It is clear from the pluralization of subject position, the pluralization of ideas of self and belonging, and the pluralization of the self as text and its constituent contexts in his thinking. Krieger has long seen the aesthetic as a liberating force, despite the criticism of the aesthetic as being a "respectable and ostensibly innocent front for a reactionary politics" (2000, 224), and there is some coherence between this position, which I feel Heaney shares, and the thinking of post-Marxist philosophers Ernesto Laclau and Chantal Mouffe.

For Laclau and Mouffe, what they call the democratic revolution is a project that they see as the ultimate political goal of those who espouse democracy, or at least a developmental emancipatory type of democracy. While remaining within the broad framework of Enlightenment thinking, especially its political project of "the achievement of equality and freedom for all," their work posits a new conception of human subjectivity, at odds with the traditional view of the "unitary subject as the ultimate source of intelligibility of its actions." They are taking into account the different strands of class, culture, politics, ideology, and the unconscious, which all combine to create identities. While still granting the agency of the individual, they construct a politics of the future based on the recognition of all of these strands that make up identity, so that "no identity is ever definitively established, there always being a certain degree of openness and ambiguity in the way the different subject positions are articulated." This conception, which has strong echoes of Deleuze and Guattari's notion of the rhizome, acknowledges "the particular, the multiple, the heterogeneous in effect" and crucially sets up "a new kind of articulation between the universal and the particular" (Mouffe 1993, 12, 13). Immediately, we can see this openness and ambiguity in Heaney's reluctance to address the binary of his own political identity in the chip shop and also his desire to transpose the plurality of Irishness and Englishnesses that we saw so carefully delineated in the last chapter on to the political arena of identity. Like these writers, Heaney attempts to move beyond the binaries of self and other and the particular and universal; his mode of thinking is far more nuanced and plural.

Heaney is a very contextually aware writer, and in his effort to align poetry and politics in an emancipatory manner, he is conversant with contemporary critical practices in the area of Irish studies, and he makes the explicit point that in postcolonial criticism, the theoretical mode that is the most popular method of interrogating Irish writing, there has been much said about the role of "the other." However, he goes on to ask whether "the moment of the through-other should now be proclaimed" (2002, 379). In this mode, as we saw, in literature, there is a sense of fluency and plurality of identity, a parallel to the political subjectivities of Laclau and Mouffe; Heaney, in attempting to set out this sense of pluralism, looked to literary exemplars, in particular to the poets and thinkers of Eastern Europe, who were attempting to give voice to personal utterance while under the hegemonic scrutiny of oppressive regimes. Thus, in *The Government of the Tongue*, he sets out a paradigm for his own discussions of poetry and politics in the context of what has been experienced by writers such as Miroslav Holub, Zbigniew Herbert, and especially Osip Mandelstam, in whom he was particularly interested, given that he "died unrepentant as a prisoner in one of Stalin's labour camps" (Quinn 2008, 140–41). Heaney speaks of these poets as exemplars who have to "survive amphibiously" in a political world that places demands on them, but also need to act in accordance with their own "moral and artistic self-respect" (1988, xx), and the resonances for a poet writing out of the turmoil of Northern Ireland are very clear.

It is significant that he feels the contrasting pulls of the emotions and the rational even as he is writing about these strong precursors, to use Harold Bloom's term, and it is equally thought-provoking that the adverb used to qualify the aim of survival is *amphibiously*, which is defined as the ability to survive in different conditions and to move fluently between them. The use of the adjective *demeaning* is also significant, as he seems to feel that the demands to offer univocal support for one position is demeaning his lyrical voice as well as his own commitment to poetry. This idea of the pulls of politics as demeaning the poet can be related back to his injunction that poetry should not simplify, because it is precisely what a politically sanctioned, ideologically driven poetic response would be, as it would be sanctioning that very sense of suasive aesthetic ideology of which we have been speaking by using these tropes of the aesthetic to sanction the organic bonding of a people to a place.

In contradistinction to such a simplified view of poetry, Heaney sees it as creative of a more pluralistic and nuanced subjectivity, as opposed to an entrenched one, and I would propose an adequation between this position and the radical democratic politics of Laclau and Mouffe, who see such a subjectivity as necessary for "the plurality and the opening which a radical democracy requires" (1985, 178). Heaney's amphibious subject is surely a correlate of "the subject as a decentred, detotalized agent, a subject constructed at the point of intersection of a multiplicity of subject positions," which Mouffe sees as necessary for her new brand of radical democratic politics. This fluidity of identity is necessary if subjects are to engage with the differences and dissensus that are fast becoming the norm in Western society. The politics of Laclau and Mouffe look to a fluid and cosmopolitan social sphere, in which relationships between particularity and universality are debated and critiqued and where ideas of justice and emancipation are evaluated on an ongoing basis. In such a political construction, "no identity is ever definitively established, there always being a certain degree of openness and ambiguity in the way the different subject positions are articulated" (Mouffe 1993, 12).

When Heaney talks about subjectivity, and about his feelings regarding living in Belfast at the beginning of the Troubles, he talks about the "weary twisted emotions" that are "like a ball of hooks and sinkers in the heart" (1980, 30). He needs a type of thinking that can acknowledge the role of these emotions, while at the same time transcending them, though never consigning them to a lesser role in discourse. In other words, he wants to locate them in a field of force, and in much of his writing it is the political position that is being sketched out, whether he is talking about the overtly political or the literary dimensions of that politics. Therefore, while those emotions of fear and anger are expressed in all their complexity, he still looks for that pluralistic perspective within which they are articulated. Thus, in his "Christmas 1971" section of the "Belfast" essay, he speaks of how, despite the state being officially "British," a little goodwill toward "the notion of being Irish" would take "some of the twists out of the minority" (ibid., 32), and even the use of the somatically charged *twists* is indicative of the emotional charge that is at work here.

Nevertheless, to stop here would be to acquiesce to the political and ideological givens that have created his subjectivity, and it would not be allowing the complexity and plurality of response that the poetically sanctioned field of force can enable. Thus, while granting the tribal and communitarian intensity of the binary antagonism against the other, he is still striving to access the through-other. He speaks of candles being put in the windows for Christmas and remembers Louis MacNeice; W. R. Rodgers, whose *Collected Poems* have appeared in time for Christmas; and John Hewitt, whose poetry has been an exploration of the "Ulster Protestant consciousness." He goes on to place them in a wider field of force, noting that, as Northern Protestants, they each explored their relationship to Ireland. He uses the Joycean metaphor of Ireland as "an old sow who eats her farrow" here, but immediately goes on to deconstruct it by commenting that he has never seen it occur and that what usually happens is that "the young pigs eat one another's ears" (ibid., 32–33).

Here we see his poetized thinking and the field of force in action. Emotions, atavisms, resentments, all the different factors that can twist people into acts of violence and racism and that can ultimately descend into forms of ethnic cleansing, are brought into connection with writers who look at the same issues from a fictive perspective and who are able to "understand [them] otherwise," in Kearney's terms. It is clear in this paragraph, as one of the strongest literary metaphorizations of Ireland—James Joyce's comment that Ireland is an old sow who eats her farrow (1993, 228)—is deconstructed by Heaney, who notes that the farrow itself is plural and active, and the old sow is no longer a factor. Here is the result of this teasing through of the emotional and rational interactions of Heaney's responses to the violence: a plural metaphor of Ireland, where the young pigs interact with each other and are no longer victims of their mother. They have become active agents of the future, and each interaction, each act of eating of metaphorical ears, is a particular example of an act of plural identity, and the universal figure of the mother is no longer hegemonic. It could be seen as a reorientation from the past of the mother Ireland figure to a future of equality and the toleration of difference. We are not very far from the perspective on transformed relationships between the particular and universal that we saw in the work of Laclau and Mouffe.

Heaney has more to say about the fluidity of relationships between the singular and universal. He makes the point that the imaginative arts, when faced with the brutality of the historical onslaught, are "practically useless." However, speaking about the biblical story of the woman caught in adultery, an example to which we will return at the end of this chapter, Heaney stresses that while "no lyric has ever stopped a tank," nevertheless there is a power in poetic writing that is "unlimited," and he compares it to the "writing in the sand" in the Bible, "in the face of which accusers and accused are left speechless and renewed" (1988, 107).

Again, there is the parallel with a specific type of politics, one that looks to difference and plurality as opposed to sameness and a monological ideological subjective position. For him, poetry is a form of knowledge, parallel to Krieger's view of it as a critique that can open up a sense of understanding otherwise in the discourses of politics and history. We have already spoken of how poetry can access aspects of the real and of the emotions, and for Heaney it is a strong motive force in its operation, as it can enunciate visceral emotions because it shares them as a starting point, which can lead to a form of political knowledge as well. This politics is all the more real, as it takes note of the visceral and emotional responses that are often part of the political and ideological motivations of acts in the political sphere, but are seldom made overt in the symbolic order.

There is also an ethical dimension at work here, as Heaney cites Simone Weil's dictum that if poets or artists know in what way a society is unbalanced, then they should "add weight to the lighter scale." She sees this process as ongoing, similar to the flight of justice, "that fugitive from the camp of conquerors" (Heaney 1995b, 3), and the ethical force of poetry is foregrounded in a discussion of his own reaction to various political crises in Northern Ireland. His attraction to Weil is significant, as she is another advocate of the notion of poetry as a form of knowledge that is useful in dealing with oppositions that are seemingly intractable. As Joan Dargan has shown, the "artfulness of the opposition is an instance of the poetic thinking that continually lifts Weil's prose out of the ordinary and makes of it a thing inspired" (1999, 112).

Part of the complexity of his view of poetry rests in the idea that it is of value in society but also in itself: "I credit poetry, in other words, both for being itself and for being a help" (1995a, 11–12), and this sense of help is, I would suggest, to create that plural subjectivity of which we have been speaking. It is a point to which he returns, referring to Greek poet George Seferis, who felt that, in a time of personal and political crisis, "poetry was strong enough to help," while John Hewitt is seen as bringing the "imagining faculty" into the domain of politics (1995b, 191, 195). The same pattern is discerned in the work of Lowell, who succeeded in "uniting the aesthetic instinct with the obligation to witness morally and significantly in the realm of public action" (Heaney 1988, 133).

This uniting of the aesthetic and the ethical again echoes the ideas of Krieger, Laclau, and Mouffe, who see ethics as a necessary dimension of the literary, and the political, respectively. The "movement from democratic to popular demands presupposes a plurality of subject positions" (Laclau 2005, 84), and this subject position does not preclude antagonisms and social division "but, on the contrary, considers them as constitutive of the social" (Laclau 2007, 114). For all these thinkers, such conflict and antagonism are a fact of life, and any political position must take note of them. So, just as the binary of the old sow and her farrow has been deconstructed into the plurality and particularism of the interactions of the pigs themselves, a similar "democratic matrix" is the aim of Mouffe, who stresses that a project of radical democracy "requires the existence of multiplicity, of plurality, and of conflict, and sees in them the *raison d'être* of politics" (1993, 24). Such conflict is seen by these thinkers as creative of new forms of identity, and Heaney's conception of the through-other is an example of this type of new perspective on old ideas, as the binaries of self and other become fused in a dynamic new formulation that grants the original positions of each, but locates them in a transformative context. That such a construction is also part of a political discourse in the realms of philosophy and political thinking lends it even more credibility in terms of Heaney being seen as a thinker about politics.

Just as de Man offered such a searching critique of aesthetic ideology because he was all too aware of its suasive attractions, so Heaney, having seen how foundationalist concepts of identity could cause such havoc in his own society, is anxious to suggest alternative formulations. His field of force, by encompassing the conflicting perspectives, moves toward new forms of identity and the promotion of hybridized democratic identities that "does not necessarily mean decline through the loss of identity: it can also mean empowering existing identities through the opening of new possibilities"

(A. Smith 1998, 181). These new possibilities are being set out in the different structures of thought that we see Heaney creating, as he talks about issues of identity in Northern Ireland. He is in the process of creating "a multiplicity of subject positions," and he is doing so by creating his field of force or what Mouffe would term a "democratic matrix" (1993, 18).

For Heaney, then, thinking as poetizing is a relevant way of engaging with politics, as he is dealing with the present through the aesthetic, and the poetic force field allows him to place each in juxtaposition with the other so that he is gesturing toward a politics to come, or a "democracy to come," to use Derrida's term. For Derrida, like Heaney, Laclau, and Mouffe, it is the "we" of the democratic project with which it is so difficult to come to terms, as he observes that it calls for "the infinite respect for the singularity *and* infinite alterity of the other," and respect for the equality "between anonymous singularities" (1994, 65). Heaney's ideas of the through-other and the field of force are very much part of a commitment to the future, as opposed to a solidifying of the givens of the past. The piglets nibbling each other's ears symbolize this rhizomatic sense of the future; the sow eating her farrow has a certainty as to its outcome, but the piglets' movements are more random—in this case, the outcome is far from certain. Thus, Heaney is partaking in a "progressive movement of nations, states, and peoples in a transformational enterprise aimed at negotiating the effectivity of a democracy to come" (Derrida 2002, 97). The discourses of Derrida and Heaney aim to "let the future open," because it is an essential aspect of "democracy as democracy to come" (Derrida and Stiegler 2002, 21), and in both cases they see politics as signifying something far deeper: "It is necessary also in politics to respect the secret, that which exceeds the political or that which is no longer in the juridical domain" (Derrida, Brault, and Naas 2001, 55).

In Heaney's work, the key to his poetized political perspective is inclusivity. Thus, in an oneiric paragraph, he can refer to reading Martin Luther King's "I Have a Dream" speech, and talk about the optimistic vision of a democracy to come with which that speech is imbued, while in almost the same breath he recalls a dream he had of seeing a wounded man in his shaving mirror, "his bloodied hands lifted to tear at me or to implore." For him, dreams, when they move from the unconscious private world to the public realm, can be powerful forces for emancipation or for destruction, and his nuanced poetized thinking about politics attempts to grant the complex reality of this process. The political world as it exists is composed of antagonistic binaries, and time and time again, we will see Heaney recontextualize these binaries into a more nuanced, fluent structure, where they are free to interact to create a different sense of the future. Thus, he explains, "at one minute you are drawn towards the old vortex of racial and religious instinct, at another time you seek the mean of humane love and reason." His solution is poetry, but as we will see it is poetry that looks at politics in a different way. He writes in English and he speaks English, but he does not share the "preoccupations and Perspectives" of an Englishman, and while he teaches English literature, that tradition is not really his home—as we have already noted, he lives off another hump as well (1980, 33, 34).

Consequently, we see the movement from the poetic to the political, and it is such a seamless one that on first reading, it may be missed. He begins by showing how a poem is a way of bringing the different terms of the binary positions together, and the crucial role of the unconscious in poetry, and in aesthetic thinking, is signified by his use of the adjective *somnambulist*, as this term suggests that openness to the beyond, to what Derrida has termed the secret, which exceeds the rational and makes the poem itself an inclusive field of force where the different areas interact in a democratic matrix.

However, in the next sentence, he makes the political connections between the feminine clusters of "image and emotion" and Ireland and between the masculine qualities of "will and intelligence" and England, thereby connecting poetry and politics, especially the politics of identity, in his seminal description of his own poetic practice. However, in Heaney's thinking, there is no sense of one identity subsuming the other or of the scope of poetry being attenuated for narrow political ends. Rather, the two identities, and their associated qualities, are set up in a new structure that is oriented toward a future where they exist in a new structure. It is an ongoing strand in Heaney's writing, one that figured in his Nobel Lecture, *Crediting Poetry*, where he talked about the partition of the island of Ireland as well as an "equally persistent partition of the affections in Northern Ireland between the British and Irish heritages." He went on to hope that politics could devise institutions that would "allow that partition to become a bit more like the net on a tennis court, a demarcation allowing for agile give-and-take, for encounter and contending" and would result in a future where the "vitality that flowed in the beginning from those bracing words 'enemy' and 'allies' might finally derive from a less binary and altogether less binding vocabulary" (1995a, 23).

This position is parallel to Derrida's democracy to come, as well as to Laclau and Mouffe's democratic revolution, as difference, antagonism, and conflict are all built into the democratic matrix that Heaney is postulating. His border is porous, a boundary point between self and other that serves as a signpost for the through-other. That all of this is achieved in two ostensible discussions of poetry would further connect Heaney with the thinking of Heidegger, who says that poetry is "politics in the highest and most authentic sense" (Young 1992, 76), and again it must be taken into account that Heidegger was also someone who was involved in an aestheticization of politics, given his involvement in the Nazi Party in the 1930s and the dark consequences of this involvement.

As we saw in chapter 3, Protevi sees a lot of Derrida's thinking as based on a political physics similar to that paradigm that was outlined above, where "making sense," the creation of meaning, is achieved through the "forceful interaction of vectors in a field of force and signification. This general text of force and signification is the site of struggle for the 'democracy to come'" (2001, 13), and throughout Heaney's thoughtful placement of different identities into new structures is very much a feature of his poetizing politics. Repeatedly, he opens up a discursive and political space that allows self and other to become through-other in his writing, and to my mind this stance is very much a political one.

Significantly, however, he never looks to prioritize one identity over the other, as his poetizing intelligence always looks for the forceful interaction of vectors, as he attempts to prepare for the democracy to come. Just as the two dormant munitions on the sampler can be brought into fruitful interanimation, so the name of his childhood home can enact the same process. The place-name "Mossbawn" can be derived from two different linguistic and etymological sources; if the Irish language sense of the words is taken, it means "white moss, the moss of bog-cotton," whereas if the English language etymology is taken, it means "the planter's house on the bog" (Heaney 1980, 35). What is most significant here is that, even at this very early stage of his thinking, Heaney politicizes both land and language as he struggles to outline his own position. Clearly aware of the dangers of aesthetic ideology, and of the ease with which the complexities of poetry can be subsumed within a foundationalist ideology of identity, he is careful to stress that one's identity is often a matter of choices.

Indeed, he makes it clear that for him, and indeed by extrapolation for everyone, political identity is really driven by a form of hermeneutics wherein signs, be they linguistic or cultural, are read in an attenuated, ideologically motivated, and singular manner. The question mark in the middle of the quotation, where he posits the possibility of a second meaning, is semiotically significant, as he never comes down on one side or the other. His home place may mean "the planter's house on the bog," or it may mean "the moss of bog-cotton"; it is this both/and epistemology that is significant, as these two meanings interact in the force field of which we have been speaking, a structure wherein identities are less binary and less binding and hence, looking toward the future, whose borders may be a lot more permeable. What is very obvious is that Heaney, while acutely aware of the power of aesthetic ideology to attenuate meanings according to its own foundationalist desires, is also aware of the emancipatory power of such associations, a point made consistently by Krieger, who feels that there is an obligation on any thinker about poetry to "dwell upon that resistance [to ideological closure] as a special feature of literature" (1994, 47). Poetry as apophantic discourse is ideally placed to achieve this by looking at associative layers of meaning as well as purely logical and grammatical ones. Heaney's poetizing politics is an ongoing, and largely successful, attempt to avoid "killing the future in the name of the old frontiers" (Derrida 1994, 169).

Heidegger, in *Poetry, Language, Thought*, similarly asserts the value of poetry as an expression of wholeness: "To be involved in saying is the mark of a saying that follows something to be said, solely in order to say it. What is to be said would then be what by nature belongs to the province of language. And that, thought metaphysically, is particular beings as a whole. Their wholeness is the intactness of the pure draft, the sound wholeness of the Open, in that it makes room within itself for man" (1971, 135). Heidegger and Heaney connect any sense of wholeness with speech—either the vocable or the saying—and both writers express the centrality of poetry in the revelation of the full nature of what it means to be human. This sense of fluid wholeness, which still maintains a discernible relationship between each particularity and the universal whole, is something that is central to the epistemology of poetizing as thinking. Literature, in short, is "counter theoretical," where, by "theoretical" Krieger means "ideological"—and "in these ideological days, it is the pressure to resist, as well as the role of literature in supplying it, that is sorely needed" (1994, 87, 75).

The idea of the poem as vocable is another restatement of the field of force, and, interestingly, it is focused not on the problems of the past but on the possibilities of the future, where the names of places, and the political and identitarian traditions for which these names stand in synecdoche, may be located in a structure that allows the different traditions to interact in a transformative manner. Heaney, grounded as ever, images this structure as an "assenting, equable marriage between the geographical country and the country of the mind," and just as the geography and history of a place can become a given for the mind, in the manner of aesthetic ideology, so also can a more enabling and a more open sense of the geography of the mind be imposed on the practicalities of place, thereby creating a more inclusive political, historical, and geographical structure. Cultural politics "are inflected in important ways by media (and the mediascapes and ideoscapes they offer)" (Appadurai 1996, 45), and so much of Heaney's work involves using the power of poetized thinking to open up hitherto unseen and unexpressed aspects of philosophy and politics. "Poetry is a limit of reason that philosophy finds unthinkable" (Bruns 1997, xv), and Heaney's writing demonstrates this concept very clearly across the range of his prose.

So, much of his writing on other poets gently, firmly, and consistently makes this point about the need for fluid political structures, for fields of force, that encompass the different antagonisms of self and other at all levels. His critique of poetic positions is often, by extension, a critique of political agendas that have been carefully wrapped in the warm clothing of the aesthetic. Therefore, when talking of the poets John Montague and John Hewitt, he makes the point that Hewitt's vision "is bifocal, not, as in Montague's case, monocular." He points out that both look for ancient symbols, but that Montague's is on "Knockmany Dolmen," which is part of the "insular tradition," while Hewitt's megalithic symbol is "a broken circle of stones on a rough hillside, somewhere," and he explains that this "somewhere" is a conflation of "the Rollright Stones on the border of Oxfordshire, mingled with the recollection of 'Ossian's Grave,' Glenaan, Co. Antrim." Heaney goes on to define this disparity in terms of how "two fidelities, two spirits that, in John Donne's original and active verb, interinanimate each other" (1980, 147). This interinanimation is another cognate term in the vocabulary that we have been using to describe the structures of Heaney's thinking on politics as, rather than eliminating or transcending differences, such a perspective "provides a way to link differences to each other without resolving the conflicts and tensions they produce" (D. Carroll 2000, 124). In this instance, poetry is used as a way of showing how connections, which may seem to be politically or culturally motivated, are in fact always chosen and are always validated by a form of cultural hermeneutics that prioritizes one reading and invalidates all others. Hewitt's validation of an imagined "somewhere" acts as an avatar for his own political investigations of the value of the linguistic and cultural sign and symbol in the political.

For him, poetry has always been written in the context of the political. He recalls that, as his early books were being published, alongside a golden generation of writers like Derek Mahon, James Simmons, and Michael Longley, Ian Paisley was already "in full sectarian cry," and "hair-raising bigotries were propounded," and he notes that it was all out in the open and not seen as in any way wrong. The poets who were publishing in this climate did not need to reveal the acts of the political power as they did in Eastern Europe, where violence and repression were less overt, but, instead, "they assumed that the tolerances and subtleties of their art were precisely what they had to set against the repetitive intolerance of public life" (1988, xxi). Heaney's work has always been written with one eye on the political context within which it has been produced. He is all too aware that much of what motivates political action is never addressed by political discourse, and, as I have been suggesting, his thoughts on this subject are in parallel with a strand of the European philosophical tradition that has focused on language and the epistemological aspects of language. He cites Jung's idea that one way to overcome an insoluble conflict is to outgrow it by developing "a new level of consciousness." He goes on to develop this concept by showing how Jung suggests that we develop mechanisms to look at the "affect" of suffering or violence on us but try to avoid becoming identified with this affect. Heaney goes on to describe a consciousness that can regard "the affect as an object," as a way of both acknowledging and at the same time refusing to be controlled by this affect, which Heaney sees as a "disturbance, a warp in the emotional glass which is in danger of narrowing the mind's range of response to the terms of the disturbance itself" (ibid., xxii). One could see it as another expression of his field of force, as there have been a number of instances cited in this chapter where he takes the emotional and rational aspects of an event and locates them in a structure that allows for conflict and interaction and that interinanimate, to use his own borrowing from John Donne, each other.

This interinanimation is his way of achieving that Jungian higher consciousness, which we will later see recast in his own term *further language*, as atavisms and emotions are acknowledged but are also constantly critiqued by the more thoughtful dimensions of the mind, and it is this interaction of the poetic and the politic that he admires. Consequently, when he writes about Zbigniew Herbert's "Mr Cogito," what he most admires is not the fact that it is dissident poetry, but that its whole intent is to "devastate those arrangements which are offered as truth by power's window-dressers everywhere"; he notes that Herbert's poetry can hear the "screech of the fighter bomber" behind the "righteous huffing of the official spokesman." From Heaney's perspective, this poetry is not just content to expose; rather, it wants to go beyond the collective versions of experience and to plumb the depths of the "individual's perception and endurance," which he sees as an "attentive listening post" (ibid., 61). Here poetry, far from being complicit with the political, is in fact an agent of critique of the political. In the relationships between the particulars and the universals of which Laclau and Mouffe speak, poetry is very much focused on the particular individual and how such organicism effects (and affects) the individual.

We already referred to Heaney's discussion of the woman caught in adultery in *The Government of the Tongue*. Heaney's focus is on the individual's intervention in a communal (political) act of punishment of the woman through the act of writing in the sand, an activity that seems ephemeral in the extreme, as such writing is, by definition of its medium, transient and impermanent. However, Heaney sees that the drawing of these characters is like poetry in that it is a "break with the usual life but not an absconding from it"; it does not propose a solution, nor does it propose to be "instrumental or effective." Instead, "in the rift between what is going to happen and whatever we would wish to happen," it focuses attention and concentration "back on ourselves," and in its greatest moments, he suggests that it would attempt, in Yeats's famous aphorism, "to hold in a single thought reality and justice" (ibid., 108). The real and the just are at the core of poetic thinking and are also at the core of poetry's interinanimation with politics.

To conclude this chapter, it is appropriate to return to the views of Murray Krieger, in relation to the power of literature to withstand ideology by critiquing the ideological aspect of language as it is used in politics and in some ideologically motivated versions of the aesthetic. It has been my contention that Heaney has traveled along the same conceptual path as Krieger, seeing poetry as a counterweighting force to the ideological and seeing its nuanced use of language, as well as its unparalleled access to the real of communication, as a way of critiquing ideology, of calling it to account and of understanding it otherwise. For Krieger, the poetic act "represents the failure of the period ideology to sustain the enclosure it would enforce" because what poetic thinking does is to "find the fissures of disbelief and slips in to explore and exploit them" (1989, 29). This sense of poetry as ideological critique, and as a focus on the individual in all of his and her conscious and unconscious complexity, is very much how Heaney sees it and how he thinks about the connection between the aesthetic and the politic.

5

The Place of Writing —the Writing of Place

This chapter will look at the ambiguous relationship between place and writing in the thinking of Seamus Heaney. In the last chapter, we looked at how the aesthetic can be used to validate a monological, monofocal, and motivated connection between a people, a language, and a place. In this chapter, we will examine the careful and nuanced manner in which Heaney treats the connections between place and people in his work. Heaney is well aware of the attenuating influence of the "appetites of gravity" as he describes them (Heaney 1975, 43), which fuse a people to a place, and he is also aware of the linguistic and ideological structures that bring this situation about. One thinks of Heidegger's sense of homeland, "the blessing of its destined assignment" (2010, 157) and the poisonous political affiliations sanctioned by this very motivated sense of a homeland.

This essentialist sense of identity is exactly the ideological position of which Heaney has stood accused in the context of *North*, where he writes from within the perspective of those individuals who see their homeland as almost sacred. There are, as we have seen, elements of anger and resentment in Heaney's attitude to unionist politics and to some British policies in Northern Ireland. He told Seamus Deane, in an interview in 1977, that he was writing from the perspective of a "slightly aggravated young Catholic male" (Deane 1982, 66). As previously noted, the expression of visceral emotion is very much part of Heaney's view of the scope of poetry as a discourse, and accessing this aspect of the real has been important to the depth and truth of his work. However, to isolate such poems, or indeed such comments in interviews, and to see them as Heaney's own and only opinion, is to perpetrate an egregious version of the authorial fallacy. The voice of a lyric persona is not necessarily the opinion of the author—in *North*, for example, Heaney voices himself as England at one stage in "Act of Union," but no one has accused him of secretly wanting to become a country (1975, 49–50).

We have already seen that Heaney has been accused of such a perspective and that he has been seen as a tribal voice, with Heaney himself talking about his early work as a "slow obstinate papish burn" (Deane 1982, 67). Much of his subsequent work has been read in this light. Conor Cruise O'Brien, a critic who had been very sensitive to nationalist rhetoric and ideology, spoke of *North* as being about "the tragedy of a people in a place: the Catholics of Northern Ireland" (1975). Dillon Johnston, in a book entitled *Irish Poetry after Joyce*, makes the point that Heaney's poetry posits some "radical connection between the land and the language it nurtures" (1985, 142), while Elmer Andrews, who has written a number of books on Heaney, makes the point that in Heaney's place-name poems, "language is pushed toward a magical relationship with the things it is speaking about" (1988, 55). Maurice Harmon also reads many of the poems as a fusion of land and language: "The processes of the natural world are linguistic codes. . . . 'Anahorish' is a vowel meadow" (1992, 73). Blake Morrison made the following points about the poem "Kinship," in *North*, where he notes that, like "Punishment," this poem "ends up speaking the language of the tribe, brutal though that language may be." He goes on to suggest that it is one of "several points in *North* where one feels that Heaney is not writing these poems, but having them written for him, his frieze composed almost in spite of him by the 'anonymities' of race and religion" (1982, 68).

Although much of this criticism is based on one section of one book of poetry, it has become something of a commonplace that Heaney is a Northern Irish, Catholic, nationalist poet who is inevitably imbued with this ideology and whose work reflects it. As has been argued in previous chapters, such is Heaney's poetizing thinking that he will include these unconscious, and at times atavistic, pulsions in his overall field of force, but these poems need to be taken as part of this pluralistic intellectual structure. It is clear from his own ruminations about his own home place, and its ideation in his mind, that his understandings of place and politics are far more complex. In this chapter, his philosophy of place will be explored, and it will become very clear that, far from being governed by his given place and his given tradition, he is also more than prepared to critique such ideologies of place and those appetites of gravity about which we have already spoken. This complex perspective can be seen in the poem about Grotus and Coventina, validating the power of words to affect the somatic being of a reader, as it notes:

> And when he remembered the stone where he cut his name
> Some dried-up course beneath his breastbone started
> Pouring and darkening. (1987, 40)

Here we see the power not of place qua physical coordinates on a map, but rather of place as an ideological construct, created through the power of language.

According to Heaney, it was on a visit to Hadrian's Wall that he first saw images of Coventina—"more of a mud maiden than a marble nymph" (Heaney and O'Driscoll 2008, 294)—and the carving of these altars in far-flung places meant that every time water was poured, the juices of memory flowed in the minds of the Roman legionnaires, and they were reminded of home. Hence, place is especially potent when it is culturally inscribed, and here we are touching the territory of aesthetic ideology again. What makes the poem even more interesting in the present context is the next line, where, having described the effect of the lines on the visceral emotions of the persona in the poem, there is a sudden deictical swerve as he says, "more or less the way / The thought of his stunted altar works on me" (1987, 40). This swerve signifies that place is very often a thought, an ideation, as much as a physical entity, and in these lines we see the homology of physical location, visceral emotion, and ideological cognition, and it is within this nexus that Heaney's ruminations on place will be located. His discussion of the world, like all other discussions, is mediated by the word, by other words, and all of their connections, said and unsaid.

Speaking about this poem, and about its classical frame of reference, Heaney stresses that it is not an attempt by him at high culture for the sake of it—he reminds his interlocutor that he is one of the last generations to have learned Latin at school, and it is the sound of the words that attract him, as much as their referential associations; there is that capillary action at work again. He speaks of the "immediate aural and oral pleasure" that is to be obtained from saying these words, as he puts it, "the consonants and vowels melt in your mouth like hard-boiled soft-centred sweets," and that visceral element of language, the comfort of rhyme and rhythm, is significant, but so also is the intertextual generic dialogue with other poets and poetry. And significantly for the purposes of this discussion, he goes on to expand on this thought, saying that it is a "category of knowledge, of reality, of human understanding, of durable value" (Heaney and O'Driscoll 2008, 295). The durability in question is the ability of poetry to embody the rationality and cultural context of words, in this case the classical associations of the terms and their more globalized and reflective perspective.

However, he is also referring to the sensory, somatic, and visceral dimension of words, as found in the aesthetic, where the real of situations is accessed by poetry. Poetic language, which is not bound by temporal narrative constraints to the same extent as prose, "takes place in such a way that its advent always already escapes both toward the future and toward the past." The lyric is able to capture emotion, nuance, feeling, and some refractions of the unconscious, though, of course, it can never carry the full rational weight of explanatory, analytical discursive prose. Agamben feels that "only language in which the pure prose of philosophy would intervene at a certain point to break apart the verse of the poetic word, and in which the verse of poetry would intervene to bend the prose of philosophy into a ring, would be the true human language" (1991, 76,

78), and here he is very much in accordance with both Heidegger's idea of poetizing thinking and Heaney's own spatial and conceptual linguistic structures in his various fields of force.

The core of these structures, as we have seen, is their fluidity and the sense of a movement of ideas, emotions, and feelings that poetic language can capture, so that the symbolic and the real, and the conscious and the unconscious, can mutually reflect on each other. This sense of the movement of language beyond the normative rules of grammar and syntax is suggested in Agamben's ideas on the centrality of enjambment. It involves the movement of thought beyond the linear or stanzaic structure of a poem, so that the run-on line across stanza and syntax creates a mutually defining structure of signification through which aspects of the real can be enunciated in a way not available to normal prose, where the structures of thought are determined by line length as well as rules of grammar and syntax. Enjambment allows for a motivated placement of words in sentences and clauses across a stanzaic gap, a placement that can signify in itself. Agamben sees enjambment as crucial to the definition of poetry as the "discourse in which it is possible to set a metrical limit against a syntactic one (verse in which *enjambment* is not actually present is to be seen as verse with zero *enjambment*). Prose is the discourse in which this is impossible" (1995, 39; emphasis in the original).

Enjambment refers to different structures cutting each other transversally, and, of course, it can be seen as another field of force wherein expression is achieved by the utterances, as well as in the interstices between them. The type of language and thinking that I see in Heaney's work embodies this sense of the run-on line and also the conflation of different structures that help to generate meaning. There would seem to be an aporetic relationship at work here, as Agamben notes that if "poetry is defined precisely by the possibility of enjambment," then it follows that "the last verse of a poem is not a verse. Does this mean that the last verse trespasses into prose?" (1999a, 112). Developing this point, I would suggest that there is a type of prose that is infused with those somatic aspects of experience that are accessed by poetic language, and it is this type of writing that Heidegger, Derrida, Lacan, and Heaney have used to attempt to express aspects of the real and the somatic aspect of experience in their work. The suppleness of their thought is in part owing to the complexity of the forces involved, but it is also signified by the manner in which they all use language.

For Heaney, the somatic "taste" of words is not a mere poetic affectation: he is serious about the value of the signifying importance of this aspect of words; this poetized aspect of language is part of his aesthetic epistemology of poetry. In this regard he echoes Derrida, who stresses that it can never be the case that the figurative sense of language, which traditionally derives from "the poetic resources of language," should be subordinated to the "purity or propriety of the philosophical concept." He goes on to explain how for him, "poetry and thinking are given originarily one to the other"; "they approach each other always already, without the one being older than the other, and without one being presumed simply to derive from the other." Derrida believes that the field of force that "gives poetry to thinking and vice versa, is the opening of a path, the path through which Being sets out on its voyage, and that voyage itself, have neither proper nor figurative sense" (Malabou and Derrida 2004, 131).

As we will see, this path is one upon that Heaney will happily travel, in his depiction of poetry as a form of discourse that is intellectually mobile and flexible. Like Derrida, he sees poetry as central to thinking, as it allows for the articulation of the rational and the emotional in a poetized form of language. Heaney, in his articulation of the place of writing, sets up a sense of place that is mobile and weightless, capable of being opened up and displaced at the same time: it is the understanding otherwise of place. One could well cite Derrida's words as a credo for this process: "Poetry and thinking travel together, but their voyage is without truth; unguarded, it is totally exposed to the accident, to overturning" (ibid., 261). Language, both literal and metaphorical, is at the core of any signification of place, be that signification rational or emotional.

Therefore, I would maintain that instead of being a response to the specific place, to Hadrian's Wall and its muddy reminders of home, "Grotus and Coventina" is, rather, a response to the words *Grotus* and *Coventina* and to the sound of these words as they strike his senses, and once again we are in the realm of the real and of poetry as a form of thinking, and enunciating, of the unsaid. And in this enunciating of the Grotus and Coventina myth, there is also the hauntological echo of the Greek word *omphalos* to be heard, as it is the sound of the word that is central to the effect, and affect, of the image. As Heidegger put it, "Thinking is the poetizing of the truth of Being in the historic dialogue between thinkers" (1975a, 57), and here it is the place of the mind that is the real topic of this poem. What the altar in the poem symbolizes is that place is, paradoxically, transient and mobile. Associations with place are very much created through language and ideology, and the actual place qua location is of comparatively little importance. This reading may seem like arcane philosophizing, but it is easy to prove by example. At the height of the Northern Irish conflict, Northern Protestants would come to Lansdowne Road to cheer for other Northern Protestants playing for an Irish rugby team against England, while lustily singing "God Save the Queen" as their national anthem. In the area of European Union (then the European Economic Community) farming policies, Northern Ireland was happy enough to be seen as part of the island of Ireland when it came to farm quotas and grant schemes. IRA hunger strikers died for political status and for a politics that refused to recognize the power of either the British or the Irish government over an Ireland that was not united. Now, Sinn Féin parliamentarians are represented in Irish and British Parliaments (taking expenses, if not their seats, in the latter institution, and taking both in the former), thereby recognizing both.

Many of these identifications with place are almost impossible to represent, as they involve emotional attachments and asymmetric senses of value and, as such, are best expressed in poetry as genre and in poetry as thinking. Poetized thinking allows for the saying of this unsaid through the image of place: "The unsayable being precisely what language must presuppose in order to signify" (Agamben 1993b, 4). Jacques Rancière makes the telling point that "poetics is from the beginning political" (2004, 11), and in this sense poetry as thinking is equally political as it attempts to tease out the real of the politics of place in the place of politics. As opposed to the physical place, it is the naming and the cultural commodification of place that create the ideological charge that has caused so much of the attachment to place in politics and culture. Certainly, the aesthetic has a role in such a process, but as noted in the previous chapter, a particular strand of the aesthetic can also act as a critique of such a process.

Accordingly, Heidegger sees poetry as that aesthetic activity that most closely "correlates with the task of thinking," but at the same time he situates poetry with politics and philosophy as "fundamental cornerstones in establishing the polis" (Simon 2011, 187), and it is this complexity that Heaney brings out in his own discussion of place, and of the ideality of place, something that is often far more potent. "Language, by naming beings for the first time, first brings beings to word and to appearance" (Heidegger 1971, 71), and if language can do this, then it also has the ability to mediate the way in which beings react to word and appearance. This mediation is definitely true of place, and Heaney's poetic thinking will be focused on his own place and on how it has become enculturated into myth. His perspective validates a turn to poetry to assist thinking to overcome the aporias of modern thought (Watkin 2010, 118), and one of these aporias relates to the issues of identity, belonging, and the centrality of place and home in this process.

Rather than reinforcing essentialist equations between a culture and a place, poetic thinking can transform those relationships, thereby achieving an emancipatory political effect. Instead of just identifying with one place, and telling the story of a people in that place, poetry is also able to create, through language and imagery, another place "where the mind could take shelter from the actual conditions" (Heaney 1984a, 6). Rather than being the mouthpiece of his tradition, a *vox loci* whose gift "like a slingstone" should be "whirled for the desperate" (Heaney 1975, 71), Heaney will instead adopt a position analogous to Maurice Blanchot's, who sees the writer as belonging to a language that "no one speaks, which is addressed to no one, which has no centre, and which reveals nothing" (1982, 61–62).

Actually, one could see this process as a gradual movement from a territorial to a deterritorial perspective and from the enunciation of a sense of place to the enunciation of a sense of space, and we will trace this progression in his aesthetic thought. Indeed, "forms of content and forms of expression are inseparable from a movement of deterritorialisation that carries them away" (Deleuze and Guattari 1987, 87). Part of this transition is the idea that place can actually be two different places at the same time, both culturally and politically speaking, and he addresses this sense of identity in *An Open Letter.*

As we have already noted, he wrote this text in response to his inclusion in Morrison and Motion's *The Penguin Book of Contemporary British Verse*, in 1983, telling the editors that his "anxious muse" has to refuse "the adjective" (meaning the proper adjective *British* in this context), though even here there is the qualification that his muse had been called British before and had acquiesced, but this time has become like the "third wish" in fairy tales; it is now he feels the "crucial test" (Heaney 1983b, 7). Speaking about this text, Heaney makes the point that he felt "more awkward than indignant." However, Heaney is only too well aware that the issue of identity is a serious political one; he knows that people were killing and being killed because of "matters related to the British and Irish words," and he is also very aware that "there was a political as well as a cultural context to be taken into account" (Heaney and O'Driscoll 2008, 418, 417).

This political and cultural context of which he speaks is one that has preoccupied his thinking and writing over a long period of time. Indeed, one can trace this process of the deterritorialization of place from his very first essay in *Preoccupations*, where he says, "Mossbawn, the first place, widened." This widening of Mossbawn is significant to our discussion of place, and it is a process that is part philosophical and part poetic. Philosophically, an interrogation of any sense of fundamental attachment is something that is to be recommended; however, that sense of attachment is something real that is in need of conceptual unpacking if it is ever to be properly understood and fully comprehended. Habermas, for example, sees philosophy as the guardian of rationality, but poetry is not "the dark age that it supersedes but that which accompanies it and keeps it awake. Poetry is a limit of reason that philosophy finds unthinkable" (Bruns 1997, xv). As Blanchot argues, their relationship is complex, but quite productive, as poetry is a question for philosophy that "claims to provide it with an answer, and thus to comprehend it (know it). Philosophy, which puts everything into question, is tripped up by poetry, which is the question that eludes it" (1986, 63). This interconnection is something that, as we have seen, is strong in Heaney's work, and in this chapter the poetics and thinking of place are conflated in his sense of the place of writing, and the use of Mossbawn as the initial locus of this thought process indicates just how important this theme is in Heaney's thinking. In the previous chapter, we looked at the two meanings of "Mossbawn" that were postulated: the "planter's house on the bog" or else the "moss of bog-cotton," and their interanimation is part of that process of widening with which he is engaged. Here, he is looking at the plurality of perspectives, that field of force about which we have been speaking. However, the pluralization of the "first place" Mossbawn is, I would contend, paradigmatic of his thinking on the vexed issues of home, place, language, and politics, and I propose to trace his thought process in this chapter.

Talking to Dennis O'Driscoll about Mossbawn, Heaney speaks of an early sense of what could be seen from there, as the originary point of his perspective on the world. He noted that the windows were small and low set and that from the back window, the yard and the byre could be seen, along with the front hedge, and beyond them to the southwest "Slieve Gallon on the horizon," which he calls "our hill of longing." Significantly, the chestnut tree is very much at the center of his first place, and along with the sense of belonging and comfort there is also a sense of longing: home is paired with the horizon in a structure that we have seen is part of Heaney's thought process; hence, the memories of Mossbawn are more complex than they seem on first reading. Already, even as he remembers the stirrings of vision and of his perspective on the world, there is a nascent field of force created around his descriptions of his home, a field marked out by the trees, hedges, and the hill of longing. The Heaney family moved houses when he was a teenager, to a house called "the Wood," near the village of Bellaghy, and O'Driscoll posed the question as to whether he regarded the loss of Mossbawn as "a cornerstone" of his poetic imagination, and the response is emphatic: "definitely." He tells of how being away at boarding school and only being at home on school holidays meant that he was never properly "moulded" into the Bellaghy ground, as there was a sense of "at-homeness missing." Significantly, given the widespread consensus that Heaney is very much a poet of home and of place, he makes the point that this "out-of-placeness of those in-between years mattered as much for the poetry life as the in-placeness of childhood" (Heaney and O'Driscoll 2008, 15, 24, 25).

I would contend that this longing is the case, as it set up that oscillating dialectic in his thinking between place and space, fullness and emptiness, and at homeness and out of placeness, which was to develop into that poetized thinking that looked for fields of force as opposed to points of certainty. If we were to set out the coordinates of that constellation, a process that is crucial to the widening of that first place, then one of them is found in those early recollections in *Stepping Stones*, significantly entitled "Bearings," where he first mentions the little chestnut tree in the front garden. In an essay from *The Government of the Tongue*, entitled "The Placeless Heaven: Another Look at Kavanagh," he looks at this given of his childhood, one of the core signifiers of that sense of at homeness of which he has been speaking, from a different perspective, which will set up another constellation. This tree was planted by one of Heaney's aunts, Mary, in a jam jar in 1939, and when it sprouted it was transplanted into the boxwood hedge, where it grew steadily. Because this aunt had a particular fondness for the young Heaney, and because this tree was the only one that was actually growing in a garden of pretty mature shrubbery, which "appeared therefore like given features of the world," he came to identify his "own life with the life of the chestnut tree" (1988, 83).

It would seem that I am offering argumentative hostages to fortune here, in the discussion of a particular thing that attaches him to a particular place, but it is not the case. It is not the tree per se but its ideological and emotional associations that have made it special and significant for him. In his discussion of the tree, he makes it clear that it is these associations that motivated him, and these associations are foregrounded by the language of others. The tree had been planted in the year when Heaney was born, and so it grew as he grew. The context of the tree is also significant; the rest of the garden was mature, so the chestnut tree was the only growing plant in the garden and was "watched in much the same way as the other children and myself were watched and commented upon, fondly, frankly and unrelentingly" (ibid., 3).

What is most significant here is that the connections with the tree are all metaphors for the connection with his aunt; it is as if the tree is an organic symbol of the connection between them, and the tree qua tree is not the main element in the connection with Mossbawn. It was a place where he knew comfort, love, and that sense of at homeness of which he spoke. In this sense, what he is describing is a generic phenomenon, one described by Martin Heidegger in *Being and Time*, as the "tranquillized self-assurance, 'being-at-home' with all its obviousness" (1996, 176). For Heidegger, the centrality of dwelling is part of this sense of at homeness, and indeed it could be Heaney who states that "we believe we are at home in the immediate circle of beings. That which is, is familiar, reliable, ordinary" (1971, 53), such is their connection on this issue. The loss of such groundedness has long been seen as a concomitant of modernism and of postmodernism, and the question has been posed as to the nature of this "'dwelling,' this 'at-homeness,' which we, in modernity, are said to lack" (Young 2001, 125) and also of the related term "not-being-at-home" (Heidegger 1996, 177).

Heaney's own early deliberations on place can be located within this more abstract discussion, a discussion that, like Heidegger's case, is contextually constituted by his memories of the seismic dislocations of European populations during the war. Heaney notes that in his early teens, the new owners of Mossbawn chopped down the trees, including the chestnut tree. Interestingly, he tells that it was not in any way problematic for him at the time, but that it was in later years that he began to think of both the tree and the space where the tree had been, or would have been, and in his mind's eye he saw it as "a kind of luminous emptiness, a warp and waver of light," and once again he began to identify with that space, which was now "a placeless heaven rather than a heavenly place" (1988, 3, 4).

This luminous passage forever gives the lie to accusations of Heaney as being in thrall to aesthetic ideology or to seeing his politics as being worn on his poetic sleeve. In the context of the adequation suggested by this study between the aesthetic thought of Heaney and Heidegger, it is interesting that Jeff Malpas makes the point that in Heidegger's later work, his view of the fourfold tended to see the axis of earth and sky as being "more closely associated with space (and also language)" (2012, 57), which would certainly accord with Heaney's view of the signifying powers of the empty space associated with the former site of the tree.

Instead, he would seem to agree with Agamben that "the place of thought and feeling is in the poem itself" (2007, 71). He provides a deeply reasoned account of the need for uprooting, be it physical or ideological, one's planted givens into something else, something that is capable of transformation and change: a transformation of place into space. Instead of Heaney being some poetic apologist for a foundational version of aesthetic nationalism, he is rather a far more nuanced thinker who, while well aware of the pull of the "tight gag of place" (Heaney 1975, 59), is intent on critiquing it and loosening the gag in order to allow for freedom of speech. Again, one can site the connection with the thought of Heidegger, who, having discussed his sense of "being-at-home," goes on to state that "not-being-at-home" as a condition "*must be conceived existentially and ontologically as the more primordial phenomenon*" (1996, 177; emphasis in the original). Poetic language has the ability to make this interaction of presence and absence creative of a more nuanced, more complicated, sense of place. In Heaney's poetized thinking, poetic technique "is expressly intent upon the possibility that this music—the tang and texture of English—can order experience as music itself does" (H. White 2008, 33), because poetry embodies an "extreme intensity of mysteries, interrogations and oppositions" (Blanchot 1995, 123).

In Heaney's view, the new place was all idea, as mind, thinking, and ethics all combine to create this utopic vision of a heavenly place, of an imagined realm, a space of literature in Blanchot's term, from where the old place can be observed, understood, and critiqued. In this sense, it is also redolent of Derrida's idea of a *non-lieu*, a non-site, which was mentioned in the introduction. Speaking to Richard Kearney about philosophy, Derrida says that his "central question is from what site or non-site (*non-lieu*) can philosophy as such appear to itself as other than itself, so that it can interrogate and reflect upon itself in an original manner" (1995, 159), and what Heaney is looking for is such a space from where place, and the ideology of place, can be critiqued. He is looking for a perspective from which to analyze and scrutinize politics and for a structure that allows for the interaction of place and space in a fruitful manner. Again, Derrida has touched on this theme, talking about the "space of writing" in general and going on to see it as a space wherein exists "the power to say everything, to break free of the rules, to displace them, and thereby to institute, to invent and even to suspect the traditional difference between nature and institution, nature and conventional law, nature and history" (Derrida and Attridge 1992, 37). Such a freedom is important for Heaney, who wants both to express the attractions of place, and the at homeness of a language and a place, and at the same time to articulate the need to be wary of not merely succumbing to the attractions of this narrow form of the aesthetic; he wants these perspectives to inform and interinanimate each other as opposed to eliding each other.

Once again, he is examining issues that have been at the heart of the European intellectual tradition. We have already seen that Heidegger has spoken about at homeness, and his views on the *Heim* and the *Volk* have been affected by his early immersion in Nazi ideology, where these aesthetically sanctioned fusions had strong political consequences. Here, place had become monofocal, as the gag was pulled very tight indeed. Blanchot, like Heaney, sees literature as the genre where the seeming certainties of place can be critiqued by imaginary conceptions of space. For Blanchot, it is the transformative potential of art that brings this critique about. He points out that whereas in the real world things are viewed as objects in order to be grasped and classified and categorized, in imaginary space "things are *transformed* into that which cannot be grasped. Out of use, beyond wear, they are not in our possession but are the movement of dispossession which releases us both from them and from ourselves" (1982, 131). In Blanchot's mind, literature is primarily an interrogative discourse that poses questions of the political and ideological: "Literature begins at the moment when literature becomes a question" (1981, 21).

In the context of Mossbawn, the question is posed by the signification of space, by the longing of the horizon, and by the spectral presence/absence of the chestnut tree. So Mossbawn, the first place, did not actually widen; rather, the perspective of the writer and thinker on the place brought about a more broad and complex representation of this place through an apophantic discourse that allowed for such interactions. Clearly, he felt that one's first place cannot, and should not, remain one's only place, and it was the chestnut tree that was the focal point of this process. It appeared in *Electric Light*: "Wild as the chestnut tree one terrible night / In Mossbawn, the aerial rod like a mast" (2001, 48). It signifies both a place and a space, as the radio aerial that connects the Heaney home to the wider world is located on the branches, an aerial that brings the wideness of the world to Mossbawn and is in a way responsible for the widening of that first place. He spoke of this in his Nobel address, *Crediting Poetry*, explaining how his family's den-like life in Mossbawn, "ahistorical, pre-sexual, in suspension between the archaic and the modern," was permeated by the outside world, as passing trains caused the water in a bucket in their scullery to "ripple delicately, concentrically, and in utter silence." Interestingly, as well as this symbol of place being permeated by the outside, so also was the space around them: "The air around and above us was alive and signalling too," as the wind stirred an "aerial wire attached to the topmost branch of the chestnut tree." The wire came into their kitchen and into the radio where the voice of a "BBC newsreader" spoke "out of the unexpected like a *deus ex machina*" (1995a, 9, 10).

However, it was not only the tones of Standard English that were part of the process of widening, but also the voices of Europe, even though they could not be fully understood:

> I grew familiar with the names of foreign stations, with Leipzig and Oslo and Stuttgart and Warsaw and, of course, with Stockholm. I also got used to hearing short bursts of foreign languages as the dial hand swept round from BBC to Radio Éireann, from the intonations of London to those of Dublin, and even though I did not understand what was being said in those first encounters with the gutturals and sibilants of European speech, I had already begun a journey into the wideness of the world beyond. This in turn became a journey into the wideness of language, a journey where each point of arrival—whether in one's poetry or one's life turned out to be a stepping stone rather than a destination. (ibid., 11)

It is language that ushers in the wideness of which he is speaking, and the image of a series of arrivals and departures stands as another enunciation of the field of force where it is the interaction of different elements that creates meaning. These words are pure signifiers; they are language understood qua sound, but not understood as meaning at first; these are sounds that have a visceral appeal to the ear, to the auditory imagination, like "Grotus" and "Coventina." The image of the stepping-stone is thematically appropriate here, as stepping-stones consist of a number of places and spaces, with the space between each stone as part of the structure.

At this point, Heaney is very close to Blanchot and his sense of *The Space of Literature*, where literature is seen as a point of nullity: "If literature coincides with nothing, for just an instant, it is immediately everything, and this everything begins to exist" (1982, 22). The "short bursts of foreign languages" and his encounter with the "gutturals and sibilants of European speech" are important signifiers of this widening of Mossbawn as a place and space of poetic and philosophical origin, for as Agamben says there is an experience of language "for which we have no words, which doesn't pretend, like grammatical language, to be there before being," and he terms this discourse "the language of poetry" (1995, 48). It is an experience of language as other, as a form of communication that we cannot understand, even though we know it is signifying on some level. It is an alternative understanding of language, a feeling, a sensation, of difference through language; it is a conceptual displacement from any claim that our own language is the only way in which to speak or say the world.

Poetic language has an ability to express and access aspects of experience that are silenced in normal discourse, as it belongs "neither to the day nor to the night but always is spoken between night and day and one single time speaks the truth and leaves it unspoken" (Blanchot 1982, 276). Writing about the spaces that are part of the stepping-stones, Heaney makes the point that poetic language has allowed him to uproot from the appetites of gravity, and the next line in *Crediting Poetry*, after the piece quoted above, validates this point: "I credit poetry for making this space-walk possible" (1995a, 11). The foreign words become part of his memory of Mossbawn, just as much as the chestnut tree and the boxwood hedge.

Just as place has become part of a structure that also includes space, so the place of writing is seen as an alternative way of expressing place in Heaney's thinking, and it is to a text entitled *The Place of Writing* that our discussion now turns. This text comprises three lectures, given April 11–15, 1988, which inaugurated the Richard Ellmann lectures in modern literature at Emory University, in Atlanta. The title is one toward which a lot of Heaney's thinking had been building, and it expresses his philosophy about the relationship between the text and the territory: "We are more and more aware of writing as a place in itself, a destination in art arrived at by way of art." Art, the aesthetic, the poetic imagination, is what transforms the place and what "imposes its vision upon a place rather than accepts a vision from it," and this sense of the power of poetry to shape our sense of place is almost Heideggerian, as Heaney sees poetry as making space for different conceptions of place, because "once the place has been brought into written existence, it is inevitable that it be unwritten" (1989, 19, 20). This notion parallels Heidegger's view that the "work as work sets up a world" and that the work "holds the Open of the world" (1971, 44), and it also presages a change of outlook in Heaney's own attitude to the writing of place (Russell 2014, 212).

For Heidegger, it is part of a dialectical relationship between the work of art, in this case the poem, and the earth. "The work moves the earth itself into the Open of a World and keeps it there" (1971, 45), but only as that "which is by nature undisclosable, that which shrinks from every disclosure and constantly keeps itself closed up" (1971, 46). For Heidegger, a work of art, in its work-being, is an ongoing dialectical tension between the terms *world* and *earth*, between ideas of revelation and unconcealment associated with the world, and ideas of the concealment and reserve associated with earth. One could see parallels here between Heaney's dialectical interanimations of the writing of place and the place of writing, and for both thinkers it is poetry as breath, as language, that allows it to happen. Heidegger sees art as that which allows an interpretation and a sensing of the truth of the world through what he terms "a founding leap" (*Ursprung*); for Heidegger, "art lets truth originate" through this *Ursprung* (ibid., 77).

As Heidegger explains, truth is present "only as the conflict between lighting and concealing in the opposition of world and earth" (ibid., 60). Both writers are talking about how place needs to be subject to space in order to liberate new dimensions of meaning, both aesthetically and politically. It is important that writing, which can create claustrophobic bonds between race and place, can also be, as we saw Krieger argue, a structure through which polysemic layers of the meaning of place can be uncovered and a form of truth can be uttered.

Heaney is alert to this closed relationship between writer and place, where "he or she becomes a voice of the spirit of the region" (1989, 20); however, it is more the writing of place than the place of writing. The place of writing is a more open discourse, where place becomes displaced in language, and as we have seen, Blanchot views this as a creative process though which "everything begins to exist" (1982, 22). To widen any place, the wideness of language and of difference must be allowed scope to influence the meanings created for the place in writing. Thus, rather than being bound by one of the two received meanings of his own place, the "planter's house on the bog" or the "moss of bog-cotton," and going on to create a mythos and a politics of the place based on that narrow view of language, instead he chooses to set up "a country of the mind rather than the other way round," where the country, and the narrow language and ideology of that country, "has created the mind which in turn creates the poems" (1989, 21).

This country of the mind is one, as imagined in the quincunx and his images of the triangle, where different meanings of place exist in a dynamic tension that in turn creates new and fresh levels of meaning for those places. Going on to talk about Yeats and his ability to impose his own vision on a place, he makes the point that the place of writing can be seen, in one sense, to be "the stanza form itself, that strong-arched room or eight iambic pentameters," which Yeats used in much of his later signature poetry (ibid., 29). This view of the stanza as a place of writing has a distinguished history. At the beginning of his book *Stanzas: Word and Phantasm in Western Culture*, Agamben cites an epigraph from Dante: "And here one must know that this term (stanza) has been chosen for technical reasons exclusively, so that what contains the entire art of the canzone should be called stanza, that is, a capacious dwelling or receptacle for the entire craft. For just as the canzone is the container of the entire thought, so the stanza enfolds its entire technique" (1993c, vii). This passage reminds us strongly of Heaney's views on the stanza as a place of writing, which argue that the aesthetic is a process whereby work is involved. Heaney describes work in the traditional sense used in physics, where it is seen as moving "a certain mass through a certain distance," and in terms of place, and the politics of place, the distance involved is that which separates the topographical place from the written place, and this distance is another aspect of that constellation wherein meanings intersect and interact, as "the mass moved is one aspect of the writer's historical/biographical experience, and each becomes a factor of the other in the achieved work. The work of art, in other words, involves raising the historical record to a different power" (1989, 36).

The sophistication of this construction of "understanding place otherwise" locates Heaney firmly within the ranks of contemporary Continental philosophy and theory. He is well aware that cultural nuances also have political implications, but is similarly keen to stress the distance between the cultural and political ramifications of place. In the context of this discussion, it should come as no surprise that Heaney took a stand on the controversial issue of the flying of the Union flag over city hall in Belfast. There had been eight weeks of street protests—with sporadic outbreaks of violence—since Belfast City Council voted on December 3, 2012, to fly the Union flag at city hall on designated days only. In an interview with Erica Wagner, Heaney made the point that loyalists should be allowed to fly the flag, as "each side is entitled to its pageantry" (Wagner 2013). He refuses to conflate the literary and the political, as in his aesthetic thought, the writing of place will never conflate with the place of writing. The ethical duty of writers and thinkers is to widen that sense of the first place and to make sure that the distance between the first place and other places is worked through. The different flags would symbolize those different concepts of place, that sense of being in two places at once as discussed in connection with Wordsworth and a number of other writers. The transformation into the political sphere is a fine example of Krieger's point that the aesthetic can often work as a deconstructive lever in the reified sphere of political and ideological positions. It is not a huge leap from his literary two-mindedness to a more political incarnation of this idea, and the flag, as an emblem of territorial ideology, is a significant example of how symbols can be significant in the political realm. One could see the flag issue as another version of the mentality that set out the quincunx as an ideal of Irish identity—both literary and political.

This two-mindedness is why the work of MacNeice, as we have seen, is significant for Heaney, as his prenatal mountain was a conflation of different forces and influences on his personality and on his writing. He is also an avatar of Heaney's own theories about the multiple meanings of place that are accessed in the place of writing, as in "Carrick Revisited," what Heaney terms the "whole parallelogram of cultural and ancestral forces operating in MacNeice's life is discovered and thereby, to a certain extent, re-dressed," once again using a geometrical structure in order to contextualize what he means. Here, the mountain is held in "equilibrium" with the England of MacNeice's schooling and the "plumb, assured, unshakable fact of an Ulster childhood" (Heaney 1989, 44, 45). This dynamic equilibrium, wherein the different traces and connections that help to write our sense of place are all granted their effect and affect, is very much what Heaney values. Indeed, he makes this very point when he speaks of the Northern Irish writers whose thought and work attract him. He sees them as being able to "take the strain of being in two places at once, of needing to accommodate two opposing conditions of truthfulness simultaneously," which can be seen as constitutive of his own inclusive and nonbinary mode of aesthetic thought. Because he and other Northern Irish writers "belong to a place that is patently riven by notions of belonging to other places," he is attuned to plurality of belonging and to seeing identities not as monolithic but as composed of interwoven differential strands: each person in Ulster lives first in the Ulster of the actual present and then in one or other Ulster of the mind (Heaney 1984a, 4).

It is this sense of "two-mindedness" (Heaney 1995b, 202) that serves as a possible paradigm of the desired relationship. The ideal place of writing, a place that is more idea than topography, allows for this plurivocal, ethical attitude, and it is this dialectic of immanence and transcendence that allows him to survive amphibiously in the contemporary political situation. The unwriting of monological associations with place is very much part of the place of writing, as he puts it: "If one perceptible function of poetry is to write place into existence, another of its functions is to unwrite it" (1989, 47), and this unwriting is part of his third lecture.

He refers to his own poem "The Disappearing Island" (1987, 50–51), which recalls the mythical tale of Saint Brendan the Navigator, who landed with his monks on a barren island in the western ocean. For them, it was a "place of refuge, a locus of penitential discipline and potentially a home where they might settle for good." Yet after their first night of respite on its shores, the island "turned over, revealed itself as a wakened sea-monster and promptly disappeared into the waves." It is a profound image of the writing and unwriting of place, and it explains how different meanings of place can seem to be natural and given but ultimately prove to be ideological constructions. Such constructions can either leave people firmly embedded on one side or the other, in cultural or political terms, or else force them to tread "the tightrope" of "uncertainty in a line that stretches between two opposing truths" (Heaney 1989, 54). This point is where the place of writing becomes internalized, as this "line" is another field of force, on which the mind travels, moving from one meaning to the other, while all the time struggling to keep a sense of balance, and this idea of balance, of the balancing of opposite and contradictory forces as being one of the core functions of the aesthetic, is one to which he will turn in his Pete Layer Memorial Lecture at the Wordsworth Summer Conference in Grasmere Cottage, entitled *Place and Displacement*.

Even the title here is redolent of Heaney's view of structure as dynamic and oscillating, and it harks back to *The Place of Writing* and to his idea that poetry both writes and unwrites senses of place, and ultimately of identity. The position of Wordsworth, who was writing at the time of the French Revolution, is one that resonates particularly with Heaney's own placement in the bodies politic and cultural. Wordsworth had always been a strong advocate of the Revolution and of its emancipatory and egalitarian imperatives. However, in the 1790s, this passion for liberty came into conflict with his love of England, and when the latter declared war upon revolutionary France, it brought about a crisis of great intensity for him, as his love for his native place came into conflict with his sense of the rightness of the revolutionary paradigm:

> He is displaced from his own affections by a vision of the good that is located elsewhere. His political, utopian aspirations deracinate him from the beloved actuality of his surrounding so that his instinctive being and his appetitive intelligence are knocked out of alignment. He feels like a traitor among those he knows and loves. To be true to one part of himself, he must betray another part. The inner state of man is thus shaken and the shock waves in the consciousness reflect the upheavals in the surrounding world. (Heaney 1984a, 3)

Here Wordsworth is in two places at once: he is English and loves his country, but he is still an admirer of the globalizing imperative of the Revolution with its ringing assertions of *The Declaration of the Rights of Man and of the Citizen*. This discussion of the pulls of ideology and thought on the meanings of a place is no idle academic matter for Heaney, and he makes this plain as he draws the parallel between Wordsworth and writers in contemporary Northern Ireland.

These writers also take the strain "of being in two places at once, of needing to accommodate two opposing conditions of truthfulness simultaneously," or they belong to a place that is "patently riven between notions of belonging to other places." Each person, he feels, lives in two Ulsters simultaneously, one "of the actual present" and then in "one or other Ulster of the mind." Consequently, people are adept at being in a place but not of that place, just as Wordsworth was present in his congregation, but "withheld assent from the congregation's prayers for the success of the English armies." We have already noted the working distance that separated political dimensions of place from dimensions of the aesthetic, and the same is true of his sense of two-mindedness. He speaks of how the cultural movement was parallel to the political movement but still separate from it. He makes the very clear point that to locate the roots of one's identity in the "ethnic and liturgical habits of one's group might be all very well," but allowing one's responses to be programmed by that group "was patently another form of entrapment" or, to put it another way, of allowing one's first place to remain one's only place (1984a, 4, 6, 7).

Instead, the aesthetic needs to act as a form of critique of such conceptions of rootedness and narrowness; it understands them otherwise, and once again for Heaney this point is expressed in a fluid structure, where the poet is seen to be stretched between "politics and transcendence, and is often displaced from a confidence in a single position by his disposition to be affected by all positions, negatively rather than positively capable." The sense of being affected by multiple positions is carried on in his discussion of Derek Mahon's poetry and its enunciation of Hugh O'Neill through what is termed the "civil beauty of Penshurst," home of the Sidney family (Heaney 1984a, 8, 12). O'Neill, as we have seen, is seen as the last truly Celtic or Gaelic chieftain, who fought the armies of Queen Elizabeth in the Nine Years' War (1593–1603). However, he can also be seen as a more liminal figure, as he had been fostered by the Sidney family in their home in Penshurst for eight years before returning to Tyrone, where he led the rebellion against the very Tudor aristocracy that fostered him. Again, we see someone riven by a sense of belonging to two different places and whose very name embodies this bifurcation, as to the English, he was the Earl of Tyrone, while to the Irish he was "the O'Neill."

Heaney, in pointing out this sense of two-mindedness, of bifurcation, and of the plurality of place, has no bland solutions to offer. His poetized thinking is alert to the nuances and is capable of constructing fluid and flexible structures of identity, but he has no ready answers. For him, poetry functions in the interstices of a structure of what "is going to happen and whatever we would wish to happen," allowing us to concentrate fully "back on ourselves." Heaney sees this focus on the individual as part of a context that is crucial to the mode of knowledge that is poetry, as at its "greatest moments," it would attempt, in Yeats's phrase, "to hold in a single thought reality and justice," and he is also interested in how it occurs, because the modalities of expression, as well as its effect (or affect), are always important to him. Once more, it is a structure that is fluid, balanced, and in dynamic tension. "Poetry is more a threshold than a path," and this sense of the importance of the threshold in contemporary aesthetic thinking will be developed in the coming chapters. Heaney's view of the threshold echoes his triangular and quincuncial structures in that it is the movement and the oscillation and mirroring of the different motions across the threshold that are of significance. This sense of motion and dynamic process mirrors his sense of poetry as a mode of knowledge that allows for a dialectic of experience that he sees in terms of being "summoned and released" (1988, 108). This idea of poetry as a threshold, as a point of entry and exit into more than one dimension, is typical of Heaney's poetizing thought, and it also reflects the idea that identities and perceptions of place are more about modes of entry and exit than they are about actual topographical or physical locations. Such concentration on the self, and such a dynamic process of summoning and releasing, "does not limit itself to distinguishing what is inside from what is outside but instead traces a threshold (the state of exception) between the two" (Agamben 1998, 19). Agamben, as we have seen, also looks to the threshold as a symbol, and indeed this term has a distinguished history in European thought.

Immanuel Kant often spoke of the idea of borders between different disciplines or modes of identity, and as Agamben has explained, in Kantian terms, what is in question in this bordering is "not a limit (*Schranke*) that knows no exteriority, but a threshold (*Grenze*), that is, a point of contact with an external" (1993a, 65). Speaking about space, Jean-Luc Nancy has remarked that this spatiality "is the space of freedom, inasmuch as freedom is, at every moment, the freedom of a free space" (1993, 145), and Agamben, also talking about identity and structures, makes a parallel use of the term in his own writing. Speaking about place and space, Agamben first thematizes the threshold in *The Coming Community*, in a piece entitled "Outside," where he talks about "the event of an outside." It is through this liminal border that the belonging of an entity to a set, or its identity, is determined. This limit does not, however, open on to another determinate space: "The outside is not another space that resides beyond a determinate space, but rather, it is the passage, the exteriority that gives it access" (1993a, 66).

Poetry is just such a passage. It is a "point of contact with an external space that must remain empty," and for both Agamben and Heaney, it is the openness of the space that is important, as the interaction of points of contact, and the summoning and releasing process, will fill it in parts so that new structures of meaning may be created through the crossing and recrossing of this threshold. Agamben notes that ideas of the outside have been expressed through the symbol of a door in many languages, and he cites the two seminal languages of the European intellectual tradition, where the sense of the "outside" is expressed by a word that means "at the door," as "*fores* in Latin is the door of the house, *thyrathen* in Greek literally means 'at the threshold'" (1993a, 63, 66). If the first place is to widen, there must be a space outside it into which it can widen, and, logically, there must also be some mode of access to that space, both physically and intellectually. For Agamben, both the outside space and the mode of access to it are conveyed in the term *threshold* (Murray and Whyte 2011, 190), and this composite meaning is relevant to our final example of the widening of Mossbawn and its locus as a place of writing.

At the conference of the European Federation of Associations and Centres of Irish Studies, held at the University of Vienna on September 3–6, 2009, Heaney delivered a reading and a lecture based on the conference theme, which was Irish/European cross-currents and exchanges. The title of this lecture is germane to our discussion: "'Mossbawn via Mantua': Ireland in/and Europe, Cross-Currents and Exchanges" (2012), as it sets out a form of attunement between his own place and the city in northern Italy and, by extension, between Irishness and European intellectual and cultural traditions. Heaney begins by talking about how Coleridge looked to poetry as a way of retrieving the novelty and freshness of old familiar objects, and he also refers to Joyce's remark in *A Portrait of the Artist as a Young Man*, when he aphorizes that the "shortest way to Tara is via Holyhead," meaning that emigration and a broader perspective are the best ways to come to a real (and I use the term in the Lacanian sense) knowledge of Ireland. As Heaney puts it, "From the viewing deck of Europe ordinary Irish things were presented and represented to the mind in an unusual way" (ibid., 19). Hence, this European perspective allows him to look awry at Ireland and see it in a new context. Here the threshold between inside and outside, between first and other place, between the chestnut tree and the absent space, is expressed in the imagery of place, but of a written as opposed to a topographical place. The "Mantua" that acts as a threshold to, and from, "Mossbawn" is not the contemporary topographical city in northern Italy, but rather the birthplace of Virgil, one of the seminal figures of the European literary and intellectual tradition. The rhizomatic connection is motivated by writing rather than by place, by the idea of Mossbawn and by the idea of Mantua, and by a connection between Heaney the writer and Virgil the writer as opposed to any connection between the two actual places themselves (apart from the fortuitous alliteration). In this sense, he is looking to this place as a liberating space that will allow for a new perspective: it is "the space of poetry—space without place: the space of exile, the region of the foreign and the strange" (Bruns 1997, 117).

In this lecture, Heaney sets out five different areas of influence that he feels have had this effect for him, and again the structure, the number of items, and the interplay between them are what are interesting here, given our discussion of his initial quincunx and the connection of it with Heidegger's fourfold. Clearly, the place of writing is a plural structure, and it is one where different influences interact and intersect, and we could be talking about the quincunx again, or about the different Englishnesses, or about the sense of surviving amphibiously, which dominated the last chapter. We are now familiar with the structural process he uses as he sets out parameters, and then focuses on the relations and interstices between them. In this case, he sets out different threshold experiences between different aspects of the European intellectual tradition, and by so doing he is making a connection between his first place, Mossbawn, and the other of European writing, what Heidegger has termed "the Open." In a typically opaque summation, Heidegger explains that in taking possession of the Open, the "openness holds open the Open and sustains it. Setting and taking possession are here everywhere drawn from the Greek sense of *thesis*, which means a setting up in the unconcealed" (1971, 59).

The unconcealed here is analogous to the Lacanian real, in that it attempts to voice the hidden dimensions of language and thinking, such as the influence of different aspects of a tradition on a writer, or of different aspects of contexts on a text, to use Derrida's terminology. Heaney explains this notion clearly, as he sets out how Mossbawn, as a place of writing, became entwined with other European places:

> As a title, "Mossbawn via Mantua" is meant to echo Joyce and to suggest how the Irish home ground can be reviewed in the light of certain European perspectives—classical, medieval, and modern. These planes of regard allow us to get a closer view of that ground by standing back from it and help to establish a different focus, a more revealing angle of vision. I'm thinking of Mantua first and foremost as the birthplace of the poet Virgil and I juxtaposed the name of his region with the name of my own birthplace because it so happened that the invitation to speak at this conference arrived just after I had finished a sequence of short autobiographical poems which depended significantly on Book VI of Virgil's *Aeneid*. In this, too, I was following the example of Joyce, since each poem in the sequence echoed and paralleled episodes in that most haunting book in much the same way as Joyce had echoed and paralleled books of Homer's *Odyssey* in the different chapters of his novel *Ulysses*. (2012, 19)

Once again, there is a reference to Frost submerged in this quotation, as Frost has famously made the point that "education doesn't change life much. It just lifts trouble to a higher plane of regard" (2009, 156), and this attitude has strong parallels with Heaney's own views. His own higher planes of regard involve those shifting contexts of European history as well as the different modes of enunciation and the connections between voice, language, and imagination.

It is these connections between voice, language, and imagination that underlie this second quincunx, as in this one, Mossbawn/Mantua would occupy the center, and the other European places and traditions would occupy the other points of the structure. Once again, it is a field of force wherein the hidden, concealed aspects of identity are allowed to be glimpsed and expressed. It is an agalmatic relationship, as through its interactions that which is hidden or occluded is revealed.

The place of writing is very much determined by words, languages, and traditions, and I am using the plural here in a very deliberate manner, as it is this plurality that allows for the widening of a sense of place and identity. The voice coming down the aerial is now supplemented by the voices from Europe that Heaney is invoking. It is no accident that the idea of translation is significant here, and we will probe this notion in more detail in the next chapter. For now, it is sufficient to note that many of the voices invoked have become available to him only through translation, and the Mantua connection is specifically motivated by translations that he had completed (at the time of writing) of book 6 of Virgil's *Aeneid*. Here, we "are at that thrilling moment when the place of writing shifts its locus into psychic space" (Heaney 1989, 68).

Translation, in its broadest sense, is the voice of the other, and it can offer some access to aspects of language and thinking from different traditions that may have become occluded in the paradigm of the self. In all of Heaney's European perspectives, there is this sense of adding to the native tradition, or of offering different perspectives on the home tower, to revert to the quincunx again. The parameters of his influences are interesting, and all locate Heaney as an aesthetic thinker very much within the European intellectual tradition. He is keen to retain aspects of his givens, and of the autochthonous tradition, but is reluctant to let it be the limit of his horizon of expectation. Instead, the different European locations, or places of writing, will cast new light on his own writing of place and will also look to understand otherwise his own tradition and identity.

These five European places of writing that form this second quincunx are the Greco-Roman and Judeo-Christian heritage; the northern "barbarian" tradition; the Hyperborean perspective, which includes Eastern European influences; the influence of Dante Alighieri; and the influence of translation. These five areas all conspire to pluralize the European influence and experience, as well as offering reflected and refracted light on Ireland, as each influence in some way illuminates aspects of the Irish experience as part of a broader and changing European contextual framework. Thus, the Greco-Roman and Christian traditions are "foundational" to the way we think and to the way that "we in Europe imagine and make meanings of our experience." These traditions provide "the first co-ordinates of the western mind, its common vocabulary," a system of "longitude and latitude," whereby "the individual can locate himself or herself in culture and consciousness" (Heaney 2012, 20). To see Ireland as part of a Christian tradition is hardly remarkable, as this aspect of Irish experience has long been a synecdoche for Irishness as a whole. However, in a manner redolent of the Irish quincunx, Heaney is setting out this influence as just one coordinate of the place of writing that is Ireland, and he goes on to see this aspect as challenged and influenced by a number of other traditions.

Among them are the traditions of the Vikings and the Germanic peoples, whose influence on Europe is strong and whose influence on Irish history is recorded by Heaney in *North*. Heaney calls these traditions "equally familiar and accessible" but "less official." They comprise the barbarian element in European culture, "all that babble beyond the pale": all those tribes "north of the Alps and north of Hadrian's Wall, all that is symbolized by the runic Germanic letter or the Irish ogham stone rather than the lines of Roman script" (ibid.). It is typical of his transgressive style of the writing of place that he imagines the relationship of the Germanic, barbarian culture to the culture of the Greco-Roman world through an Irish comparison, as the "pale" is the area of Ireland in medieval times where the English language and law were fully enforced, whereas beyond this area, beyond the pale, the native Irish culture held sway. Therefore, the influence of Europe on Ireland is balanced by this Irish way of describing a European phenomenon: a further complexity in the writing of place and in the place of writing and of understanding place otherwise.

His third place of writing here is what he calls the Hyperborean, an imagined area by the Greeks beyond "Boreas, beyond the north wind," and in Heaney's literary atlas it is inhabited by Eastern European poets with whom he came into contact through translation and who helped him to make sense of his "own situation in the turbulent Ireland of the 1970s and 80s." He mentions three poets by name: the Russian Osip Mandelstam, the Polish Zbigniew Herbert, and the Lithuanian Czesław Miłosz, all of whom were "dual citizens of the republic of letters and the republic of conscience." The fourth area is a very specific one; it is the province "invigilated" by Dante Alighieri, and his influence on Heaney is very much located in the political place of writing. Heaney learns from Dante's *Divine Comedy* that one way to represent "the vehemence and complexity of a riven society" is to allow those individuals most violently and fatally involved in it to "speak for themselves and bear witness to their own experience," which led him to write his "Station Island" sequence, wherein he encountered a series of ghosts, some people who had been killed in the violence, and some figures from the historical past "who acted at one moment as accusers, at another as counsellors, at yet another as confessors and ultimately, therefore, as comforters" (Heaney 2012, 20, 21). The associations of people and place, of traditions and place, and ultimately of violence and place are all conflated here in this image, and the lesson of Dante is clear in the plurality of voices that Heaney hears in "Station Island." This influence is also true of his use of the Dantean *terza rima* form of loose three-line stanzas, which he borrowed from Dante and suggests a form that deals with elevated issues of transcendence and the afterlife.

The final place of writing is translation, the topic of the next chapter. Here it is that aspect of the European experience that becomes available to Heaney through other languages that have been rendered into English—again, it is like those voices speaking in strange languages on the radio in Mossbawn, but now, through translation, they are comprehensible. Indeed, the European dimension of the place of writing would be impossible without translation, both in its philosophical sense of revealing notions of alterity to notions of the self, and vice versa, and in the practical sense of the linguistic processes of transference from source language to target language. It is the broader sense of the term that is of significant interest; as he puts it, the main influence has been "indirect, a matter of example, of being shown how to deal with conditions on the home ground, of translation in a wider, looser, more general sense as 'carry over'" (ibid., 21–22), and he has told O'Driscoll that much of the motivation for his considerable translation output was in response to political circumstances, with Dante, Aeschylus, Virgil, Sophocles, and Horace all being used to describe a place that was riven with political tension. Without doubt, his translations and European influences all allow for a widening of perspective on Mossbawn and for the inscription of his first place of writing as a European place, which has important ramifications for his own sense of poetry as a form of thinking.

In this structural outline, Heaney is placing Mossbawn in connection with the "Open," and with what Heidegger would also call the "neighbourhood," which is a relational structure wherein he situates the seeming opposites of poetry and thinking: "poetry and thought, each need the other in its neighbourhood, each in its fashion, when it comes to ultimate" (1982b, 70). The term *neighbourhood* is significant here, as surely what Heaney is doing in "Mossbawn via Mantua" is tracing out the locus of the European neighborhood of Irish writing. The initial invocation of Joyce is noteworthy here, as of all the writers and thinkers within the Irish tradition, he was the one who most overtly located that tradition within a broad European context, as the names of his most famous characters embody that tradition, from the colonial Gibraltar of Molly Bloom, to the European Jewish Diasporic other of Leopold Bloom, to the mythically inspired vowel shift that created "Dedalus" from "Daedalus," and of course the title of his most famous book, *Ulysses*. The Pan-European relationship is traced out specifically in this essay, but generally in much of Heaney's writing is a statement of relation and, as such, parallels the Heideggerian sense of the neighborhood.

Significantly, for our discussion, Heidegger used this term across a number of his works, but most often when attempting to describe the relationship between poetry and thinking, a topic that is at the core of this analysis and, I would maintain, is also at the core of Seamus Heaney's project. His thinking and poetizing resonate with the work of Heidegger, whose whole philosophical thrust rests "upon the supposition that poetry and thinking belong within one neighbourhood," and here we are in the same territory, or place of writing, as Heaney, because what Heidegger realizes is that poetry manages to locate and voice the concealed and the Open in ways that purely rational thought is unable to achieve. Poetry allows access to aspects of the real, so that when Heidegger states that the "lofty poetry of all great poetic work always vibrates within a realm of thinking," the word *vibrate* is deliberate, as it signifies all that is appetitive and somatic about language as it is used in poetized thinking. For both writers, the shape and sound of the words convey meaning in a way that they can never do in other verbal discourses; for Heidegger, this complex, more nuanced level of thinking "goes its ways in the neighbourhood of poetry," because, as he stresses, "thinking cuts furrows into the soil of being." He elaborates on this notion by paraphrasing Nietzsche: "Our thinking should have a vigorous fragrance, like a wheatfield on a summer's night" (ibid., 80, 69, 70). In all of these statements, the senses and the body are core to the process of thinking. The aesthetic, as the realm of language, emotion, and the body, is essential for any thinking that would attempt to come to any fullness of description of the human experience, and the same is true of place. Heidegger's cutting of furrows, Nietzsche's fragrant wheat field, and Heaney's concentric ripples of water in the scullery bucket all bear witness to the role of the body and of sensation in the fullness of human experience. If thinking is ever to fully come to terms with the complexity of the experience of living in the world, then it must be poetized thinking that allows access to this realm of experience. All three, I would contend, share this vision of aesthetic thinking.

To articulate place, our sense of place, the ideation of place, and the voicing and signifying of place is not easy, nor is it easy to trace all of the associations that accrue to the place of writing, as these relationships are complex. Language can become lost in the attempts to express this complexity, which is why poetry, with its lyrical charge and its relative freedom from narrative constraints, is able to symbolize and signify the plurality of place and, more important, the plurality of the contexts within which conceptions of place are created. Poetry is a particularly potent method of articulating this kind of thinking about place and its writing: "The neighbourhood of poetry and thinking is concealed within this farthest divergence of their Saying." Even the term *neighbourhood* has connotations of a relationship between people and place and, indeed, between different places: "Poetry moves in the element of saying, and so does thinking. When we reflect on poetry, we find ourselves at once in that same element in which thinking moves, we cannot here decide flatly whether poetry is really a kind of thinking, or thinking really a kind of poetry. It remains dark to us what determines their real relation, and from what we so casually call the 'real' really comes" (Heidegger 1982b, 90, 83). In the context of the place of writing, the "real" here is that writing, as well as being creative of fundamental associations between a people and a place, can also be constitutive of idealized and plural conceptions of that relationship.

Hence, for Heaney, the image of the chestnut tree and his sense of belonging and comfort in the den of Mossbawn are equally balanced by the space that was left when the tree was cut down and by his leaving of Mossbawn: place and space are intertwined for him. The same can be said of the associations of the places of writing of which he speaks, as the tree is shot through with connections and associations with his aunt, and it stands, both in presence and in absence, as a symbol of her connection with him. Likewise, his attraction to Mossbawn itself is held in balance with the influences of the outside world that came in through the sounds on the radio. Place and space are set out in a field of force so that all influences are given some form of voice, and the reconceptualized poetic space becomes "a new clearing for thought" (Watkin 2010, 34). Poetized thinking is the discourse where place and space can be seen as parts of a contextual structure where the aesthetic can act as a form of critique of the political and of the ideological and can dislocate the signification of place from any seemingly umbilical relationship between place, people, and language.

Although poetic language has been guilty of aestheticizing place within a particular ideology and politics, where the affect of language can make a place seem to be uniquely connected to a particular ideological position, Heaney's poetized thinking unpacks this position, and his fusion of the poetic and the philosophical allows him to offer a perspective of the place of writing as connected to place in that immanent mode of belonging while at the same time having something of a transcendent perspective that allows him to see place as "pure idea" and as space. Such thinking is very much part of the European philosophical tradition:

> Even poetry seems here to experience the originary event of its own word as *nothing*. The poetic and philosophical experiences of language are thus not separated by an abyss, as an ancient tradition of thought would have it, but both rest originally in a common negative experience of the taking place of language. Perhaps, rather, only from this common negative experience is it possible to understand the meaning of that scission in the status of language that we are accustomed to call poetry and philosophy; and thus, to understand that which, while separating them, also holds them together and seems to point beyond their fracture. (Agamben 1991, 74)

In a parallel manner, place and space are similarly connected through their expression and through language. It is part of Heaney's strength as an aesthetic thinker that the place of writing and the writing of place inform each other, have strong connections with each other, contradict each other, but in the end mutually define and interinanimate each other.

Poetry and thinking are very much connected in Heaney's writing, and in this connection he follows in the footsteps of Heidegger, whose emphasis on poetry and poetic thinking was foundational to the tradition that was able "to hand philosophy over to poetry" (Badiou 1999, 74). In his discussion of the place of writing, and in his use of what we might call the space of writing as a way of bringing this concept to a fuller meaning, Heaney combines poetic thinking with philosophy in order to come to a fuller understanding of the concept and ideology of place. This space is one where poetry and philosophy, and where poetic and philosophical language and discourses, are fused in a poetized thinking. He has examined place in an Irish context, looking at his own first place, Mossbawn, as we have seen, and it is to a different but related perspective on this first place that our discussion now turns.

6

Translations

The Voice of the Other

In keeping with his view of poetry as encouraging complex and dialectical transformations of the actual, this chapter will discuss how Heaney grants both the effectiveness and the plurality of identifications of Irishness through a further structure, translation. Heaney has spoken a lot about complex structures of meaning and identity, and he has stressed the importance of plurality and influence in his thinking, and in his writing. We have seen his political amphibiousness as well as his displacement and dislocation of foundational attachments to place. We have also seen that he is keen to use the aesthetic as a tool through which to critique such perspectives. In this chapter, another of his complex and fluid structures of signification will be examined, structures that reinforce the view that for Heaney, complexity and mobility are two of the most significant aspects of his work. Translation has long been a significant topic in philosophical discourse. Its etymology speaks to its importance in a culture where meaning and language are diffuse, plural, and different: *trans*, meaning "across," and *latum*, the past participle of *ferre* (to carry), suggests a transportation of meaning, a physical displacement. The German übersetzen implies the same, so we are looking at a sense of movement of meaning, and a possible transformation of that meaning in the process; translation involves "transaction and as transfer" (Derrida and Venuti 2001, 175), and it is in this more expanded epistemological sense of the term that this chapter will analyze Heaney's work in this genre.

Translation, according to Lawrence Venuti, with its allegiance both to source and to target cultures, "is a reminder that no act of interpretation can be definitive" (1998, 46), and it can be seen as "another way of recognizing a summons to translation at the very threshold of all reading-writing" (Derrida and Venuti 2001, 175). In terms of its mode of operation, and according to Benjamin "translation is a mode" (1968, 70), every translation makes the attempt to transfer meaning from one language to another, and this transference is, by definition, an interpretation, as there are numerous problems whose resolution defines the task of the translator. The connections between source language and target language need to be teased out, and the habitus of the source language needs to be transferred across the divide to the habitus of the target language, even though the habitus of the target language may well be very different. Issues of archaism, dialect, idiolect, and intentionality must be addressed; generic aspects of the work in question need to be dealt with, and there are, indeed, many problems to be overcome.

I would suggest that one could see translation as a paradigm of the process of poetized thinking and reading. Normally, the reading process involves a dual movement. One reads a sentence, in the Anglophone culture, from left to right, stopping at the period. However, there ensues a parallel revision of the sentence, as units of meaning are now revisited in terms of understanding after the syntactical movement has been terminated by that full stop. It is a complicated process in itself, but reading poetry is far more challenging. In prose the units involved are syntactical and semantic; in poetry the structures include the syntactical, the semantic, the stanzaic, and the phonetic. All of these structures intersect and interact in an apophantic discourse that results in the idea of the full stop as a point of closure of meaning being deconstructed by the stanzaic and linear enjambment and by connections of rhyme and rhythm, which allow meaning to be created through association as opposed to sequence. One could see these different structural paradigms as yet another field of force, and when one factors in translation as well, then the structure is all the more complex and fluid.

Besides, there are no guide rails for the process; instead, there are only the previous works of translation to act as mentors. However, as Heidegger puts it, "Every translation is already an interpretation. Every interpretation must first of all have entered into what is said, into the subject matter it expresses" (2004, 174), so there are issues of immanence and transcendence to be taken into account as well. Clearly, there is a lot more at stake here than merely getting a dictionary and looking for a word-to-word adequation. As Susan Bassnett, probably the foremost authority on translation studies, has stated, translation is "therefore a dangerous act, potentially subversive and always significant. In the 1990s, the figure of the subservient translator has been replaced with the visibly manipulative translator, a creative artist mediating between cultures and languages" (1991, 9). This view is echoed by Ricoeur, for whom the act of translating either involves the "transfer of a spoken message from one language to another" or, in a broader sense of the term, is "synonymous with the interpretation of any meaningful whole within the same speech community" (2006, 11). Unlike Ricoeur, however, I do not see these two pathways as being mutually exclusive; indeed, I would argue that as we take a message from one language to another, the languages act as necessary supplements to each other, as the very choice of words, phrases, and sentences is underlined by processes of selection, interpretation, and ideology.

I think it is fair to say that all of the Western intellectual traditions, and specifically the European intellectual and literary traditions, are governed and enabled by translation. Beginning with the Greeks, their work was translated into Latin and thence, gradually, into the European vernacular languages and thence to English. The term *translator*, as we know it today, arises from the Latin verbs *transfero*, *transfere*, *transtuli*, *translatum*, which evolves into the terms *transla-tare*, *translater* in the romance languages of the Middle Ages (hence the later English *translate*). In the fifteenth century, "the Italian humanist Leonardo Bruni became the first modern thinker to devote an entire scientific treatise to the art of translation, entitled *De Interpretatione Recta* (1420)" (ibid., xiii). So much of our foundational knowledge in philosophy, literature, science, and theology is owing to ongoing processes of translation. Indeed, many of the theorists addressed in this text have been read in translation, and it is through translation that the work of such thinkers in the realm of Continental philosophy has become so influential in the Anglophone world. However, it would be an error to see this process as a transparent one whereby eternal truths are passed across different languages in an unchanged manner.

Heidegger has looked at the ontological status of translation in this regard, dealing, albeit in a negative manner, with the appropriation of Greek words by Roman-Latin thought: "*Hupokeimenon* becomes *subiecturn*; *hupostasis* becomes *substantial*; *sumbebekos* becomes *accidens*." Heidegger does not view this process as ideologically neutral, indeed far from it. He argues that what happened here is "a *translation*, of Greek experience into a different way of thinking. *Roman thought takes over the Greek words without a corresponding equally authentic experience of what they say without the Greek word*. The rootlessness of Western thought begins with this translation" (1971, 23; emphasis in the original). For Heidegger, the movement from Greek to Latin is a paradigm of what he terms the "rootlessness of Western thought," and for him this process is a profoundly negative one that moves from an almost holy language, which is connected with the thingness of earth, to a more unconnected form of language, which does not share the quasi-mystical qualities of the original Greek: "Roman thought takes over the Greek words without being able to take over the corresponding, authentic experience of what they say; thus they took over the words (*Wörter*) but they were unable to take over what they say (*Worte*)" (Kockelmans 1986, 114).

In other words, this rootlessness takes place when linguistic practices, which "refer to presence and a core with assembled properties," are translated into "linguistic practices that refer to substance and accident. So the first move in the translation resulted in the substance/accident mode" (Simon 2011, 191). For Heidegger, it is problematic that our only access to a "two-thousand year-old tradition" of Western metaphysics is mediated through a form of language and translation that has made it "timeworn, shallowed, threadbare, and rootless" (2004, 75), because the translation is "no longer supported by the original experience" (Harries 2009, 91).

Heaney, on the other hand, while always valuing the centrality of place, seems to have a more positive view of the gradual transcending of the physical place through a language, and in this sense Heaney's views on politics and place, which have already been discussed, underline this sense of fluidity and lack of a single origin. The widening of Mossbawn is very much conducted under the aegis of such concepts of a more benign notion of roots that can be uprooted in some way, and in this chapter the role of other languages in the field of force that constitutes Heaney's own work will be foregrounded. Perhaps one can see this distinction between the valuing, respectively, of the rooted and the rootless as metonymic of the politics of each of these thinkers. Heidegger's valorization of roots, of a fixed identity and of privileged notions of gathering (*Versammlung*), can be seen to underwrite his own attraction to National Socialism, with its appeal to the monological concept of the *Volk*. Heaney, who in section 1 of *North* has expressed the seductive attractions of such an identity politics, nevertheless in his general work eschews the siren song of the tribal in favor of a more nuanced and cosmopolitan enunciation of identity. For him, the rootedness of place is always invested with other versions of itself, versions that are often voiced through translations into other namings and other languages.

Indeed, translation as process could be seen as a working model of Heaney's own complicated structures of signification, as what is involved in translation is never simply the singular movement of a concept from a source language to a target language with the signified meaning kept completely intact across the movement of the different signifiers. Instead, the movement of thought is transformational, and it is this crossing, this "movement of the "*trans*—translation, transference, transport, transformation," that serves as a paradigm for the "movement of thought between points of origin and arrival that are always being deferred, differed one by the other" (Kamuf 1991, 242).

Richard Kearney makes the point that "to think, to speak is always to translate, even when one speaks to oneself, when one discovers the traces (and one cannot subsist without them) of the Other in oneself" (Ricoeur 2006, xx). In a sense, the binary opposition between self and other is made more complex and deconstructed by translation, as meaning is immediately pluralized, and this process is exponential between languages. It is also operative within the same language, which has now seen new layers, and aspects of the other—other languages, other identities, other philosophies, other senses of place—grafted onto it through the translations of different ways of thinking and of representing the world. In this way, translation inaugurates a new relationship with the self, and this relationship, like the European languages that came down the aerial wire in Mossbawn, is an agent of change and transformation.

In previous aspects of this discussion, I have been making a case for forms of adequation between the thought of Heaney and the thought of Derrida, and nowhere is their symphysis more overt than in the whole area of translation as a form of knowledge, as a poetized mode of thinking. Derrida sees deconstruction as a breaking of rigid barriers and of a transferral of thought across boundaries; Heaney sees poetry as offering the same intellectual route, and this notion is highlighted in his thoughts on, and use of, translation. Derrida, too, is interested in translation, and in one of the very few programmatic definitions he has ever offered of the term *deconstruction*, he uses translation as the vehicle through which to convey something of what he means. Deconstruction, he says, consists "only of transference, and of a thinking through of transference, in all the senses that this word acquires in more than one language, and first of all that of the transference between languages." Indeed, he continues that, if ever pressed to offer a single definition of deconstruction, something which he strongly resisted throughout his life, he would say "simply and without overstatement: *plus d'une langue*—both more than a language and no more of *a* language" (1989, 14–15; emphasis in the original).

Here the connection between translation and deconstruction is manifest, but it has been a long-running submerged trope in Derrida's thinking. One of the core tenets of his mode of reading has been the primacy, indeed the necessity, of interpretation and a resultant deep suspicion of meaning in any mode of discourse that is seen to be "self-explanatory" or "commonsense." Meaning, in a deconstructionist sense, is always created by a process of reading—a reading alert to the nuances of different elements that combine to create meaning and signification. For Derrida, his famous aphorism "*Il n'y a pas de hors-texte*" (There is nothing outside the text) (1997, 158; emphasis in the original), which has been seen as a clarion call to textualist relativism, is in fact a statement that all meaning is textual, in the sense that all meaning needs to be interpreted—one could say all meaning is achieved through a process of translation. Derrida has never claimed that external reality is no longer a factor, or that there should be no access to it. What he was arguing was that to read a text as a single meaning, to read a text as a monological activity that had a single teleological goal, or was guided by "the tranquil assurance that leaps over the text toward its presumed content, in the direction of the pure signified" (ibid., 159), was not something in which he believed, and it was a mode of reading that he felt needed to be challenged. He felt that this perspective attenuated the possible plurality of texts and occluded voices of difference—be these gender, class, ideology, or ethnicity—that should be heard as part of the discourse.

This explanation may be seen as an aberrant reading of Derrida, but six years after he initially set out his view on the hermeneutic basis of all meaning construction, he felt obliged to stress that deconstruction was never an attempt to outlaw context or reality. In fact, in *Limited Inc.*, he made the direct point that "there is nothing outside context" (1988, 136). This developed position suggests that all meaning is socially created and that there is a context within which every utterance, in every discourse, needs to be located. In other words, meaning is never simple or pure but is haunted by an interaction of text and context, and it is in this very interaction, this interinanimation, between text and context that Heaney's poetizing thinking is grounded; indeed, it is the interpenetration and interaction of text and context that bring about the widening of his first place, and I would see it as part of that broader sense of translation of which we have been speaking. We have already mentioned an aspect of this point in the first chapter where we analyzed in some detail his adequation of Mossbawn with ancient Greek mythology. We remember the way in which he equated the sound of the repeated Greek word *omphalos* with the sound of water being pumped outside his front door.

This spoken word has a strong resonance with the sounds of unknown and strange-sounding "sibilants of European speech" crackling down the aerial located in the chestnut tree of Mossbawn, sounds that are credited with beginning Heaney's intellectual journey into the wideness of "the world beyond" and "the wideness of language" (Heaney 1995a, 11) and sounds that are associated with the Lacanian real, with that which has significance and influence but cannot be easily expressed. As Derrida has put it, listening to the other is a central aspect of self-definition, as it is "the ear of the other that signs. The ear of the other says me to me and constitutes the *autos* of my autobiography" (1985, 51). It is through the lens of the other that the self is created, and in this case the sounds of European languages, as symbolic of the European intellectual tradition, have been formative aspects of Heaney's development.

Just as he is not generally seen to have a significant body of prose, similarly Heaney's translations constitute a surprisingly significant amount of his overall work. As well as an increasing number of poetic translations in his later collections such as *The Haw Lantern* (1987), *Seeing Things* (1991), *Electric Light* (2001), *District and Circle* (2006), and *Human Chain* (2010), Heaney has a number of stand-alone works of translation: *Sweeney Astray* (1983c), a translation of the Old Irish poem *Buile Shuibhne*; *The Midnight Verdict*, a book of translations of Ovid and Brian Merriman (1993); and *Laments*, cotranslated by Stanislaw Barańczak, which is a series of sixteenth-century poems that are laments by the Polish poet Jan Kochanowski (1995) for his daughter, Urszula, who died suddenly. In 1999 he published his translation of *Beowulf.*

Heaney is also known for his two translations from the work of Greek writer Sophocles: *The Cure at Troy* (1990) is based on *Philoctetes* and *The Burial at Thebes* (2004b) on *Antigone*. Given the context of this discussion, which locates Heaney as an aesthetic thinker in the European tradition, his choice of *Antigone* as a text, when it had already been translated a number of times in Ireland, is significant, as since the 1980s Irish adaptations and translations have been produced by Frank McGuinness, Tom Paulin, Aidan Carl Matthews, Brendan Kennelly, Conall Morrison, and Owen McCafferty. Since the aesthetic entered the realms of epistemological discussion, this play, with its contestation of the political by an individual, and with its assertion that there is an intersubjective humanity that supervenes all political laws and demands, has been written about by a significant number of European intellectuals. In a book entitled *Interrogating "Antigone" in Postmodern Philosophy and Criticism*, Steve Wilmer and Audrone Žukauskaitė make the point that this text has been a central aspect of the European canon over the years:

> Sophocles' *Antigone* is one of the most important cultural texts in Western civilization. It has been reinterpreted not only by classicists but also by poets from Hölderlin to Heaney, novelists such as Virginia Woolf and Grete Weil, philosophers including Hegel, Heidegger, and Derrida, the psychoanalytic theorists Jacques Lacan and Slavoj Žižek, feminists and gender studies theorists Irigaray and Butler, and playwrights and theatre practitioners including Artaud, Brecht, Cocteau, Gide, Kantor, and Fugard. *Antigone* has received more than fifty translations into the English language in the last century and many adaptations all over the world. (2010b, 1)

For Heaney, the contrast between the political and ethical, between self and other, and between a simplistic version of identity and a more complex one all resonate with his own philosophical concerns. That these concerns reverberate with the concerns of the European aesthetic tradition is hardly surprising at this stage. Given the diverse languages of that tradition, the fact that translation is a significant aspect of the European tradition is, again, hardly surprising.

It is clear from his output that Heaney has had a preoccupation with translation for a significant part of his career. In *Stepping Stones*, he cites a number of translations as central to his development as a poet. In the early days of "the Group," a writing workshop in Belfast, founded and directed by Philip Hobsbaum, from 1963 to 1966, and later directed by Heaney himself, translation was important. Heaney recalls how translations figured among the readings encouraged by Hobsbaum, including one by Victor Hugo (Heaney and O'Driscoll 2008, 75), while Heaney also recalls the effect of Andrey Voznesensky's poetry in translations in a book called *Antiworlds*, which he thought was "marvellous." He also explains that he had been looking at Penguin translations of Eastern European poets since the 1970s but adds that their "historically aware, hard-bitten, eastern-European aesthetic meant more to me in the 1980s" (ibid., 101, 114–15).

Therefore, when Irish politics were very troubled, and when issues of identity were becoming quite fraught, the translations of these writers encouraged him to "be true to poetry as a solitary calling, not to desert the post, to hold on at the crossroads where truth and beauty intersect." He also explains how the translations of Robert Lowell were influential on his own work, noting that without his reading of Lowell's version of the Brunetto Latini canto in *Near the Ocean*, "there would have been no 'Ugolino' in *Field Work*" (ibid., 297, 218).

As already mentioned, it is through his renditions of ancient Greek plays that his worth as a translator has become more generally acknowledged, and, again in his revealing interview with O'Driscoll, Heaney points toward the philosophical underpinning of this work as a translator and to why he saw it as such a central part of his writing career. While in Harvard, he noted the availability of good translations of the classics, and he cites one that he bought by chance as going on to be of permanent interest. This book was William K.

Guthrie's *The Greeks and Their Gods*, where Heaney first read about the connection between Hermes and "herms," which were standing stones. Hermes as god of travelers was "connected with cairns at crossroads and stoneheaps of all sorts" (ibid., 293).

Heaney's association of herm and Hermes is transformative, as the field of force that connects a very mobile and unlocated god with a standing stone is one that encapsulates how, through the processes of translation and transformation, place is metamorphosed into space through the structures of language and myth. The association between the stone heap and the immaterial idea of a god is a strong metaphor for how translation uproots seemingly culturally embedded concepts and gives them a new, if unpredictable, life. Heaney sees translation as another form of poetized thinking that is creative of this space wherein different identities are set in comparison and contrast. The transformation of the word is crucial to the transformation of the philosophical world that that word has created. By pluralizing words and languages, and by infusing the language of the self with translated aspects of the language of the other, this new space, this field of force, is created. The terminal *es* that changes *herm* into *Hermes* is a translation in itself, wherein the airy figure of Hermes is translated into piles of stones and conversely where piles of stones are given a cultural signification through this linguistic connection with the transcendent.

This sense of a different language created by translation is something about which Agamben has also spoken, referring to the language of poetry in general, but in a manner that is also applicable to prose translation. He speaks of how binaries, such as internal/external and subjective/objective, can be addressed in the aesthetic through "the area of illusion," in whose "potential space they will subsequently be able to situate themselves both in play and in cultural experience." He goes on to say how this localization of culture and play is, therefore, neither "within nor outside of the individual," but in a "third area" that is distinct both "from interior psychic reality and from the effective world in which the individual lives" (1993c, 59). Agamben sees this space as created by the aesthetic, and the role of the aesthetic as a signifying vehicle of identity has been an ongoing trope in the European intellectual tradition. This obscured phantastic space, this third space, leads Agamben back to his point of departure: "a space he sees as common to poetry and philosophy, as well as common to another dichotomy, that between enjoyment and knowledge" (de la Durantaye 2009, 64).

Hillis Miller also envisions such a space through his discussion of the term *anastomosis*, which is a variety of "crossings, displacements, and substitutions, as inside becomes outside, outside inside, or as features on either side cross over the wall, membrane or partition dividing the sides" (1987, 7). It is thus another form of different or fluid space, and one can see a parallel movement in the work of Derrida. In "Living On: Borderlines," he probes the epistemology of the border between text and context in a broadly analogous manner, as he talks about borders in terms of permeability, noting that no context is "saturatable any more" and that "no border is guaranteed, inside or out" (1987, 78). Therefore, a third space between them is an option, and it is in this space that aspects of the real can be encountered, and the aesthetic is the discourse where such a space or area can be created.

Translation is another way of problematizing the seemingly fixed conceptions of borders, be they linguistic or political, and of creating this third space. Writing about *An Duanaire, 1600–1900: Poems of the Dispossessed* (Ó Tuama and Kinsella 1981), a book wherein poems in the Irish language appeared across the page from their English translations, Heaney spoke approvingly about how the translations "lead our eyes left across the page, back to the Irish" (1988, 31). In other words, the value of the translation was in this third space between the two languages, as the mind of the reader oscillated between the source and the target language. One could see this space as another form of threshold, which allows for a sense of openness to the other. At this point, he is also gesturing toward a line from his Nobel lecture, where he speaks of the need to "accommodate two opposing notions of truthfulness simultaneously" (1995a, 4), as this accommodation of oppositions is what translation does, at a linguistic and philosophical level. Self and other are blurred, as the voice of the other permeates the language of the self and makes it more inclusive. This movement, across the page and across languages, is symbolic of a broader philosophical movement wherein cultures become open to alterity.

Here is one example of a process that Derrida sees as programmatic across cultures, as his neologism *différance* describes precisely such a shuttling movement (reminiscent of the one discussed in chapter 3), which is "no longer conceivable on the basis of the opposition presence/absence. *Différance* is the systematic play of differences, of the traces of differences, of the *spacing* by means of which elements are related to each other." He goes on to describe this spacing in a manner that is redolent of Heaney's reading of the movement from the Irish to the English translations of the poems in *An Duanaire*. He sees it as "the becoming-space of the spoken . . . which makes possible both writing and every correspondence between speech and writing, every passage from one to the other" (2004b, 27). This becoming-space has strong connections to Agamben's third area as a locus where new identities and dimensions of language can come into being, and, as this chapter progresses, Heaney, too, will be seen to coin phrases that signify such a space. Indeed, his concept of the "through-other," of which we have spoken at length, is just such a phrase, as it seeks to transcend the static boundaries of self and other, as the stone heap becomes the transcendent figure of Hermes, whose airy lightness is again symbolized by a heap of stones in an ongoing shuttling oscillation.

Heaney's translations are similarly informed by their ability to enunciate the voice of the other and in the process conveying increasingly more complex dimensions of selfhood and identity. Heaney's concept of translation is transformative in that meaning is rendered as a process of interpretation as opposed to a fixed essence. This creative idea of translation allows him to engage with the matter of the past, while at the same time taking up a form of critical distance from that past. In *Negative Dialectics*, Adorno stresses the role of art in negotiating such a critical distance that avoids the twin dangers of wiping the past away completely or else of coming under its sway by taking it as a cultural *datum*—the entrapment of which Heaney spoke earlier. Adorno notes that the past or traditional mode of thought can be seen as "quasi-transcendental," inasmuch as any new ideas must be viewed from the perspective of their originating milieu; to critique a tradition, one must of necessity engage with that tradition but from an altered perspective—one must look at it awry. This altered perspective was why Adorno saw his own project as a "transition to interpretation" (1973, 54, 55), and it seems clear that Heaney's interaction with the "appetites of gravity" within his own tradition can be seen as part of an analogous process of immanent critique.

In a parallel context, the importance of literature in the achievement of critical distance has also been voiced by Derrida, who has spoken of how, in literature, "philosophical language is still present in some sense," but he goes on to stress the important point that here "it produces and presents itself as alienated from itself, at a remove, at a distance." Interestingly, he goes on to argue that this distance "provides the necessary free space from which to interrogate philosophy anew" (1995, 159), and one could well see translation as serving precisely the same purpose, as it offers a transcendent perspective on an immanent phenomenon to which we, as readers, belong and through which, in many ways, we are constituted. Part of Heaney's goal as a writer is to create such a "free space," an idea similar to the already mentioned third space, in order to better encompass the alterities of identity "at a distance," which is precisely the aim of *Sweeney Astray*.

Sweeney Astray was originally published by the Field Day Company in Derry in 1983 (it was also published by Faber in 1984). Heaney saw the publishing of this translation with Field Day as significant. He talks of a bit of "submerged naughtiness" in this act of publishing, noting that it connoted a "kind of all-Ireland event situated just within the North" and also observing that he had translated the place-names into their modern equivalents. He went on to express the hope that he did this translation so that "the Northern

Unionist or Northern Protestant readership might, in some minuscule way, feel free to identify with the Gaelic tradition" (Corcoran 1998, 261). Once again, it is toward concepts of alterity that aspects of this poem are directed; he is far from writing only from within his own tribe. At this juncture, processes of transferral and transformation come into being as Heaney attempts to use the critical distance of the translation to achieve some form of ethical rapprochement with possible readers of his work and to create new dimensions of selfhood and alterity among those readers, even if only to an incremental degree.

Seamus Deane has made the point that for him, Field Day's raison d'être has been an involvement with "a particular experience of what we may call translation." However, Deane's sense of translation, as predicated by a "traumatic political and cultural crisis" that causes "individuals and groups" to "forge for themselves a new speech," seems narrower than Heaney's. This view seems to see translation as confined to tribal or communal speech; it is the new dialect of the tribe talking to the tribe. It operates in a worldview that sees self and other as "a clash of loyalties which is analysable but irresolvable." It is a worldview that sees the communities in Northern Ireland as condemned to "rehearse positions from which there is no exit" (Deane 1990, 14, 15). Heaney's aim, on the other hand, would seem to be a restructuration of language so that the tribe can talk to the other through an acknowledgment of the essential hybridity of language itself. For Heaney, to translate is metonymic of the ethical imperative: it is the quintessential form of dialogue with the other through the creation of a space or structure where this dialogue is possible.

Speaking further about the impetus behind *Sweeney Astray*, Heaney stresses the importance of translation as an opening of language and ideology to the voice of the other: "One of my motives for translating *Sweeney Astray* was to say to unionists in the North, 'Look! Ulster may be British but here was Sweeney, a king in County Antrim. The ethos of the places that you think of as Plantation places was Irish in Sweeney's day. There was and is another culture here. Listen! You have to listen to this'" (Murphy 2000, 94). In this translation, he is setting out a space for a plurality and complexity of relationships between culture and place, and it connects with his comment that loyalists and unionists should have the right to their flags in contemporary Northern Ireland. Seeing flags as cultural signifiers, not unlike different texts, Heaney wants to create this third area in which both sets of traditions can intermingle. The imperative to "listen" in the above quotation is as central to Heaney's project as the ear of the other is to Derrida's, as it is only by listening to the voice of the other that the narrowness of selfhood can be broken down. The fact of translating *Sweeney Astray* from Irish to English allows members of the Unionist community not only to read it, but in a way to claim it, as it is now active and signifying in their own language.

The very use of the language of that other, English, is a factor here and allows for a critical distance in its enunciation. Through translation, Heaney can comment on his own place, and its past, while remaining distant temporally, linguistically, and politically from that place. John Wilson Foster has pointed out that for Heaney, translation is a seminal aspect of his vision of the world and consequently of his writing. Describing Heaney's reaction to the political situation in Northern Ireland, he says that Heaney did not speak *out* about issues: "He spoke *in*, which is what a poet in his truest office does. Events are absorbed and internalized, re-issued and sometimes recognizable in their translation only by our disciplined reading" (1995, 3). This transforming and reissuing aspect of translation has to do with an expressed desire of Heaney's to deal with political material. In an interview with Barry White, he made the point that writers of his generation attempted to transcend their Catholicism and Protestantism: "I would prefer not to talk in those terms because they are terms I deplore." He went on to say that the desire on the part of writers of his generation was "to get through the thicket, not to represent it" (1989, 9). Crucially here, he is prescribing a political and ethical imperative to writing, in that the role of the writer is to transform perceptions in order to find some way out of the thicket of internecine sectarian violence. This prescription would seem to further distance Heaney's creative ethics of translation from that of Deane, who seems to see writers from both traditions as impenetrably caught up in that very thicket.

In the same interview, Heaney makes the point that there are those individuals in each community who "live near their roots," and he goes on to suggest that "firm roots are terrific," but, and this point is crucial, "they can also hamper you transforming yourself," and the only way to get through the thicket of polarized communities is by "rethinking what you know and transforming yourself" (B. White 1989, 9). Translation allows this transformation by permitting us to see the thicket from a new perspective, and this change of perspective, necessary for a change of language, is a crucial development in Heaney's own thinking-through of translation as a mode of thinking and as a mode of knowledge. In many of his translations, he finds this Adornoesque quasi-transcendental perspective on another culture through the process of voicing a text in a different language. The imperative underlying translation, that shift, through language, into a different way of thinking, is very much a philosophical position, and throughout his career Heaney has taken the opportunity to use translation to hold one type of cultural thinking up to another in order to look at the self through the lens of the other, and vice versa, thus creating this third area or third space that we have been discussing. For Heaney, it is always about the language, but also about more than the language, to paraphrase Derrida. He looks at the third area or space that connects different cultures. Agamben delineates this third space "between subject and object" and locates it "in liminal spheres" (de la Durantaye 2009, 64).

So, when Heaney is writing about Christopher Marlowe's "Hero and Leander," under the significant title of "Extending the Alphabet," he comments on how "Herewith affrighted Hero shrunk away, / And in her lukewarm place Leander lay." His reading of this translation immediately looks for those transformational impulses that cut across borders and boundaries of space, time, and language and enable that different way of thinking that is at the core of the epistemology of translation. He observes that this lukewarm place "that

Leander slips into under the bedclothes" (which describes the empty space in a bed just after a warm body leaves it) "was probably never warmed again in exactly the right way until Molly Bloom jingled the bedsprings more than three hundred years later." It is central to Heaney's poetizing use of translation to look at the cultural transformations and differences in thought processes that can be put together in such a constellation that will effect, and affect, some sort of change. He goes on to talk about Marlowe's translations of Ovid that he undertook as a student, and he speaks of these works as having a "wiliness and sexiness and scholastic panache" that would have been "as much at home among the cleveralites of James Joyce's university wits in *A Portrait of the Artist as a Young Man* as they must have been among the scholars of sixteenth-century Cambridge," and he goes on to compare "Hero and Leander" to the world of Joyce's "Anna Livia Plurabelle" and to the "hithering-thithering whims of a self-possessed mind" (1995b, 31, 32, 30). It is interesting that he associated one of the qualities of a self-possessed mind as moving across and back over borders and boundaries, and of course it is the very motion that he used to describe the intellectual movement within his quincunxes. The alphabet and the real world to which it refers are both extended in these translations from Cambridge wits to those university wits of a fictive Dublin in the early 1900s.

The concept of extension is at one with the hithering-thithering eye of the reader looking across the page from source language to target language and back again, as each oscillation extends the boundaries of each language for the responsible reader, a topic to which our discussion will turn in the conclusion of this book. We have seen this perspective shared by Derrida, in his metaphor of the *navette*, which negotiates meaning through a movement to-ing and fro-ing across the textile. This is hithering-thithering by another name, and, epistemologically, both writers are stressing the importance of movement in any kind of philosophical thinking. Meaning, it seems to both, resides in that process, and whether it is across the translated page or between binary oppositions, it is the hither-and-thither movement that is creative of lasting forms of signification. Accordingly, for

Heaney, it is this extending of language into a further language that is one of his goals as an aesthetic thinker. Therefore, he speaks of the real value of the work of Zbigniew Herbert in translation as being a sense that his writing has the ability "to lean, without toppling, well beyond the plumb of its native language" (1988, 55).

As we will see in his introduction to *Beowulf*, this leaning out beyond the plumb of the native language is what translation validates and enables, but it also opens the mind to ethical dimensions that may not be available within the native tradition and culture. Thus, while still conscious of poets of a broad English-speaking canon, like Yeats, Frost, Pound, Eliot, and Auden, translation, says Heaney, has also enabled readers to be introduced to new literary traditions, and he cites the example "of the passionate spirits of Russian poetry in the teens, twenties and thirties of this century" (ibid., 38).

The sense of thinking differently about the place of writing, and about the role of the aesthetic with respect to the political, is fore grounded in the experiences and lives of those Russian and Eastern European writers such as Marina Tsvetaeva, Anna Akhmatova, Osip and Nadezhda Mandelstam, Boris Pasternak, Nikolay Gumilev, Sergei Esenin, and Vladimir Mayakovsky, who have all become heroic names. They are important because they translate the business of poetry from the conditional mood to the mood of the indicative. He sees these poets as ethical as they have "toed the line," and not just "the verse line but the line where courage is tested, where to stand by what you write is to have to stand your ground and take the consequences." This courage is what he means by their writing being in the indicative mood, as to even write under these conditions is to state a fact, the fact that writing, that the aesthetic, is of value and will continue to speak the truth to power. In this sense, they pose a "shadow-challenge to poets who dwell in the conditional, the indeterminate mood," a mood that characterizes so much of the poetry in the Anglophone world (ibid., 39).

The ethical need for poetry to resist a monological political system is at the core of this influence, and the exemplars for Heaney come from the voices, however silenced and downtrodden, of the poets who spoke for individual freedom in the face of an oppressive communist regime. He learns this lesson through translation and is, and has been, very much opposed to the suasive power of nationalism, or indeed of any other "-ism," to such an extent that he has often been accused of political diffidence. However, such an accusation mistakes and conflates the poetic and the political and has little understanding of Heaney's conception of the aesthetic as a crowbar that picks away at the standing and stolid monuments of one-dimensional ideology through the nuanced thinking of poetry and, in this case, of translation. This poetic thinking is that third area of which Agamben spoke, and it embodies the stretching of the bounds of language into a further language, something that Heaney admired in Herbert's work, and it will be further developed in his introduction to his translation of *Beowulf.*

Heaney has spoken of the difficulties he faced when attempting to take this foundational aspect of the canon of English literature and to translate it into an idiom with which he felt comfortable. The task of taking on such an established text would seem daunting, but once again Heaney's poetized perspective sees things in a different light. He admits that the poem is seen as the cornerstone of the canon, and he cites the general consensus that "it was written (as Osip Mandelstam said of *The Divine Comedy*) 'on official paper.'" He also comments on the modalities of previous translations, and on the multiplicity of academic approaches to the text, before stressing the importance of Tolkien's reading, which foregrounded the text as a work of literature, as he sees the *Beowulf* poet as "an imaginative writer" (Heaney 1999, xi). I will not examine the modalities of Heaney's translation or the academic reception of that translation, as it has been comprehensively outlined in Conor McCarthy's work *Seamus Heaney and Medieval Poetry* (2008). Instead, I wish to look at how this text underlines the epistemology of translation that we have been examining in his work by further widening notions of Mossbawn, both as text and as context, and by offering another example of the hithering-thithering process of linguistic and cultural identities.

It is interesting that from the outset, Heaney is keen to pluralize the poem and to dislodge it from its position as a cornerstone of a monological view of the canon of English literature. In a manner that exemplifies the drive toward complication of response that I have argued is typical of his aesthetic, he makes the valid point that "as an English poem it's a problematic poem, because it's actually European": "Its subject is somebody from the south-west of Sweden coming down into Denmark and helping the Danes, then returning to the south-west of Sweden and clearing a dragon out of that place. It is written in England, perhaps in Northumbria, but then Northumbria itself was a hybrid enough place, also because of the Irish culture of the Scoti, those Irish monks who came down from Iona and settled there in Lindisfarne" (Murphy 2000, 95). It is this relentless probing of borders and limits, this stepping through origins to uncover their ultimate permeability, that makes Heaney's work so ethically important. He offers a constant critique of received ideas about language, belonging, and hegemonic conceptions of culture. As well as translating the other, he will also translate senses of selfhood through a similarly penetrating critique, so it is as if *Beowulf* itself is that third area, or third space, as it has already a site of that hithering-thithering imagination of which he has been speaking.

Thus, his description of the halls, sites of refuge, and comfort in the dangerous world of the poem is very much of a place of plurality: "Within these phantasmal boundaries, each lord's hall is an actual and a symbolic refuge. Here are heat and light, rank and ceremony, human solidarity and culture; the *duguð* share the mead-benches with the *geogoð*, the veterans with their tales of warrior-kings and hero-saviours from the past rub shoulders with young braves—Þegnas, *eorlas*, thanes, retainers—keen to win such renown in the future" (1999, xv). Here there is no single entity awaiting the appearance of the monster, but rather an intricate and varied group, all interacting with each other and all combining to create the dynamic of the hall through their actions and stories. Heaney sees the poem as also composed of two different "psychic fabrics," with the pagan warrior ethic being filtered through the distanced perspective of a Christian poet; it is a text "in which conflicting realities find accommodation within a new order." Thus, in this reading, the poem can be seen as a third space where paganism and Christianity interact, and by extension Heaney will look to translation to put different cultures into dynamic interaction. He has already done so in *Crediting Poetry*, where he speaks of how the cries of the Geat woman who laments as "the flames consume the body of her dead lord" immediately call to mind for him the crying women who have been portrayed in "late-twentieth-century news reports" from Rwanda or Kosovo (ibid., xvii, xxi). The cultural transfer is significant for him, as it allows the meaning of the poem to translate to the contemporary present: for monsters, the contemporary psyche substitutes dreams and the unconscious, the pain of death, the decline of old age, and the fear of the unknown.

Connection and rhizomatic association are always important for Heaney, as we have seen, and it is very much his way of dealing with binary adversarial positions. Indeed, his account of finding his way into *Beowulf* is synecdochic of his whole intellectual progression from cultural givens to a recreation of that culture in the form of a third space or area. He speaks of those givens as the binary opposition of Irish and English languages and cultures, and he speaks of his given "cultural and ideological frame" (ibid., xxii), which saw Irish as the language he should have been speaking but which had been taken from him by the processes of colonization. We have already briefly mentioned, in chapter 3, how he found the word *lachtar* was actually an Irish-language word. This word became a "rapier point of consciousness" for him, pricking him with a sense of loss and tempting him "into binary thinking about language." He now goes on to explain that, conditioned by his sociocultural and political context, he had "tended to conceive of English and Irish as adversarial tongues, as either/or conditions rather than both/and," and he had become aware that this type of thinking would enmire him in the givens of his society, whereas what was required was a new structure that would transform the "either/or" into a "both/and" paradigm. It was only when he had gotten to this stage of development that he could begin to look at "a more confident and creative way of dealing with the whole vexed question—the question, that is, of the relationship between nationality, language, history and literary tradition in Ireland" (ibid., xxiv).

However, this binary thinking is dislodged and uprooted in his original discussion of the term. This original discussion took place in his pamphlet *Among Schoolchildren*, and he made broadly the same point as he does in the introduction to *Beowulf*, realizing that what he thought was an English word was in fact Irish in origin and that it "lived upon our tongues like a capillary stretching back to a time when Irish was the lingua franca of the whole place." Here, translation has become epiphany, as this word, and its linguistic history, confirms the "resentful nationalism" of his "Catholic minority experience" (1983a, 9). The use of the term *lingua franca* is clearly intended to convey the sense of an originary Irish-speaking area, whose presence is invoked by the concept of the origin of the signifier *lachtar*. However, the term *lingua franca* (literally, "Frankish language") is defined as meaning "a hybrid language," and as such gestures toward the field of force that is the influence of different languages, traditions, and cultures on the language we speak.

This new reading of *lachtar* provided him with a way of thinking differently about the root and origins of this word: rather than seeing it as an example of how he was robbed of his language, this term, and another that will also be discussed in the introduction to *Beowulf*, allowed him instead to see the political and cultural effects of ongoing translation and transformation. This new perspective is indicated by his use of the term *lingua franca*, but the seeds were sown in lectures from Professor John Braidwood, a lecturer in Queen's University, who pointed toward similar signifiers of translation and hybridity across the two cultures and the two languages, noting, for example, that the word *whiskey* is the same word as the "Irish and Scots Gaelic word *uisce*, meaning water," and that the River Usk in Britain is "therefore to some extent the River Uisce (or Whiskey)." Heaney now began to think of this stream as a kind of "linguistic river of rivers issuing from a pristine Celto-British Land of Cockaigne, a riverrun of Finnegans Wakespeak pouring out of the cleft rock of some prepolitical, prelapsarian, urphilological Big Rock Candy Mountain," and once again we are in the presence of a structure that is fluid and inclusive. This new structure had the effect of momentarily collapsing the "Irish/English duality, the Celtic/Saxon antithesis," and he now began to see what he terms an "elsewhere of potential that seemed at the same time to be a somewhere being remembered." I would suggest that this elsewhere, this third space, can be located at the widened space of Mossbawn, and he notes tellingly that the place on the map where "the Usk and the *uisce* and the whiskey coincided" was definitely a place where "the spirit might find a loophole," like an "unpartitioned linguistic country": a place where one's language would not be "simply a badge of ethnicity or a matter of cultural preference or an official imposition, but an entry into further language" (1999, xxiv, xxv).

This idea is another aspect of his poetized thinking, or of his thinking differently, as Heidegger would put it. It is, I would argue, also a cognate of Agamben's third area or space and of Derrida's dictum of "more than a language." In this context, Heaney is looking for a language that will acknowledge the real of hybridity, of that riverrun of context, culture, translation, and accretion that makes all language an opening to the other as opposed to a closed-off enunciation of a particular cultural or ideological position. What Heaney finds here are the interactions and flows of those structural paradigms that we have seen him create across different works throughout his career. The further language is the language of the through-other; it is the language of the place of writing and the writing of place, and in his translation of *Beowulf* he will demonstrate how such an emancipatory language can be achieved.

He has written, in the introduction, of how difficult he found it to find his voice in this translation of the poem and to achieve some form of linguistic foothold in it, though he says that he always considered *Beowulf* to be part of his "voice-right," and it was the word Þolian, meaning "to suffer," that provided one aspect of this sense of ownership of the text. This word, glossed in C. L. Wrenn's standard edition of *Beowulf*, sent a frisson through his linguistic antennae, as it was a word often used in his own locality, a point illustrated by a quotation from his aunt, speaking about a bereaved family: "they'll just have to learn to thole" (ibid., xxiii, xxv). At this juncture, the "either/or" binarism is being replaced by a "both/and" sense of ethical translation, as both linguistic and cultural strands coexist in a new linguistic and philosophical formulation. Finding this attunement between the world of the poem and the world of his childhood was a point of contact into a "becoming space" within which he could fruitfully build his inclusive structure.

This process proceeded apace when he read the same word—*thole*—in the work of John Crowe Ransom, and he goes on to trace the spatial and temporal journey (a translation in the literal sense of *transferre*, a "carrying across") made by this word. He traces its progress north from England to Scotland, and thence to Ulster, via the planters, into the local dialect of the native population, and then across the Atlantic, as some Scots Irish emigrated to the American South in the eighteenth century. Through tracing this word, and its many translations, from his aunt's vocabulary to the verbiage of *Beowulf*, and finally to the language of a modern American poet, Heaney has moved from the "either/or" to the "both/and" mind-set, a mind-set that had its origin in the "multi-cultural odyssey" of *thole* (ibid., xxvi). It was also yet another of his mobile structures, another field of force, wherein the connections were more important than the actual points being connected: it was not the word per se but the multiple origins and identities of the word that interested him in his quest to bring literary structures into the realm of the political.

Just as *thole* gave him a sense of cultural inclusion in *Beowulf*, so his translation would begin with another example of a further language that would make us see *Beowulf* differently. The initial word of the poem, *Hwæt*, has been generally translated as "lo," "hark," "attend," or "listen." As he looked for the mot juste to translate *Hwæt*, Heaney remembered another voice of his childhood, and it was this voice that allowed him to achieve the correct timbre that he needed if he was to do justice to the poem (the voice of the other) and to his own tradition (the voice of the self). He speaks of relations of his father's called Scullions, on whose name he had punned, calling them "big-voiced scullions" in *Field Work* (1979, 17), as when they spoke: "the words they uttered came across with a heavy distinctness," as "phonetic units" that were "weighty and defined." When he began to translate *Beowulf*, and to ponder how he wanted the words to "sound" in his version, he framed the lines in "cadences that would have suited their voices, but that still echoed with the sound and sense of the Anglo-Saxon" (1999, xxvi, xxvii).

It is through the voice of Peter Scullion that Heaney has been able to imagine the sound of "the first twenty-five or thirty lines" of the poem. This voice again foregrounds the somatic, bodily aspect of language, the sound, and the feeling of the aptness of that sound to what he wants to say. He felt that the writing had to be such that "his large, dignified simple utterance would carry it" (Murphy 2000, 95), and here we see the apotheosis of his idea of the broadness of translation with respect to significations of self, identity, and belonging. Through the initial monosyllable *so*, he is inserting a deconstructive lever in an English hegemonic culture, which traces its lineage back to *Beowulf*: "In Hiberno-English Scullion-speak, the particle 'so' came naturally to the rescue, because in that idiom 'so' operates as an expression that obliterates all previous discourse and narrative, and at the same time functions as an exclamation calling for immediate attention. So, 'so' it was" (1999, xxvii). Here, the translation of English literature and Irish experience gave rise to a new form of discourse, where self and other were allowed to interact and to mutually transform each other. This *so* is emblematic of the becoming space of his aesthetic thinking, and it is a space that connects with another of his conceptual formulations, the through-other.

One could see Heaney's *so* as his version of Joyce's *Patrick W. Shakespeare*, as both terms allow their writers to experience a sense of ownership, familiarity, and belonging in what has traditionally been the language of the colonizer. In this context, both writers are deconstructing the hierarchy of colonizer-colonized and at the same time inaugurating a new order that offers a further language in which they both belong, in different ways, and of which they are, to some degree, creative. Derrida has made the point in relation to power structures that rather than promoting "a suppression of all hierarchy," or inciting "a simple change or reversal in the terms of any given hierarchy," "the *Umdrehung*," or revolution, "must be a transformation of the hierarchical structure itself" (Derrida 1978, 81), and Heaney's translation of this poem achieves this goal through the choice of the initial word and through the insertion of another word that has significant associations with himself and with his own pluralized poetic first place.

This insertion is the fullest example of his initial project of widening the conceptions of his first place, Mossbawn, as in this Anglo-Saxon poem, his home, or at least the *bawn* part of the signifier, will appear four times, referring to Hrothgar's hall, Heorot:

> Line 523: . . . in strongroom and bawn (1999, 37)
> Line 721: . . . and arrived at the bawn (ibid., 49)
> Line 1304: . . . to the afflicted bawn (ibid., 91)
> Line 1970: . . . inside his bawn (ibid., 135)

Heaney sees the use of this word, deriving from the Irish language "*bó-dhún*, a fort for cattle," and also meaning, in Elizabethan English, a fortified dwelling built by settlers to defend themselves against the native Irish, as significant, as it suggests that sense of siege mentality that connects the worlds of Heorot and the early Irish settler culture, and so "it seemed the proper term to apply to the embattled keep where Hrothgar waits and watches." The significance of this use of words is to be found in the imperative that has been identified as a core tenet of Heaney's philosophy: that poetry should not simplify. Using what is a term mired in the colonial enterprise, in a poem that was written hundreds of years before the term was part of the lexicon, meant that he is dislodging this term from its roots, in that Heideggerian sense of translation as uprooting. He goes on to explain and explore just how wide the bawn in Mossbawn has become:

> Indeed, every time I read the lovely interlude that tells of the minstrel singing in Heorot just before the first attacks of Grendel, I cannot help thinking of Edmund Spenser in Kilcolman Castle, reading the early cantos of *The Faerie Queene* to Sir Walter Raleigh, just before the Irish would burn the castle and drive Spenser out of Munster back to the Elizabethan court. Putting a bawn into *Beowulf* seems one way for an Irish poet to come to terms with that complex history of conquest and colony, absorption and resistance, integrity and antagonism, a history that has to be clearly acknowledged by all concerned in order to render it ever more "willable forward / again and again and again." (ibid., xxx)

The final quotation is from a poem of his own, "The Settle Bed," from his collection *Seeing Things*, some lines of which have already been cited and which deals ostensibly with a "settle bed" that was a family heirloom, an "inheritance" that was "upright, rudimentary, unshiftably planked / In the long ago." As such, it stands for the cultural givens that can often limit the development of the future through the rootednesss in a previous generation's ideologies. In this poem, Heaney reimagines a series of weightless settle beds flying through the air and makes a thematically telling point, which we cited in chapter 3, that "whatever is Given / Can always be reimagined" (1991, 28, 29). In other words, it is the present that determines the legacy of the past, and that legacy can be transformed by the kind of aesthetic and poetized thinking that is the topic of this book.

Indeed, we have already noted the significance of this quotation in chapter 3 in an examination of his structures of complex meaning. One could see the whole project of Heaney's poetized thinking and, in this specific instance, of his sense of translation, as embodied in this metaphor, as the thick solidity of the settle bed is translated into something "tumbled from heaven," given a defiance of gravity and reimagined in a different way: here is Mossbawn becoming a bawn in *Beowulf*; here is the rootlessness of intellectual thought of which

Heidegger spoke, but it is a rootlessness that has a strongly positive connotation for Heaney; here is the third space full of altered images that make us think differently. It is this project of reimagining the historical, cultural, linguistic, and societal givens that I see as central to his aesthetic thinking and to his specific use of translation.

The complexity of his position is worth reemphasizing. The bawn in *Beowulf* is itself a field of force, encompassing his own "first place" and the conflation of Irish and English meanings of that place, "the moss of bog-cotton" and the "planter's house on the bog," but not attempting to choose either one of the binary options, but rather allowing them both to interinanimate each other in a transformed context. This use of the word encompasses his sense of allegiance to the native Irish givens of his traditions, but also his literary connection with Spenser and Raleigh (about whom he has written eloquently in *The Government of the Tongue* [1988, 113–14]), with whom he shares a strong connection through poetry and through an intricate relationship with Ireland. The process of taking these plural inheritances, and reimagining them, is at the center of his ongoing project of translation. The language of the other allows for a pluralization and widening of significations of the self, and in his introduction to *Beowulf* Heaney enunciates this process very clearly. For him, an inheritance is a given that needs to be constantly reimagined. An inheritance is not a monological object passed down through time, and it should not be something that acts as a transcendental signifier through which the future is sifted and attenuated; instead, it is a text that should be, of necessity, transformed by its altered context and consequently can be seen as a type of fuel that can propel the drive to a more inclusive future.

In *Specters of Marx*, Derrida makes a similar point about the fractured aspect of an inheritance, which, far from issuing from a fixed center, and from containing an unequivocal meaning, "is never gathered together, it is never one with itself" (1994, 16). This complicated notion of an inheritance is precisely what Heaney had in mind when he spoke of taking a long and difficult time to be persuaded that he "was born into its [*Beowulf*'s] language" and that "its language was born" into him (1999, xxii), and given that he had begun thinking about this in 1981, it was a long time indeed. Derrida's perspective allows for the influence of the present, and of the future, in interpreting the past, because the present is shaped by factors that were never available in the past. In other words, he takes cognizance of the fact that messages need to be interpreted, that ideologies are subject to change, and that it is through the act of reading, an act that, by definition, takes place in the present, that the past is given voice. Hence Derrida's point that, in interpreting the past, one must "filter, sift, criticize, one must sort out several different 'possibles' that inhabit the same injunction" (1994, 16).

Heaney's readings of Mossbawn as home place, and as poetic first place, validate this sense of choice and responsibility, as he voices his commitment to a complex and fluid conception of identity in which each of the different strands will have its place in the whole structure. The term *bawn* allows the conflation and interaction of all of these different meanings and, by extension, of all of these different constituents of identity. O'Driscoll put it to Heaney that Terry Eagleton saw his achievement in translating *Beowulf* as "the final, triumphant reversal of (your) cultural dispossession," and Heaney, while seeing this comment as a "grand statement of the case," nevertheless retorts that it "makes the right point" (Heaney and O'Driscoll 2008, 440). Translation here has provided a more complete sense of ownership, but of course it has also changed the nature of the poem itself and the ownership that Heaney now feels is partly owing to the negotiation between Irish and English cultural and linguistic signifiers that he has achieved in the translation, and partly owing to the becoming space that he has created that is paradigmatic of Derrida's *Umdrehung*, or revolution, as cited earlier.

While *Beowulf* is often seen as the most significant of Heaney's translations, his work on Greek drama is also highly important, as it, too, allows for a juxtapositional perspective to be brought to bear on his own culture and on the problems experienced by that culture. While finding an Irish connection with *Beowulf*, apart from the overarching European context, was something that Heaney had to work on, the opposite was true in the case of his translation of *Philoctetes*, which he called *The Cure at Troy*, as his attention was drawn to the issue of justice in the play by a colleague at Harvard, Michael Blumenthal. The conflict between justice and loyalty, or between the givens of a tradition and the sense of individual ethics as seen in the character of Neoptolemus, is at the core of the attraction of the play for Heaney. As he explains, the "crunch that comes when the political solidarity required from him by the Greeks is at odds with the conduct he requires from himself if he's to maintain his self-respect" (ibid., 420).

In this translation, the breaking down of binaries into a further language, something that has been a common connection between Heaney and the European tradition, is given full voice. In such structures of thought, the border between self and other is very much a Derridean opening, as symbolized, in *The Cure at Troy*, by the role of the chorus, as, in this translation, the speaking voice, the "I" of the poem, seems to be located in the chorus, which he sees as a "borderline between / The you and the me and the it of it" (1990, 2). Nathan Wallace makes the cogent point that in this play, Heaney elaborates on the idea of "auratic human rights poetry" by "inserting himself into a Greek Chorus" (2015, 103–4). This point is significant, as the poem is in many ways about that binary opposition that bedevils the body politic—self and other. As ever in Heaney, there is that attunement between the Irish present (Nationalist/Unionist) and the European past (Greek/Trojan) and between politics (the struggles between different armies) and the aesthetic (the rendition of that struggle in art). While politics needs to reinforce the binary opposition, by demonizing the other in order to ensure that violence against that other can be justified, the aesthetic, as Heaney sees it, looks to find points of contact between self and other; in one discourse, the border is permanent, while in the other, it is permeable. As he puts it, poetry operates between "the gods' and human beings' sense of things"; it is a liminal discourse, a boundary or threshold point between "what you would like to happen and what will— / Whether you like it or not"; and it has the power to become the voice of "reality and justice" (1990, 2). These statements are large claims for poetry, but at this juncture of the argument, I think we can see that Heaney has always felt that poetry as a form of aesthetic thinking is extremely valuable as a way of coming to terms with our human existence, in all its complexity and difficulty.

This borderline will be very much in keeping with Heaney's idea of a frontier of writing, or the threshold, which allows some form of passage across that border that separates different groups. One could see the "gods" here as close to the Lacanian real and to the voices of a truth that cannot be accessed through the symbolic order of ordinary language but nevertheless have an effect. This comment from the chorus stresses the value of poetry as a discourse through which aspects of the real and the unconscious can be accessed, as well as being a discourse that looks to connect self and other at a visceral level.

Borders, says Heaney, and indeed Derrida, are made to be crossed, and the language of poetry will provide the mode of such a crossing. In political terms, as already noted in chapter 4, Heaney has expressed the hope that the frontier that partitions Ireland into North and South could become "a little bit more like the net on a tennis court," which would allow for "agile give-and-take," a term synonymous with his "hithering-thithering," and with Derrida's "shuttling," to signify movement and fluidity. In this poetized perspective, the border, as a limit point of one community, becomes an opening to the other community. In Heaney's terms, the voice of the chorus, a poetic voice, is a point of opening between the "you" and the "me" and between self and other. It is an intersubjective point of mediation between the gods' and human beings' "sense of things." He goes on to make the ethical role of poetry qua poetry explicit by extending the connection between the voices that enunciate this poetic vision and poetry itself: "and that's the borderline that poetry / Operates on too" (ibid.).

It is poetry (in this case poetry as translation) as genre that facilitates this ethical interaction between self and other, this sense that borders are not points of closure but rather points of opening. This conflict is at the core of *The Cure at Troy*, as in the climactic confrontation of the play, Neoptolemus, who had shared this perspective earlier in the play, "I'm under orders," and who had lied to Philoctetes in order to obtain his bow, now realizes the error of his ways and becomes a more complex character through the introduction of an ethical strand to his persona. In a colloquy with Odysseus, the gradual opposition between pragmatic tribal politics and a more open, humanistic ethics is unveiled. In response to Neoptolemus's statement that "I did a wrong thing and I have to right it," and to his further remark that he is going to "redress the balance" and cause the "scales to even out" by handing back the bow, Odysseus replies in clichés: "Act your age. Be reasonable. Use your head." The reply of Neoptolemus demonstrates the gulf that exists between the two: "Since when did the use of reason rule out truth?" (1990, 51, 52, 65, 66). Being under orders is close to surrendering to the givens of one's culture, so the invocation of reason and truth is significant, as both of these qualities would strive to transcend ideology in some way.

For Odysseus, "rightness" and "justice" are values that are immanent in the ideological perspective of the tribe or community. There is to be no critical distance between his perspectives of myth and history. He tells Neoptolemus that there is one last "barrier" that will stop him from handing back the bow, the "will of the Greek people, / And me here as their representative." He sees no sense of any transcendental or intersubjective form of justice in what Neoptolemus is attempting. When Neoptolemus speaks of "doing the right thing," he is answered by the voice of the tribe: "What's so right about / Reneging on your Greek commission?" (ibid., 66, 67). Their subsequent interchange deserves to be quoted in full as it dramatizes the conflict between a view of self and other as connected and mutually responsible and a view of self and other as disparate and in conflict:

ODYSSEUS

You're under my command here. Don't you forget it.

NEOPTOLEMUS

The commands that I am hearing overrule
You and all you stand for.

ODYSSEUS
And what about
The Greeks? Have they no jurisdiction left?

NEOPTOLEMUS
The jurisdiction I am under here
Is justice herself. She isn't only Greek.

ODYSSEUS
You've turned yourself into a Trojan, lad. (ibid., 67)

In this exchange, the critical distance (Blanchot's space of literature) already spoken of is evident in the value ethic of Neoptolemus. He has moved beyond the intertribal epistemology of Odysseus, where not to be Greek necessitates one's being Trojan. Such a perspective severely limits one's range of choices: one is either Greek or Trojan—a parallel with the population of Northern Ireland being divided into the adversarial binarisms of Catholicism or Protestantism, nationalism or unionism, or republicanism or loyalism. That such identifications, such "firm roots," exist is beyond question; what is open to question, however, is whether it is wise to see them as all-encompassing, as doing so can cause the "entrapment" that has mired Odysseus and from which Neoptolemus is determined to escape. Neoptolemus has moved into that third space, that third area, that becoming space of which we have spoken, and he dramatizes this more complex perspective throughout the play.

Hence, Neoptolemus can say, "I'm all throughother," meaning that he is becoming aware that there are not just two essential identities at work here and that he realizes that there are alternatives to the essentialist ethnocentrisms of Odysseus. He realizes that "reality and justice" are values that can have a transformative effect on one's sense of being Greek or Trojan. As Philoctetes puts it, in a moment of *anagnorisis*: "the wheel is turning, the scales are tilting back. Justice is going to be woken up at last." Neoptolemus, speaking of "justice herself," makes the point that "she isn't only Greek," and this point is perhaps the crucial message of this play. While admitting that no "poem or play or song / Can fully right a wrong," this translation attempts to stake out the ground for poetic language, or poetized thinking, to have some effect in a world where people "suffer," "torture one another," and get "hurt and get hard." While being aware of the lesson of history, which says "*Don't hope / On this side of the grave*," the chorus concludes the play by suggesting that the "longed-for tidal wave / Of justice can rise up," and if this happens, and the conditional tense is significant, then "hope and history" may "rhyme" (Heaney 1990, 48, 57, 67, 77; emphasis in the original).

The phrase "hope and history rhyme" has taken on a life of its own outside of the aesthetic in the discourse of politics, as it has been quoted by Tony Blair, Bill Clinton, and Bertie Ahern in the context of the Northern Ireland peace process: "even Gerry Adams went for the uplift factor," though Heaney, nuanced as ever, is keen to stress that it is not a closed couplet that is bland and optimistic in the face of a contrary reality; rather, while he was "grateful to see the lines enter the language of the peace process," he was very aware that these lines "belonged in the realm of pious aspiration" (Heaney and O'Driscoll 2008, 421). The point is that while they do not rhyme in the English language, there is a "further language," as indicated by the "further shore" of the quotation, where they may rhyme, and I would suggest that this further shore is the language of poetry, which can access the real. The further shore may be touched only tangentially, but it is enough, as it can act as a desired destination and as one that allows for an understanding otherwise of the nearer shore that we normally inhabit. Thus, he is able to use the ancient Greek text to comment on the contemporary violence through anachronistic references. Wallace makes the valid point that the Field Day production of the play did not end "on an ecstatic note": "When we look at the video of the original tour, we can see that the Field Day production did not close with [a] sense of other-worldly intensity either. For the final lines of the play, the chorus speaks clear-headedly; accordingly, in the Field Day production, the lights went up and the characters all stood squarely on their own feet, facing the audience" (2015, 121).

Heaney found that the genre of drama, where words are spoken by an actor or a chorus, directly to an audience in a clearly defined social setting, allowed him to adopt a different perspective from the perspective of the lyric or narrative poem; he found that the choral mode allowed for a "homiletic note" and for the anachronistic insertion of comments on the violence in Northern Ireland: "the innocent in gaols," a "hunger-striker's father" standing in a "graveyard," and a "police widow in veils" who faints in "the funeral home" (1990, 77). Interestingly, Heaney now views these "topical references" as a "mistake" as "spelling things out like that is almost like patronizing the audience" (Heaney and O'Driscoll 2008, 421). In my own view, this perspective is not correct, as the juxtaposition of two eras and different political contexts is at the core of creating that "becoming space" of translation; it suggests an attunement and a form of harmony between the two different discourses. It is also at the core of Heaney's own poetizing thought, as we have seen throughout his translations.

He does the same in a discussion of the other translation of Sophocles, *The Burial at Thebes*, which was his translation of *Antigone*. Here he explains how the image of a body, lying unburied in the play, with the corpse's sister driven wild with grief, an image that is at the core of *Antigone*, causes him to recall an Irish language poem, *Caoineadh Art Uí Laoghaire*, which consists of a lament by Eibhlín Dubh Ní Chonaill, the wife of a man killed by "English Soldiery at Carriganimma," County Cork. This poem was an "outburst of grief and anger from a woman whose husband had been cut down and left bleeding on the roadside in Co. Cork, in much the same way as Polyneices was left outside the walls of Thebes, unburied, desecrated, picked at by the crows" (2004c, 4). Although it may be less overt than the contemporary reference in *The Cure at Troy*, it is nevertheless part of that hithering-thithering motion that he sees as so central to the negotiation of meaning that is the core of poetry as a mode of knowledge. He suggests an interinanimation between the two texts, and the "communication of the existential possibilities of attunement," which allows "the disclosing of existence" to become "the true aim of 'poetic speech'" (Heidegger 1996, 152).

Interestingly, the changes in title that are operative in both translations are predicated on that sense of a contemporary resonance being given to the classical text. In the case of *Philoctetes*, he felt that a change in title could work as a pointer, a "kind of subliminal orientation"; as in Ireland, the idea of a miraculous cure was "deeply lodged in the religious subculture" (Heaney and O'Driscoll 2008, 422). Thus, the change of title was oriented toward making aspects of the play more relevant to a contemporary audience, which is very much part of the idea of creating a becoming space where these words from the past can be willable forward in order to comment on contemporary issues from a different perspective. The same is true of the change of title in his translation of *Antigone*, as he focused on the cultural charge that is associated in Ireland with burials and funerary rites in general.

This play opens after an invading army from Argos has been defeated by the Thebans under their new king, Creon. Two of the sons of Oedipus, brothers to Antigone and Ismene, died in this battle: Eteocles perished defending Thebes, but his brother Polyneices was part of the attacking army and hence was a traitor: "Their banners flew, the battle raged / They fell together, their father's sons." Creon, outraged by this treachery from one of the royal family, decrees that Polyneices shall not receive the normal purifying burial rites and places under interdict of death anyone who will attempt to provide these rites to the corpse. He decrees that Polyneices, that "Anti-Theban Theban," will not be accorded burial, but will be left to rot in the open. The results are that "the dogs and birds are at it day and night, spreading reek and rot" (2004b, 8, 44). Creon justifies this decision in a manner similar to the British authorities and their treatment of the corpse of the IRA man Francis Hughes, an issue we will look at more closely in the conclusion:

> This is where I stand where it comes to Thebes
> Never to grant traitors and subversives
> Equal footing with loyal citizens. (ibid., 11)

Once again, the binary opposition here is fixed and used as a way of justifying actions of the self that demean the other. For Antigone, the duty she has to her brother as a human being far surpasses her duty to the Theban conceptions of patriotism as laid down by Creon, and, interestingly, she cites a higher law than that of Creon or Thebes itself:

> I disobeyed the law because the law was not
> The law of Zeus nor the law ordained
> By Justice. Justice dwelling deep
> Among the gods of the dead (ibid., 20–21)

This declaration is touching the real, as her loyalty is to a vision of truth and intersubjectivity that is never really explained in the play. She is looking toward that further shore and is not allowing herself to be bound by the ties or bonds of ideology or tribal identity. Like Neoptolemus, what she sees as being of value cannot be enunciated in language—she, too, is throughother, and she, too, is bound by a wider understanding of ethics than is Creon, or indeed Odysseus, in *The Cure at Troy*. Like Neoptolemus, she is a character who is governed by a sense of the real, of that which is beneath and beyond the binary and oppositional structures of identity. It is her imagination that allows her to see beyond the binary of Thebes/anti-Thebes that "yields intuitive access to the real truth of things" (R. Kearney 1995a, 5). The real, as we noted in chapter 2, is like something stuck to the sole of the shoe (Lacan 2006, 17), invisible but felt. Antigone's sense that not burying her brother, while in accord with the political demands of her polis, is nevertheless wrong at a felt, ethical level and has the effect of the real, because it will cause an effect in the polis. Though not directly accessible, the presence of the real can be felt in poetic language, as a "narrativisation in the political unconscious" (Jameson 1981, 26).

The stress here is on the individual as defined by his or her group: one is either Theban or anti-Theban—there is no other choice available. It is a sentiment connected to the ideological position of

Odysseus in *The Cure at Troy*, where the choices of definition are binary: one is either Greek or Trojan. For Creon, the binary is parallel: one is either a patriot or a traitor, and this designation carries through in life and death—there is no other identity. Heaney, in his translations, makes space for the throughother, and both Neoptolemus and Antigone embody this perspective that looks outward toward a further language of justice and truth. The difficulty of signifying this sense of the real is clear in the use of the term *throughother* in one play and in the difficulty of understanding Antigone's motivation in the other. We have already noted the fascination that this play holds for generations of European intellectuals. Lacan has written about her situation at the end of the play, where she is locked away, and describes the impossibility of signifying her place in the Theban society as a second death. He notes that her punishment "will consist in her being shut up or suspended in the zone between life and death. Although she is not yet dead, she is eliminated from the world of the living," because she is touching an aspect of signification that cannot be accessed by the living. She is touching the real that can be very frightening, as from Antigone's point of view, "life can only be approached, can only be lived or thought about, from the place of that limit where her life is already lost, where she is already on the other side" (1992, 280).

Here she is in a place that is real but where communication with the ordinary world is cut off; Heaney, like so many other thinkers, is fascinated by this position, and I would maintain that it is this sense of the real that makes the play so popular in so many different contexts. What always remains constant in the different interpretations is Antigone's stubborn resistance to the binary oppositions of identity and her attachment to that further shore of which Heaney spoke in *The Cure at Troy*. As Žižek puts it, she stands for "the exclusive and uncompromising attachment to the Other *qua* Thing, eclipsing the Other *qua* Third, the agency of symbolic mediation/reconciliation" (2005, 344; emphasis in the original). She is the symbol of that becoming space in this play, and as such her contemporaneity is ensured as expressions of the real resonate down through the ages.

Again in this play, Heaney makes some contemporary references, noting that George Bush's "war on terror" was on his mind when he began the translation (Heaney and O'Driscoll 2008, 422). He wanted to make some reference to it in his translation. He wanted to make the connection between George Bush's views on American terrorists interned in Guantánamo Bay and with Creon's condemnation of Polyneices as an "an anti-Theban Theban" (2004b, 10). Heaney also explains how, with this contemporary perspective in mind, he inserts what he calls a "Bushism" in the play by putting the phrase "I'll flush 'em out" into Creon's mouth and also in how "the word 'patriot' is employed with a definite neo-conservative righteousness." This deliberate anachronism helps to place the translation in Agamben's third place between the original and the contemporary version; as Heaney explains, "You end up mediating between the otherness of the thing itself and the mood of the moment," and we will look at a further aspect of this attunement between the otherness of the Greek text and the realities of contemporary violence, death, and burial in contemporary Northern Ireland in the conclusion of this book (Heaney and O'Driscoll 2008, 423).

That the Greek texts allow Heaney to look awry at his own culture and to understand it otherwise is clear, and in another translation he makes this connection between the classical and Irish worlds structurally overt by taking three translations, one from Irish poet Brian Merriman whose poem *Cúirt an Mheán Oíche* (*The Midnight Court*) is then juxtaposed with two translations from Ovid's *Metamorphoses*. The overall effect is to defamiliarize each text from its context by displacing it into this new context where the original languages, Latin and Irish, are dislocated into contemporary English. Heaney explains the purpose behind this structure:

> The three translations included here were all part of a single impulse. "Orpheus and Eurydice" was done in June 1993, just before I began to prepare a lecture on *Cúirt an Mheán Oíche* (1780) for the Merriman Summer School. Then, in order to get to closer grips with the original, I started to put bits of the Irish into

> couplets and, in doing so, gradually came to think of the Merriman poem in relation to the story of Orpheus, and in particular the story of his death as related by Ovid. The end of *The Midnight Court* took on a new resonance when read within the acoustic of the classical myth, and this gave me the idea of juxtaposing the Irish poem (however drastically abridged) with the relevant passages from Ovid's *Metamorphoses*. (1993, 11)

It is this placing of the voice of the self within the ambit of the voice of the other in order to set up an intertextual, intercultural, and intersubjective structure that defines the selfhood of the Irish writer in terms of the alterity of the Greek one. The web of interconnections that makes up this triangular structure between Merriman, the Irish-speaking poet translated by Heaney, Heaney the Irish poet who writes in English, and the classical Ovid, whose works come to us only through translation, one of which has been done again by Heaney, echoes the complex structure of the two quincunxes as well as the other spatial and diagrammatic metaphors of which we have been speaking. His telling use of the term *acoustic* reinforces his focus on the sound and sensation of words as part of their meaning and also on the need to look awry at texts in order to see the real within them. One could well see Agamben's third space at work in this trio of poems, where meaning shuttles in a hithering-thithering motion between the different poems. Here is a field of force that again looks to the further shore in a further language.

Heaney's view of the importance of this composite translation can be gleaned from an essay in *The Redress of Poetry* entitled, revealingly, "Orpheus in Ireland: On Brian Merriman's *The Midnight Court*," wherein he outlines the value of this poem as "part of the Irish past" and also of the "literary conventions of medieval Europe," while at the same time noting that it is capable of being read as "a tremor of the future." He also suggests that the poem's original audience would have seen it as a parody of the traditional *Aisling* poetic form, a form in which the poet sees a beautiful woman in a dream who "drives him to diction and description" and is an allegory of Ireland. She generally tells of her ill-treatment by the English, before consoling "herself and the poet by prophesying that her release will be affected by a young prince from overseas." Heaney sees this poem as, among other things, "a blast of surrealistic ridicule directed against such a fantasy," or as a way of understanding this tradition otherwise, and given his own ongoing attempts at prizing open nationalist tropes and images, we can see how this dimension of the poem would be attractive to him. It is a way of gesturing toward that further language by using farce and surrealism: "It sponsored a libertarian and adversarial stance against the repressive conditions which prevailed during those years in Irish life, public and private" (1995b, 39, 48, 53).

The Irish poem, Heaney maintains, can be read as another manifestation of the story of Orpheus, "master poet of the lyre, the patron, and sponsor of music and song," and the different conclusions of both poems depict the different cultures involved. Orpheus, singing in the woods, is spied by a band of "crazed Ciconian women," who call him "Orpheus the misogynist" and attack him: the "furies were unleashed," and they turned to "rend the bard." The Irish parallel has a tamer ending. As the women decide to "Flay him alive" and to "Cut deep. No mercy. Make him squeal / Leave him in strips from head to heel," the poet wakes up: "Then my dreaming ceased / And I started up, awake, released" (1995b, 58, 39, 40, 33, 34). Mirroring Derrida's idea of the *navette*, Heaney tends to read one ending in light of the other, yet another of those transformative crossings of self and other, as Ovid is read through Merriman and Merriman through Ovid, as meaning shuttles across languages, cultures, pages, and centuries.

The resulting structure is a triptych, which features Ovid's account of the death of Eurydice and Orpheus's subsequent descent into the underworld, followed by two sections of the Merriman piece, and culminating in the death of Orpheus. Perhaps more than any other, this translation enacts the imperative toward viewing Ireland within a classical and European perspective. The three sections are all in English but spring from two very different source languages. The very act of reading this piece is to submerge oneself in cultural hybridity, as the Irish, Latin, and English languages interact and intersect in a structure that is sufficiently fluid to accommodate them all and within which each is understood otherwise. All three poems deal with some form of transformation, so they are keenly connected with the other concerns of his translations, and the creative juxtaposition within this triptych, I would argue, has a lot to do with Heaney's assertion that *The Midnight Court* has a "role to play in the construction of a desirable civilization" (ibid., 57). Reading these translations in their new context is a form of poetized thinking, where self and other are continually redefined in this fluid field of force.

For the aesthetic thinkers discussed in this book, the knowledge that poetic thinking and poetic language achieves is precisely this unsought, and unforeseen, adequation between different phrase regimes, between different paradigms of knowledge, and between different cultural expressions. I have been arguing that poetic language accesses the real, or aspects of the unconscious, and Heaney suggests this point as he speaks about how when writing poetry, "you're after something just at the edge of your knowledge, so you're in a much more improvisatory frame of mind." The edge of knowledge is precisely the ability of language to lean without toppling, though well beyond the plumb, that he saw in the poetry of Herbert; it is the range of the unconscious where words, thoughts, images, and emotions come to the consciousness rather than being actively summoned: "a kind of waiting for the right word to fill the space," as he puts it, which is something which he associates more "with translation" (Heaney and O'Driscoll 2008, 448).

This association is hardly surprising, as some form of explanation of the concepts of the other in the language of the self, however difficult, is at the core of the nature of translation. What is interesting is from where Heaney sees the source of this further language deriving, as he speaks about such occasions as occurring "when you waken at night, or when you're trying to get to sleep" (ibid., 448–49), and here we are in the language of the unconscious, that area of experience where feelings and experiences are repressed and can be accessed in only a random and refractive manner.

Poetizing as thinking is one way of attempting to access these areas, and a glance at the different cultures from which he translates demonstrates his desire to grant a broad swath of signifiers of identity their due through translation, through the fusion, but never the full synthesis, of languages, cultures, and habituses. One could argue about the nature of the linguistic text, and in generic terms there is a truism that says that when a poem is translated, the "poetry" is what gets lost in translation, but I would not agree. Instead, I would suggest that it is the real that is accessed in translations, as the difference that is part of all our identities, as embodied in Heaney's field of force structures, is further foregrounded, and the areas of identity that are often elided can be unconcealed, to use Heidegger's term, in the complex new language of translation.

The translating of aspects of the other into the language of the self also has a strongly political aspect. In this context, it is instructive to note that Heaney has seen much of his translating work as a response to politics and to the violence caused by politics: he has said that his translation from Dante in *Field Work*, which deals with "the starving to death of the imprisoned Ugolino in a tower in Pisa," was completed during the late 1970s as "the dirty protest in the Maze Prison," which would eventually lead to the IRA hunger strikes of 1981, was at its height. His translation from Aeschylus, "Mycenae Lookout," which appeared in *The Spirit Level*, "was done fifteen years later, after the orgy of sectarian killing which had preceded the IRA ceasefire in 1994." In the aftermath of the Good Friday Agreement in 1998, he translated Virgil's "Ninth Eclogue," which is concerned with "the frail but vitally necessary work of poetry in a time of violence," while his version of the Horace ode "Anything Can Happen" was done "in the aftermath of the 9/11 destruction of the Twin Towers" (2012, 22). The anachronistic comments on contemporary Northern Irish and world politics in his two Sophoclean translations make their political dimensions overt, while at another level the conflicts between ethics and politics, and a sense of identity that transcends the identity of the tribe, are explored in both plays.

I would see translation as a synecdoche of Heaney's poetizing thinking in general, as it is a locus of the negotiation, of the hithering-thithering, shuttling movement, between different positions that serves to signify a more complex sense of identity, which is the teleological goal of much of his writing. Here, that attempt to transpose the structures of the quincunx from the literary to the political sphere is operative, as issues of conflict, violence, and sectarian strife are reframed in a more fluid structure by being juxtaposed with another expression of related actions, in another language, from another time. Such an activity is essentially political, as in a world where self is surrounded with numerous others, there is necessary interaction between them, and thus translation is the central sociopolitical activity. As Ricoeur puts it, the future ethos of European politics, and eventually of world politics, should be one based upon an exchange of memories and narratives between different nations, "for it is only when we translate our own wounds into the language of strangers and retranslate the wounds of strangers into our own language that healing and reconciliation can take place" (2006, xx).

The use of *wounds* here is relevant, as translation across languages, and within languages, attempts to carry over the sense of pain, hurt, and loss that accrues from such wounds—the real of political strife—and it is only when there is this crossing over, and where the other is seen as an equal being along with the self, that some form of rapprochement can begin to take place. Consequently, translation is related to deconstruction, which is also "a field of transgression, of the solicitation of boundaries, the crossing of borders, the parergonality of bounded works, the possibility of something different," and one could argue that these same comments could well be made about translation as a field of force in the sense that Heaney uses it, all of which "loosens the soil for something *tout autre*, which is coming" (Caputo 1997, 25).

The *tout autre* that helped to widen Heaney's notions of Mossbawn was the language of the other, the language of Europe, and this sense that there were other languages, other perspectives, and other paradigms of human society, thought, and culture is at the core of the value of translation and of its creation of a further language wherein differences can interact in a more positive manner. We have already cited Agamben's idea of a third area or third space, wherein signification touches on the real, and a parallel concept is to be found in the work of Homi Bhabha, another thinker who has engaged with issues of colonization, language, and identity, as he sees the third space as the "unrepresentable condition of enunciation which means that meanings and conditions of culture have no primordial unity or fixity, that even the same signs can be appropriated, translated, rehistoricized and read anew." Politically, translation can be seen as a seminal agent in the changing of positions, and in the broadening and widening of ideologically given situations. For Bhabha also, translation is a "place of hybridity" where the final source of meaning is "*neither the one nor the other*" (1994, 37, 25; emphasis in the original). The ongoing play of multilinguistic signifiers in the poem is paradigmatic of this play of *différance*, which ensures, as de Man observes, that "meaning is always displaced with regard to the meaning it ideally intended—that meaning is never reached" (1986, 91). The *différance* referred to here is Derrida's neologism, wherein every concept is seen as inscribed "in a chain or in a system within which it refers to the other, to other concepts, by means of the systematic play of differences" (1982, 11). These differences are expressed in language, which has "invaded the universal problematic" (2001, 280).

Language, as the signifying system of concepts and knowledge, is likewise based on a structure of differences, the meaning of each word being related to a series of other words, both phonetically and semantically. Each word, like each concept, is related in a series of matrices to other words that are not present. The use of *displaced* in the de Man quotation is pertinent here. In translation, the "meaning" passes from language to language, there is little or no referential dimension brought into play, and so the posited linguistic repossession of the place seemingly attempted by the quasi translations at the beginning of each poem is in fact dismembered and disarticulated by the processes of language itself. Politically, the passage from language to language does provide a referent-free zone of discourse, where the ideological construction of the referent can be created anew.

Derrida, as we have noted, sees meaning as being created through a constant process of negotiation, and he uses this term with one eye on its Latin etymology: *neg-otium*, meaning "not-ease, not-quiet . . . no leisure." He sees this "[no]-leisure" as the "impossibility of stopping or settling in a position," of "establishing oneself anywhere," and this constant movement is at the core of how meaning is created and re-created through the process of translation (2002, 11, 12). It can serve as a paradigm for interpretation between self and other. Richard Kearney, in his introduction to Ricoeur's *On Translation*, makes the point that "as soon as there is language there is interpretation, that is translation. *In principio fuit interpres*. Words exist in time and space, and thus have a history of meanings which alter and evolve. All translation involves some aspect of dialogue between self and stranger. Dialogue means just that, *dia-legein*, welcoming the difference" (2006, xvii). This welcoming of difference, which is what is described in Heaney's recounting of listening to the languages of Europe on the old wireless radio in Mossbawn, is significant in translation, as the existence of responses to violence in other languages and in other times allows for Heaney to reconceptualize his own responses to a parallel situation, and it is that process, that movement, that negotiation, that is a feature of all of his poetized structures of thought. As Benjamin puts it, "Translation passes through continua of transformation, not abstract areas of identity and similarity" (1979, 117), and in the gap between these oscillations is created the third space, the becoming space, where new perspectives allow for ongoing assimilation of different concepts into that further language of which Heaney speaks. This oscillation is part of the negotiation that I see as central to the interaction between the societal and the personal, the local and the global, and the cultural and the political.

As Derrida suggests, the word must "*negotiate* its usage" (2002, 11) in debate, and this ongoing negotiation is probably the best way to view the relationship between the local and the global and between the aesthetic and the political. As Heaney puts it, again citing Joyce, "In every one of those acts of translation, therefore, you could say I was approaching terror via Holyhead" (2012, 22), and this parallels his return to Mossbawn via Mantua. Here he is using his poetizing thought to make a phonetic, and also a symbolic, connection with the work of Joyce. The original quotation on which he is chiming comes from near the end of Joyce's *A Portrait of the Artist as a Young Man*, where Stephen is writing in diary mode. He meets his friend Davin, and the following conversation ensues: "April 3. Met Davin at the cigar shop opposite Findlater's church. He was in a black sweater and had a hurley stick. Asked me was it true I was going away and why. Told him the shortest way to Tara was via Holyhead" (1993, 288). By this statement he means that the best way to understand Irish culture is to leave Ireland and look back at the country from a different perspective, a quasi-transcendental one. It is this sense of aesthetic distance, a sense of a "remove due to which it always escapes what it is" (Blanchot 1982, 205), that Joyce is advocating here. By alliterating and half-rhyming *Tara*, as symbolic of an ur-Irish identity, with *terror*, the symptom of a broken politics in Ireland, Heaney is paralleling the European consciousness and contextualization of his great forebear, in the form of a *tessera*.

Like Joyce, Heaney is looking for structures of thought that allow for interaction with the other in order to achieve new perspectives on the self. So, whether the issue is terror, identity, or the politics of selfhood, alterity, in the form of translation, can provide a path to an altered perspective, and translation is the process into this "different way of thinking" (Heidegger 1971, 23).

Conclusion

Aesthetic Responsibilities

Seamus Heaney's fame derives primarily from his poetry, and this book does not attempt to gainsay that reputation. Heaney's poetry is a resonant enunciation of the aesthetic in the late twentieth and early twenty-first centuries and will be a lasting legacy in times to come. What this book has attempted to do is to demonstrate that, as well as being a practitioner, Heaney is a philosophical thinker on the aesthetic and on its value in defining knowledge and influencing critique, both internally in terms of individual self-knowledge and also in terms of issues in the broader public sphere. I see Heaney's thinking, as set out in his essays on poetry and on the aesthetic, as being of lasting value. I also see these writings as providing an alternative context through which to read and critique his work, and I maintain that they situate Heaney squarely in the European aesthetic tradition that, after Kant and Hegel, has seen the aesthetic as a seminal factor of any inquiry into the nature of epistemology.

In Continental philosophy, the aesthetic has often been seen as that which grants access to a more physical and sensuous grasp of the world, as exemplified by Heidegger's concept of *Dasein*, the sense of "being" in the world, and the somatic consequences of it. Heaney's view of poetry as leading into a further language is in keeping with this view of the aesthetic, as I have shown. It allows for an understanding otherwise, a looking awry, the creation of a becoming space, wherein the conscious and the unconscious, the rational, the irrational, and what I have termed the arational, can all mutually inform each other.

Psychoanalytic thinkers such as Freud and Lacan have spoken in depth about the associative methods of thinking in the unconscious and in dreams. In poetry this associative mode of thinking is given its place in the creation of that aesthetic discourse through the apophantic mode of utterance that focuses on the particular and the unconscious. In philosophy this type of language is seen to have access to aspects of the real, and this very specific attunement to the unconscious dimensions of language is what I have seen as a significant aspect of Heaney's overall project as a cultural thinker. He writes about poetry in a number of ways, and we have noted how he credits it both for being itself and for being a help. I would contend that it is a help by being itself, by allowing associative and somatic aspects of language to have an effect on how we see and know the world in which we live. In this way it participates in what might be termed an aesthetic epistemology, which can influence our knowledge of the world. The language of poetry, through its connections and associations, which are not necessarily rational, allows for a different perspective on issues of politics, identity, self, and other, the notion of the border, language, knowledge, and truth.

The placement of the lived life, of the sense of being in the world, and of the value of emotion and intuition and sensation at the core of thinking has been central to his work, and I would conclude with a final example of this aspect of his poetized thinking that demonstrates yet again his connection with the modes and methods of contemporary European philosophical thinking. This example is a development of his translation of *Antigone*, and of the retitling of that translation, which was discussed in chapter 6. In a lecture that he gave to the American Philosophical Society, in April 2004, later reprinted in abridged form in the *Irish Book Review*, Heaney spoke of issues political, somatic, and literary in an essay that encapsulates his originality as an aesthetic thinker, as well as situating him within the European aesthetic tradition. The title of the essay, "Thebes via Toomebridge: Retitling *Antigone*," once more sets up a field of force and an attunement between past and present, self and other, and Ireland and Europe. The title immediately recalls our discussion in chapter 5 of his comments on Ireland and Europe in literary terms, "'Mossbawn via Mantua': Ireland in/and Europe, Cross-currents and Exchanges" (2012). In both texts, there is this recontextualization of Ireland from being part of the Anglophone world to a re-visioning in terms of its location in a European context.

Here, in an essay ostensibly about why he chose to change the title of his translation of *Antigone* to *The Burial at Thebes*, Heaney begins by speaking of a very nonliterary event, one that would seem to be very far removed from the concerns and context within which that original play was written in Greece in 442 BCE. Heaney begins by speaking about a political event in the recent history of Northern Ireland, in May 1981, where, at the village of Toomebridge, a crowd had gathered: "They were there to meet a hearse that contained the body of a well-known Co. Derry figure, and once the hearse arrived they would accompany it back to a farmhouse on a bog road some six or seven miles away, where the body would be waked in traditional style by family and neighbours. They had come to Toome to observe custom, to be present at 'the removal of the remains.'" The figure in question is Francis Hughes, a member of the Provisional IRA, who was the second of the hunger strikers to die in their ongoing protest seeking political status in prison for all republican prisoners. This protest meant that they would be allowed to have the status accorded to prisoners of war and not be labeled criminals and that they would be allowed to organize themselves in a hierarchy within the prison, a hierarchy that would be recognized by the prison authorities. The British Conservative government under Margaret Thatcher was unwilling to accede to these demands, and the resulting standoff meant that between May 5 and August 30, 1981, ten hunger strikers died, "resulting in a steady issue of emaciated corpses from the gates of the prison and repeated processions of miles-long funeral crowds through the gates of the cemeteries" (2005, 12).

In keeping with his view of situations and structures as necessarily complex, Heaney explains that his own connection to Hughes is also a familial and neighborly one, as he lived near, and knew, many members of this family. Like many nationalists, he felt a degree of sympathy for these men who were willing to lay down their lives for their beliefs, and the sight of their emaciated bodies evoked feelings of sympathy in many who "sought fundamental political change, who wanted to break the Unionist Party's monopoly on power, but who nevertheless did not consider this an end worth killing for." The complex nature of the response is one that seemed to elude the British government, as Margaret Thatcher, on the death of the first hunger striker, Bobby Sands, made a statement in the House of Commons to the effect that "Mr Sands was a convicted criminal. He chose to take his own life. It was a choice that his organisation did not allow to many of its victims" (ibid., 12, 13).

Heaney, however, saw that whatever the rights and wrongs of the actions of these men, their dead bodies, emaciated and famine-like, were potent signifiers of the power of a cause: he saw that the hunger strikes could be seen "both as an exercise in *Realpolitik* and an occasion of sacred drama" (ibid., 13). He also stressed the nuanced and carefully structured response of many in the nationalist community, who, while they might have had some sympathy with the aims of the hunger strikers, and also might have been emotionally affected by the sight of those emaciated bodies, nevertheless "still felt cautious about expressing public support for them, however noble their sacrifice. Support for their fast could be read by the IRA and others as support for their violent methods, so many people hesitated. But in their hesitation they were painfully aware that they were giving silent assent to the intransigence and overbearing of Margaret Thatcher, who stated with a too brutal simplicity that 'Crime is crime, is crime. It is not political.'" What is interesting here is that in an attempt to see this political situation from a different perspective, Heaney goes on to invoke two of Europe's most profound aesthetic thinkers: Hegel and Sophocles. In what I see as a typical European intellectual gesture, he looks for the aesthetic to shed light on the political and the ethical. Speaking about the funeral of Hughes, where his body was handed over by the authorities to his family, Heaney describes how the British army brought the hearse to one side of the bridge, while Hughes's family and members of Sinn Fein and the nationalist community were waiting to receive the body on the other side, and there was an amount of jostling as people queried by "what right did the steel ring of the defence forces close round the remains of one who was son, brother, comrade, neighbour, companion?" (ibid., 12–13). It is here that he goes on to invoke Hegel, a philosopher who might not seem to be germane to such a volatile political situation.

However, as Heaney attempts to access the real of the situation, he finds literature and philosophy very useful as a way of providing a context that is not immersed in, and immanent to, this event. Rather than see it as another manifestation of the Irish-English binary opposition (and here the word *opposition* hardly does justice to the intensity of feelings involved), he chooses to see it as another manifestation of a more lasting opposition: "If ever there was a dramatization of the contest between what Hegel called the 'Instinctive Powers of Feeling, Love and Kinship' and 'the daylight gods of free and self-conscious, social, and political life,' it was that evening when the hearse with its police escort arrived on the village street and the cordon surrounding it was jostled in fury and indignation by the waiting crowd." Rather than rehearse the political binaries that have been largely responsible for the violence in Northern Ireland, Heaney looks to philosophy and to literature as he tries to understand the situation otherwise. Citing Hegel, and the almost eternal conflict between instinct and politics, allows him to recontextualize this specifically Irish situation in a broader European context and thereby to create a field of force that will contain, and help to understand, what is taking place here. He makes the point that the struggle around the body (and it is significant that the somatic, physical body is at the center of this discussion) is not political or even ideological as he sees it; rather, it stems from a sense among the crowd, and there would have been nationalists of all persuasions in that crowd, "that something inviolate had been assailed by the state," and he goes on to define what has been assaulted as their sense of "*dúchas*" (ibid., 13).

Dúchas is an Irish-language word, and it is used in a very specific sense. Heaney, aware that many readers would not be familiar with the term, glosses it, using the terminology of Brendan Devlin, who has observed that *dúchas* is an almost untranslatable term, but he still offers this account: "In an effort to explain it in English, the Royal Irish Academy's dictionary of the common old Gaelic languages uses such terms as 'inheritance; patrimony; native place or land; connection, affinity or attachment due to descent or longstanding; inherited instinct or natural tendency.' It is all of these things and, besides, the elevation of them to a kind of ideal of the spirit, an enduring value amid the change and the erosion of all human things" (1986, 85). Significantly, Heaney chooses not to look at the political, cultural, or ideological aspects of the situation; instead, he looks at what we might term the somatic real, the sense, or feeling, or instinct, that was the motivating factor in the surge of the crowd toward the iconic body of the dead man, something that would be very difficult to signify in any symbolic order. In other words, he is looking to the real, to that which exerts an influence but is almost impossible to express, though in this case it was expressed in that crowd surge toward the body.

It is not that the crowd is, by definition, pro-IRA, nor is it the case that they will rise up against the police and soldiers; what is happening here is that levels of attachment, feeling, instinct, and unconscious affiliations with place, neighbors, and culture have all combined to motivate that crowd surge. In this context, we are reminded of his use of the word *surge* to describe the final stanza of Yeats's "Among School Children," discussed in chapter 3, where the aesthetic was again the focus of attention. The aesthetic is a significant factor here as well, and Heaney's poetizing critique recognizes it and goes on to make the connection with another text wherein issues of burial, of fair treatment of the dead, regardless of the cause of that death, are of central importance, namely, *Antigone*: "If we wanted a set of words to describe the feelings that motivate the heroine of Sophocles' *Antigone*, we could hardly do better than that, for Antigone, the daughter of Oedipus, is surely in thrall to patrimony, connection, affinity and attachment due to descent, to longstanding, to inherited instinct and natural tendency, and for her all these things have been elevated to a kind of ideal of the spirit, an enduring value" (2005, 13). Later in this essay, he sets up another of his fields of force because the following quote from Hegel came from the latter's discussion of *Antigone*, with Creon representing the law of the land, "the daylight gods of free and self-conscious, social, and political life," and Antigone representing the "Instinctive Powers of Feeling, Love and Kinship." By focusing on the body of Polyneices, a character that, while dead, influences the rest of the play in terms of theme, character, motivation, and action, Heaney is looking at the real, because Polyneices is the real of this play. His body, which rots and decays as the action progresses, is a symbol of the somatic real, which affects every aspect of life and knowledge.

By calling the play *The Burial at Thebes*, it is Polyneices, and not the binary oppositions of Creon and Antigone, that is placed center stage (though ironically he never appears onstage), and it is the notion of burial, of the final connection of the subject with the world, and of a very final form of being in the world, that becomes the core of the play: it is the ultimate example of the real, and Heaney has made this very point in his explanation of the value of his retitling of *Antigone*:

> But my real title deed to the version got written when I changed the name of the play from *Antigone* to *The Burial at Thebes*. Putting "burial" in the title signals to a new audience what the central concern of the play is going to be. Because it is a word that has not yet been entirely divorced from primal reality, because it recalls to us our final destiny as members of the species, it also reminds us, however subliminally, of the solemnity of death, the sacredness of life and the need to allow in every case the essential dignity of the human creature. (ibid., 14)

The word *creature* here brings my argument to a close. The body, the somatic, the unconscious, and the senses—all are brought together in the cluster term that is *creature*. Our "creatureliness" is at the center of our experience of the world, and aspects of that creatureliness are what generally escape signification in the symbolic order of discourse. It is the language of poetry that allows aspects of this creatureliness to be understood anew. Heaney, I have argued, is a strong exemplar of this tradition, as he writes about the centrality of the aesthetic to any serious critique of the political. He has shown the way in which the aesthetic is imperative to answering those preoccupying questions as to the role of poetry in the lived life of the individual and in the discourse of the public sphere.

Heaney's aesthetic structures, the quincunx, the parallelogram, the triangle, and the various fields of force that he finds in poetry and in translation, all combine to transform the hierarchical binaries of rational thought into the more nuanced and complicated constellations wherein many different aspects of language and knowledge can interinanimate and mutually inform each other. His focus is in and on the interaction of seemingly fixed points, their recontextualization in new contextual structures, and the Heideggerian mirroring of each in element in the others. He is, without doubt, part of that European tradition of aesthetic contemplation, and I will close with Heaney's remarks about two of his aesthetic mentors, Dante and Eliot, where he sees them each embody the role of the poet as "thinker and teacher" (2002, 174–75).

Just as the term *poet as thinker* can be applied to these two great European intellectuals, so too can it be applied to the work of Seamus Heaney. In all of his prose and translations, wherein he speaks about the value of poetry and poetic language, he embodies the persona of the poet as thinker, as he merges the practice of poetry with the teaching of its worth, of its value to the individual and society, and to its mode of knowledge. Therefore, like Dante and Eliot, Seamus Heaney is the poet as thinker, and as teacher, someone who is able to take the scission that Giorgio Agamben sees as being at the heart of European epistemology, namely, "that poetry possesses its object without knowing it while philosophy knows its object without possessing it" (1993c, xvii). Through his poetized aesthetic thinking, Heaney allows these two discourses to intersect and inform each other, to look awry at each other, and ultimately to create new meanings by transforming and interinanimating each other.

Works Cited

Adorno, Theodor W. 1973. *Negative Dialectics.* Translated by Robert Hullot-Kantor. New York: Seabury Press.

———. 1981. *Prisms.* Translated by Samuel and Sherry Weber. Cambridge, MA: MIT Press.

———. 1993. *Hegel: Three Studies.* Translated by Sherry Weber Nicholsen. Cambridge, MA: MIT Press.

———. 1997. *Aesthetic Theory.* Translated by Gretel Adorno, Rolf Tiedemann, and Robert Hullot-Kantor. London: Athlone Press.

Adorno, Theodor W., and Rolf Tiedemann. 1991. *Notes to Literature 1.* Translated by Sherry Weber Nicholsen. 2 vols. New York: Columbia Univ. Press.

Agamben, Giorgio. 1991. *Language and Death: The Place of Negativity.* Translated by Karen E. Pinkus with Michael Hardt. Minneapolis: Univ. of Minnesota Press.

———. 1993a. *The Coming Community.* Translated by Michael Hardt. Minneapolis: Univ. of Minnesota Press.

———. 1993b. *Infancy and History: The Destruction of Experience.* Translated by Liz Heron. London: Verso.

———. 1993c. *Stanzas: Word and Phantasm in Western Culture.* Translated by Ronald L. Martinez. Minneapolis: Univ. of Minnesota Press.

———. 1995. *Idea of Prose.* Translated by Michael Sullivan and Sam Whitsitt. Albany: State Univ. of New York Press.

———. 1998. *Homo Sacer: Sovereign Power and Bare Life.* Translated by Daniel Heller-Roazen. Stanford, CA: Stanford Univ. Press.

———. 1999a. *The End of the Poem: Studies in Poetics.* Translated by Daniel Heller-Roazen. Stanford, CA: Stanford Univ. Press.

———. 1999b. *The Man without Content.* Translated by Georgia Albert. Stanford, CA: Stanford Univ. Press.

———. 2007. *Profanations*. Translated by Jeff Fort. New York: Zone Books.

Alcobia-Murphy, Shane. 2006. *Sympathetic Ink: Intertextual Relations in Northern Irish Poetry*. Liverpool: Liverpool Univ. Press.

Allen, Michael. 1997. *Seamus Heaney*. New York: St. Martin's Press.

Allen, William S. 2007. *Ellipsis: Of Poetry and the Experience of Language after Heidegger, Hölderlin, and Blanchot*. Albany: State Univ. of New York Press.

Althusser, Louis. 2001. *Lenin and Philosophy, and Other Essays*. New York: Monthly Review Press.

Alvarez A. 1980. "A Fine Way with the Language." *New York Review of Books*, Mar. 6, 16–17.

Andrews, Elmer Kennedy. 1988. *The Poetry of Seamus Heaney: All the Realms of Whisper*. Basingstoke: Macmillan.

———, ed. 1998. *The Poetry of Seamus Heaney*. Icon Critical Guides. Cambridge: Icon Books.

Appadurai, Arjun. 1996. *Modernity at Large: Cultural Dimensions of Globalization*. Minneapolis: Univ. of Minnesota Press.

Ashcroft, Bill, Gareth Griffiths, and Helen Tiffin. 1989. *The Empire Writes Back: Theory and Practice in Post-colonial Literatures*. London: Routledge.

Badiou, Alain. 1999. *Manifesto for Philosophy: Followed by Two Essays, "The (Re)Turn of Philosophy Itself" and "Definition of Philosophy."* Translated by Norman Madarasz. Albany: State Univ. of New York Press.

Badiou, Alain, and Alberto Toscano. 2005. *Handbook of Inaesthetics*. Stanford, CA: Stanford Univ. Press.

Bakhtin, Mikhail, and Michael Holquist. 1981. *The Dialogic Imagination: Four Essays*. Austin: Univ. of Texas Press.

Barrell, John, and John Bull, eds. 1974. *The Penguin Book of English Pastoral Verse*. London: Penguin.

Bassnett, Susan. 1991. *Translation Studies*. London: Routledge.

Benjamin, Walter. 1968. *Illuminations*. Translated by Harry Zohn. New York: Schocken Books.

———. 1979. *One-Way Street, and Other Writings*. Translated by Edmund Jephcott and Kingsley Shorter. London: New Left Books.

———. 2008. *The Work of Art in the Age of Its Technological Reproducibility, and Other Writings on Media*. Translated by Rodney

Livingstone, Edmund Jephcott, Howard Eiland, and Others. Cambridge, MA: Belknap Press of Harvard Univ. Press.

Bernasconi, Robert. 1985. *The Question of Language in Heidegger's History of Being.* New Jersey: Humanities Press.

Bernstein, J. M. 2004. "Negative Dialectic as Fate: Adorno and Hegel." In *The Cambridge Companion to Adorno*, edited by Tom Huhn, 19–50. Cambridge: Cambridge Univ. Press.

Bhabha, Homi K. 1994. *The Location of Culture.* London: Routledge.

Biemel, Walter. 1972. "Poetry and Language in Heidegger." In *On Heidegger and Language*, edited by Joseph J. Kogkelmans, 65–106. Evanston, IL: Northwestern Univ. Press.

Blanchot, Maurice. 1981. *The Gaze of Orpheus.* Edited by P. Adams Sitney. Translated by Lydia Davis. New York: Station Hill Press.

———. 1982. *The Space of Literature.* Translated by Ann Smock. Lincoln: Univ. of Nebraska Press.

———. 1986. *The Writing of the Disaster.* Translated by Ann Smock. Lincoln: Univ. of Nebraska Press.

———. 1995. *The Work of Fire.* Translated by Charlotte Mandell. Stanford, CA: Stanford Univ. Press.

Bloom, Harold. 1973. *The Anxiety of Influence: A Theory of Poetry.* Oxford: Oxford Univ. Press.

Boundas, Constantin V. 2006. *Deleuze and Philosophy.* Edinburgh: Edinburgh Univ. Press.

Bradley, Arthur. 2008. *Derrida's "Of Grammatology": An Edinburgh Philosophical Guide.* Edinburgh: Edinburgh Univ. Press.

Browne, Thomas. 2012. *The Garden of Cyrus.* 1736. Reprint, New York: Gale.

Bruns, Gerald L. 1997. *Maurice Blanchot: The Refusal of Philosophy.* Baltimore: Johns Hopkins Univ. Press.

———. 2006. *On the Anarchy of Poetry and Philosophy: A Guide for the Unruly.* New York: Fordham Univ. Press.

Caputo, John D. 1997. *The Prayers and Tears of Jacques Derrida: Religion without Religion.* Bloomington: Indiana Univ. Press.

Carroll, Clare, and Patricia King, eds. 2003. *Ireland and Postcolonial Theory.* Cork: Cork Univ. Press.

Carroll, David. 2000. "Organicism in Literature and History: From (Murray Krieger's) Poetics to (Jules Michelet's) Politics." In *The Revenge of the Aesthetic: The Place of Literature in Theory Today*, edited by Michael Clarke, 117–35. Berkeley: Univ. of California Press.

Carson, Ciarán. 1975. "Escaped from the Massacre?" *Honest Ulsterman* 50 (Winter): 183–86.

Cavanagh, Michael. 2009. *Professing Poetry: Seamus Heaney's Poetics.* Washington, DC: Catholic Univ. of America Press.

Chaitin, Gilbert D. 1996. *Rhetoric and Culture in Lacan.* Cambridge: Cambridge Univ. Press.

Clines, Francis X. 1983. "Poet of the Bogs: Seamus Heaney, Ireland's Greatest Living Poet, Commands a Growing Audience." *New York Times Magazine*, Mar. 13, 42–43, 98–99, 104.

Cole, Henri. 1997. "The Art of Poetry, No. 75: Interview with Seamus Heaney." *Paris Review* 144.

Colebrook, Claire. 2008. "Agamben: Aesthetics, Potentiality, and Life." *South Atlantic Quarterly: The Agamben Effect* 107, no. 1: 107–20.

Cooke, Harriet. 1973. "Interview with Seamus Heaney." *Irish Times*, Dec. 28, 8.

Corcoran, Neil. 1998. *The Poetry of Seamus Heaney: A Critical Study.* London: Faber.

Critchley, Simon. 2005. *Things Merely Are: Philosophy in the Poetry of Wallace Stevens.* London: Routledge.

Cruise O'Brien, Conor. 1975. "A Slow North-East Wind." *Listener*, 404–5.

Cunningham, David, and Nigel Mapp. 2006. *Adorno and Literature.* London: Continuum.

Curtis, L. P., Jr. 1968. *Anglo-Saxons and Celts: A Study of Anti-Irish Prejudice in Victorian England.* Bridgeport, CT: Univ. of Bridgeport.

———. 1971. *Apes and Angels: The Irishman in Victorian Caricature.* Washington, DC: Smithsonian Institution Press.

Curtis, Tony. 1994. *The Art of Seamus Heaney.* 3rd ed. Bridgend, Mid Glamorgan: Seren.

Dahlstrom, Daniel O. 2011. *Interpreting Heidegger: Critical Essays.* Cambridge: Cambridge Univ. Press.

Dargan, Joan. 1999. *Simone Weil: Thinking Poetically.* Albany: State Univ. of New York Press.

Dasenbrock, Reed Way. 2003. "Poetry and Politics." In *A Companion to Twentieth Century Poetry*, edited by Neil Roberts, 51–63. Oxford: Basil Blackwell.

Deane, Seamus. 1982. "'Unhappy and at Home': Interview with Seamus Heaney." In *The Crane Bag Book of Irish Studies*, edited by Mark Patrick Hederman and Richard Kearney, 66–72. Dublin: Blackwater Press.

———. 1990. *Introduction to Nationalism, Colonialism, and Literature.* Minneapolis: Univ. of Minnesota Press.

———. 2003. "Dumbness and Eloquence: A Note on English as We Write It in Ireland." In *Ireland and Postcolonial Theory*, edited by Clare Carroll and Patricia King, 109–21. Cork: Cork Univ. Press.

de Graef, Ortwin, Dirk De Geest, and Eveline Vanfraussen. 2008. "Fascist Politics and Literary Criticism." In *The Cambridge History of Literary Criticism: Twentieth-Century Historical, Philosophical and Psychological Perspectives*, edited by Christa Knellwolf and Christopher Norris, 71–88. Cambridge: Cambridge Univ. Press.

de la Durantaye, Leland. 2009. *Giorgio Agamben: A Critical Introduction.* Stanford, CA: Stanford Univ. Press.

Deleuze, Gilles. 1995. *Negotiations, 1972–1990.* New York: Columbia Univ. Press.

———. 2001. *Difference and Repetition.* Translated by Paul Patton. London: Continuum.

Deleuze, Gilles, and Félix Guattari. 1986. *Kafka: Toward a Minor Literature.* Minneapolis: Univ. of Minnesota Press.

———. 1987. *A Thousand Plateaus: Capitalism and Schizophrenia.* Translated by Brian Massumi. Minneapolis: Univ. of Minnesota Press.

Deleuze, Gilles, and Claire Parnet. 1977. *Dialogues.* Paris: Flammarion.

de Man, Paul. 1979. *Allegories of Reading: Figural Language in Rousseau, Nietzsche, Rilke, and Proust.* New Haven, CT: Yale Univ. Press.

———. 1984. *The Rhetoric of Romanticism.* New York: Columbia Univ. Press.

———. 1986. *The Resistance to Theory.* Manchester: Manchester Univ. Press.

de Man, Paul, and Andrzej Warminski. 1996. *Aesthetic Ideology.* Minneapolis: Univ. of Minnesota Press.

Derrida, Jacques. 1978. *Spurs: Nietzsche's Styles.* Translated by Barbara Harlow. Chicago: Univ. of Chicago Press.

———. 1982. *Margins of Philosophy.* Translated by Alan Bass. Brighton, UK: Harvester Press.

———. 1985. *The Ear of the Other: Otobiography, Transference, Translation*. Edited by Christie V. McDonald. Translated by Peggy Kamuf. New York: Schocken Books.

———. 1987. "Living On: Borderlines." In *Deconstruction and Criticism*, edited by Harold Bloom, Paul de Man, Jacques Derrida, Geoffrey Hartman, and J. Hillis Miller, 75–176. London: Continuum Press.

———. 1988. *Limited Inc*. Translated by Alan Bass and Samuel Weber. Evanston, IL: Northwestern Univ. Press.

———. 1989. *Of Spirit: Heidegger and the Question*. Translated by Geoffrey Bennington and Rachel Bowlby. Chicago: Univ. of Chicago Press.

———. 1992. *The Other Heading: Reflections on Today's Europe*. Translated by Pascale Anne Brault and Michael B. Naas. Bloomington: Indiana Univ. Press.

———. 1994. *Specters of Marx: The State of the Debt, the Work of Mourning, and the New International*. Translated by Peggy Kamuf. London: Routledge.

———. 1995. "Deconstruction and the Other." In *States of Mind: Dialogues with Contemporary Continental Thinkers*, edited by Richard Kearney, 156–77. Manchester: Manchester Univ. Press.

———. 1997. *Of Grammatology*. Translated by Gayatri Chakravorty Spivak. Baltimore: Johns Hopkins Univ. Press.

———. 1998. *Monolingualism of the Other; or, The Prosthesis of Origin*. Stanford, CA: Stanford Univ. Press.

———. 2001. *Writing and Difference*. Translated by Alan Bass. London: Routledge.

———. 2002. *Ethics, Institutions, and the Right to Philosophy*. Translated by Peter Pericles Trifonas. Lanham, MD: Rowman and Littlefield.

———. 2003. "Following Theory." In *Life after Theory: Jacques Derrida, Frank Kermode, Toril Moi and Christopher Norris*, edited by Michael Payne and John Schad, 1–51. London: Continuum.

———. 2004a. *Eyes of the University: Right to Philosophy 2*. Translated by Jan Plug et al. Stanford, CA: Stanford Univ. Press.

———. 2004b. *Positions*. Translated by Alan Bass. London: Continuum.

———. 2005a. *On Touching—Jean-Luc Nancy*. Translated by Christine Irizarry. Stanford, CA: Stanford Univ. Press.

———. 2005b. *Paper Machine*. Translated by Rachel Bowlby. Stanford, CA: Stanford Univ. Press.

———. 2005c. *Rogues: Two Essays on Reason.* Translated by Pascale-Anne Brault and Michael Naas. Stanford, CA: Stanford Univ. Press.

———. 2007. *Psyche: Inventions of the Other.* Edited by Peggy Kamuf and Elizabeth Rottenberg. Vol. 2. Stanford, CA: Stanford Univ. Press.

———. 2008. *The Animal That Therefore I Am.* Translated by David Wills. New York: Fordham Univ. Press.

Derrida, Jacques, and Derek Attridge. 1992. *Acts of Literature.* Edited by Derek Attridge. London: Routledge.

Derrida, Jacques, Alan Bass, and Henri Ronse. 1981. *Positions.* Chicago: Univ. of Chicago Press.

Derrida, Jacques, and Jean Birnbaum. 2007. *Learning to Live Finally: The Last Interview; An Interview with Jean Birnbaum.* Basingstoke: Palgrave Macmillan.

Derrida, Jacques, Pascale-Anne Brault, and Michael Naas. 2001. *The Work of Mourning.* Chicago: Univ. of Chicago Press.

Derrida, Jacques, and John D. Caputo. 1997. *Deconstruction in a Nutshell: A Conversation with Jacques Derrida.* New York: Fordham Univ. Press.

Derrida, Jacques, and Elizabeth Rottenberg. 2002. *Negotiations: Interventions and Interviews, 1971–2001.* Translated by Elizabeth Rottenberg. Stanford, CA: Stanford Univ. Press.

Derrida, Jacques, and Bernard Stiegler. 2002. *Echographies of Television: Filmed Interviews.* Translated by Jennifer Bajorek. Oxford: Polity Press.

Derrida, Jacques, and Lawrence Venuti. 2001. "What Is a 'Relevant' Translation?" *Critical Inquiry* 27, no. 2: 174–200.

Derrida, Jacques, and Elisabeth Weber. 1995. *Points—Interviews, 1974–1994.* Edited by Elisabeth Weber. Translated by Peggy Kamuf et al. Stanford, CA: Stanford Univ. Press.

de Saussure, Ferdinand. 1959. *Course in General Linguistics.* Edited by Charles Bally and Albert Sechehaye. Translated by Wade Baskin. New York: McGraw-Hill.

Devlin, Brendan P. 1986. "In Spite of Sea and Centuries: An Irish Gael Looks at the Poetry of Sorley MacLean." In *Sorley MacLean: Critical Essays,* edited by Raymond J. Ross and Joy Hendry, 81–89. Edinburgh: Scottish Academic Press.

Dickinson, Emily. 1924. *The Complete Poems of Emily Dickinson.* Boston: Little, Brown.

Drakakis, John, ed. 1985. *Alternative Shakespeares*. London: Routledge.

DuPlessis, Rachel Blau. 2006. *Blue Studios: Poetry and Its Cultural Work*. Tuscaloosa: Univ. of Alabama Press.

Eagleton, Terry. 1990. *The Ideology of the Aesthetic*. Oxford: Basil Blackwell.

Eagleton, Terry, Frederic Jameson, and Edward Said, eds. 1990. *Nationalism, Colonialism, and Literature*. Minneapolis: Univ. of Minnesota Press.

Eliot, T. S. 1920. *The Sacred Wood: Essays on Poetry and Criticism*. London: Methuen.

———. 1974. *Collected Poems, 1909–1962*. London: Faber.

Evans, Dylan. 1996. *An Introductory Dictionary of Lacanian Psychoanalysis*. London: Routledge.

Fanon, Frantz. 1968. *Black Skin, White Masks*. London: Grove Press.

Faulconer, James E., and Mark A. Wrathall. 2000. *Appropriating Heidegger*. Cambridge: Cambridge Univ. Press.

Ford, Andrew. 2002. *The Origins of Criticism: Literary Culture and Poetic Theory in Classical Greece*. Princeton, NJ: Princeton Univ. Press.

Foster, John Wilson. 1995. *The Achievement of Seamus Heaney*. Dublin: Lilliput Press.

Freud, Sigmund, and James Strachey. 2010. *The Interpretation of Dreams*. London: Allen and Unwin.

Frost, Robert. 2009. *Robert Frost: Speaking on Campus; Excerpts from His Talks, 1949–1962*. Edited by Edward Connery Lathem. New York: W. W. Norton.

Gandesha, Samir. 2004. "Leaving Home: On Adorno and Heidegger." In *The Cambridge Companion to Adorno*, edited by Tom Huhn, 101–28. Cambridge: Cambridge Univ. Press.

Giles, Steve. 1993. *Theorizing Modernism: Essays in Critical Theory*. London: Routledge.

Gilsenan Nordin, Irene. 1999. *Crediting Marvels in Seamus Heaney's "Seeing Things."* Sweden: Uppsala Univ. Press.

Glob, P. V. 1977. *The Bog People: Iron-Age Man Preserved*. Translated by Rupert Leo and Scott Bruce-Mitford. London: Faber.

Grigg, Russell. 2008. *Lacan, Language, and Philosophy*. Albany: State Univ. of New York Press.

Harmon, Maurice. 1992. "'We Pine for Ceremony': Ritual and Reality in the Poetry of Seamus Heaney, 1965–75." In *Seamus Heaney: A Collection of Critical Essays*, edited by Andrews Elmer, 67–86. London: Macmillan.

Harries, Karsten. 2009. *Art Matters: A Critical Commentary on Heidegger's "The Origin of the Work of Art."* Dordrecht: Springer.

Hart, Henry. 1992. *Seamus Heaney: Poet of Contrary Progressions*. Syracuse: Syracuse Univ. Press.

Hartman, Geoffrey. 1989. "Looking Back on Paul De Man." In *Reading De Man Reading*, edited by Wlad Godzich and Lindsay Waters, 3–24. Minneapolis: Univ. of Minnesota Press.

Hawkes, Terence. 1985. "Swissir-Swatter: Making a Man of English Letters." In *Alternative Shakespeares*, edited by John Drakakis, 26–46. London: Routledge.

Heaney, Seamus. 1966. *Death of a Naturalist*. London: Faber.

———. 1969. *Door into the Dark*. London: Faber.

———. 1972. *Wintering Out*. London: Faber.

———. 1975. *North*. London: Faber.

———. 1979. *Field Work*. London: Faber.

———. 1980. *Preoccupations: Selected Prose, 1968–1978*. London: Faber.

———. 1983a. *Among Schoolchildren: A Lecture Dedicated to the Memory of John Malone*. Belfast: John Malone Memorial Committee.

———. 1983b. *An Open Letter*. Derry: Field Day Theatre.

———. 1983c. *Sweeney Astray*. London: Faber.

———. 1984a. *Place and Displacement: Recent Poetry of Northern Ireland*. Pete Laver Memorial Lecture, Grasmere, Aug. 2, 1984.

———. 1984b. *Station Island*. London: Faber.

———. 1987. *The Haw Lantern*. London: Faber.

———. 1988. *The Government of the Tongue: The 1986 T. S. Eliot Memorial Lectures and Other Critical Writings*. London: Faber.

———. 1989. *The Place of Writing*. Atlanta: Scholars Press.

———. 1990. *The Cure at Troy: A Version of Sophocles' "Philoctetes."* London: Faber.

———. 1991. *Seeing Things*. London: Faber.

———. 1993. *The Midnight Verdict*. Old Castle, County Meath: Gallery Books.

———. 1995a. *Crediting Poetry*. County Meath: Gallery Press.

———. 1995b. *The Redress of Poetry: Oxford Lectures*. London: Faber.

———. 1996. *The Spirit Level*. London: Faber.

———. 1999. *Beowulf*. London: Faber.

———. 2001. *Electric Light*. London: Faber.

———. 2002. *Finders Keepers: Selected Prose, 1971–2001*. London: Faber.

———. 2003. "Eclogues 'In Extremis': On the Staying Power of Pastoral." *Proceedings of the Royal Irish Academy, Section C: Archaeology, Celtic Studies, History, Linguistics, Literature* 103C, no. 1: 1–12.

———. 2004a. *Anything Can Happen: A Poem and Essay*. Dublin: Townhouse in association with Art for Amnesty and Irish Translators and Interpreters Association.

———. 2004b. *The Burial at Thebes: A Version of Sophocles "Antigone."* London: Faber.

———. 2004c. "A Story That Sings Down the Centuries." *Sunday Times*, Mar. 21.

———. 2005. "Thebes via Toomebridge: Retitling *Antigone*." *Irish Book Review* 1, no. 1: 12–14.

———. 2006. *District and Circle*. London: Faber.

———. 2010. *Human Chain*. London: Faber.

———. 2012. "Mossbawn via Mantua: Ireland in/and Europe, Cross-currents and Exchanges." In *Ireland in/and Europe: Cross-currents and Exchanges*, edited by Werner Huber, Sandra Mayer, and Julia Novak. Trier, Germany: Wissenschaftlicher Verlag Trier.

Heaney, Seamus, and Dennis O'Driscoll. 2008. *Stepping Stones: Interviews with Seamus Heaney*. London: Faber.

Hegel, Georg Wilhelm Friedrich. 1975a. *Aesthetics: Lectures on Fine Art*. Translated by T. M. Knox. Vol. 1. Oxford: Clarendon Press.

———. 1975b. *Aesthetics: Lectures on Fine Art*. Translated by T. M. Knox. Vol. 2. Oxford: Clarendon Press.

Heidegger, Martin. 1971. *Poetry, Language, Thought*. Translated by Albert Hofstadter. New York: Harper & Row.

———. 1975a. *Early Greek Thinking*. Translated by David Farrell Krell and Frank A. Capuzzi. New York: Harper and Row.

———. 1975b. *The End of Philosophy*. Translated by Joan Stambaugh. London: Souvenir Press.

———. 1977. *The Question Concerning Technology, and Other Essays.* Translated by William Lovitt. New York: Harper and Row.

———. 1982a. *The Basic Problems of Phenomenology.* Translated by Albert Hofstadter. Bloomington: Indiana Univ. Press.

———. 1982b. *On the Way to Language.* Translated by Peter D. Hertz. San Francisco: Harper & Row.

———. 1996. *Being and Time.* Translated by Joan Stambaugh. Albany: State Univ. of New York Press.

———. 1999. *Contributions to Philosophy (from Enowning).* Translated by Parvis Emad and Kenneth Maly. Bloomington: Indiana Univ. Press.

———. 2000. *Elucidations of Holderlin's Poetry.* Amherst, NY: Humanity Books.

———. 2004. *What Is Called Thinking?* Translated by Jesse Glenn Gray. New York: HarperCollins.

———. 2010. *Country Path Conversations.* Translated by Bret W. Davis. Bloomington: Indiana Univ. Press.

Huhn, Tom, ed. 2004. *The Cambridge Companions to Adorno.* Cambridge: Cambridge Univ. Press.

Jakobson, Roman. 1971. *Selected Writings.* Vol. 2, *Word and Language.* The Hague: Mouton.

James, David. 2009. *Art, Myth and Society in Hegel's Aesthetics.* London: Continuum.

Jameson, Fredric. 1981. *The Political Unconscious: Narrative as a Socially Symbolic Act.* Ithaca, NY: Cornell Univ. Press.

JanMohamed, Abdul. 1995. "The Economy of the Manichean Allegory." In *The Postcolonial Studies Reader*, edited by Bill Ashcroft, Gareth Griffiths, and Helen Tiffin, 18–23. London: Routledge.

Jay, Martin. 1984. *Marxism and Totality: The Adventures of a Concept from Lukács to Habermas.* Berkeley: Univ. of California Press.

Johnston, Dillon. 1985. *Irish Poetry after Joyce.* Mountrath, Ireland: Dolmen Press.

Joyce, James. 1989. *Ulysses.* Edited by Hans Walter Gabler with Wolfhard Steppe and Claus Melchior. London: Bodley Head.

———. 1993. *A Portrait of the Artist as a Young Man.* Edited by R. B. Kershner. Boston: Bedford Books of St. Martin's Press.

———. 1996. *"Dubliners": Text and Criticism.* Edited by Robert Scholes and A. Walton Litz. Rev. ed. New York: Viking.

Kamuf, Peggy, ed. 1991. *A Derrida Reader: Between the Blinds*. Hemel Hempsted: Harvester Wheatsheaf.

Kant, Immanuel. 1928. *Critique of Aesthetic Judgement*. Translated by J. C. Meredith. Oxford: Clarendon Press.

Kavanagh, Patrick. 1964. *Collected Poems of Patrick Kavanagh*. London: MacGibbon and Kee.

Kearney, Hugh. 1989. *The British Isles: A History of Four Nations*. Cambridge: Cambridge Univ. Press.

Kearney, Richard. 1988. *Transitions: Narratives in Modern Irish Culture*. Dublin: Wolfhound Press.

———. 1995a. *Poetics of Modernity: Toward a Hermeneutic Imagination*. Atlantic Highlands, NJ: Humanities Press.

———. 1995b. *States of Mind: Dialogues with Contemporary Thinkers*. New York: New York Univ. Press.

Kiberd, Declan. 1997. *Ireland: The Literature of a Modern Nation*. London: Vintage.

King, Matthew. 2009. *Heidegger and Happiness: Dwelling on Fitting and Being*. London: Continuum.

Kochanowski, Jan. 1995. *Laments*. Edited by Seamus Heaney and Stanislaw Barańczak. London: Faber.

Kockelmans, Joseph J. 1986. *Heidegger on Art and Art Works*. Dordrecht: Martinus Nijhoff.

Krieger, Murray. 1989. *A Reopening of Closure: Organicism against Itself*. New York: Columbia Univ. Press.

———. 1994. *The Institution of Theory*. Baltimore: Johns Hopkins Univ. Press.

———. 2000. "My Travels with the Aesthetic." In *The Revenge of the Aesthetic: The Place of Literature in Theory Today*, edited by Michael Clarke, 208–36. Berkeley: Univ. of California Press.

Krieger, Murray, and Joan Krieger. 1991. *Ekphrasis: The Illusion of the Natural Sign*. Baltimore: Johns Hopkins Univ. Press.

Lacan, Jacques. 1977. *The Four Fundamental Concepts of Psycho-Analysis*. Translated by Alan Sheridan. London: Hogarth Press.

———. 1990. *Television: A Challenge to the Psychoanalytic Establishment*. Translated by Rosalind Krauss, Denis Hollier, and Annette Michelson. New York: W. W. Norton.

———. 1991. *Seminar 1: Freud's Papers on Technique, 1953–1954*. Translated by John Forrester. London: W. W. Norton.

———. 1992. *Seminar 7: The Ethics of Psychoanalysis, 1959–1960*. Edited by Jacques-Alain Miller. Translated by Jacques-Alain Miller. London: Routledge.

———. 2006. *Écrits: The First Complete Edition in English*. Translated by Bruce Fink in collaboration with Héloïse Fink and Russell Grigg. London: W. W. Norton.

———. 2008. *My Teaching*. Translated by David Macey. London: Verso.

Laclau, Ernesto. 2005. *On Populist Reason*. London: Verso.

———. 2007. *Emancipation(s)*. London: Verso.

Laclau, Ernesto, and Chantal Mouffe. 1985. *Hegemony and Socialist Strategy: Towards a Radical Democratic Politics*. London: Verso.

Larkin, Philip, and Anthony Thwaite. 2003. *Collected Poems*. London: Faber.

Lecercle, Jean-Jacques. 2010. *Badiou and Deleuze Read Literature*. Edinburgh: Edinburgh Univ. Press.

Levinas, Emmanuel. 1989. *The Levinas Reader*. Translated by Seán Hand. Oxford: Blackwell.

Lewis, Michael. 2008. *Derrida and Lacan: Another Writing*. Edinburgh: Edinburgh Univ. Press.

Lloyd, David. 1993. *Anomalous States: Irish Writing and the Post-colonial Moment*. Dublin: Lilliput Press.

Longley, Edna. 1986. *Poetry in the Wars*. Newcastle: Bloodaxe Books.

Loomba, Ania. 1998. *Colonialism-Postcolonialism: The New Critical Idiom*. London: Routledge.

Lyotard, Jean-François. 1984. *The Postmodern Condition: A Report on Knowledge*. Translated by Geoff Bennington and Brian Massumi. Manchester: Manchester Univ. Press.

Macaulay, Thomas Babington. 1995. *Speeches of Lord Macauley with His Minute on Indian Education*. Edited by G. M. Young. Oxford: Oxford Univ. Press.

MacNeice, Louis, and E. R. Dodds. 1966. *Collected Poems*. London: Faber.

Malabou, Catherine, and Jacques Derrida. 2004. *Counterpath: Traveling with Jacques Derrida*. Translated by David Wills. Stanford, CA: Stanford Univ. Press.

Malone, Christopher T. 2000. "Writing Home: Spatial Allegories in the Poetry of Seamus Heaney and Paul Muldoon." *English Literary History* 67: 1083–1109.

Malpas, Jeff, 2006. *Heidegger's Topology: Being, Place, World.* Cambridge, MA: MIT Press.

———. 2012. *Heidegger and the Thinking of Place: Explorations in the Topology of Being.* Cambridge, MA: MIT Press.

McCarthy, Conor. 2008. *Seamus Heaney and Medieval Poetry.* Rochester, NY: D. S. Brewer.

Mikics, David. 2009. *Who Was Jacques Derrida? An Intellectual Biography.* New Haven, CT: Yale Univ. Press.

Miller, J. Hillis. 1987. *The Ethics of Reading: Kant, De Man, Eliot, Trollope, James, and Benjamin.* New York: Columbia Univ. Press.

Molino, Michael. 1994. *Questioning Tradition, Language and Myth: The Poetry of Seamus Heaney.* Washington, DC: Catholic Univ. of America Press.

Montague, John. 1972. *The Rough Field.* Dublin: Dolmen Press.

Morrison, Blake. 1982. *Seamus Heaney.* London: Methuen.

Morrison, Blake, and Andrew Motion. 1982. *The Penguin Book of Contemporary British Poetry.* London: Penguin.

Mouffe, Chantal. 1993. *The Return of the Political.* London: Verso.

Mugerauer, Robert. 1990. *Heidegger's Language and Thinking.* New Jersey: Humanities Press.

Mure, Geoffrey Reginald Gilchrist. 1965. *The Philosophy of Hegel.* Oxford: Oxford Univ. Press.

Murphy, Mike. 2000. "Seamus Heaney: Interview by Mike Murphy." In *Reading the Future: Irish Writers in Conversation*, edited by Mike Murphy and Clíodhna Ní Anluain. Dublin: Lilliput Press.

Murray, Alex, and Jessica Whyte. 2011. *The Agamben Dictionary.* Edinburgh: Edinburgh Univ. Press.

Nancy, Jean-Luc. 1993. *The Experience of Freedom.* Translated by Bridget McDonald. Stanford, CA: Stanford Univ. Press.

Nightingale, Andrea Wilson. 2004. *Spectacles of Truth in Classical Greek Philosophy: Theoria in Its Cultural Context.* Cambridge: Cambridge Univ. Press.

Norris, Christopher. 1988. *Paul De Man: Deconstruction and the Critique of Aesthetic Ideology.* London: Routledge.

O'Brien, Eugene. 2002. *Seamus Heaney and the Place of Writing.* Gainesville: Univ. Press of Florida.

———. 2003. *Seamus Heaney: Searches for Answers.* London: Pluto Press.

Ó Buachalla, Séamus. 1980. *The Letters of P. H. Pearse.* Gerrards Cross: Colin Smythe.

O'Donoghue, Bernard. 1994. *Seamus Heaney and the Language of Poetry.* Brighton, UK: Harvester Wheatsheaf.

———, ed. 2009. *The Cambridge Companion to Seamus Heaney.* Cambridge: Cambridge Univ. Press.

Ó Tuama, Seán, and Thomas Kinsella. 1981. *An Duanaire, 1600–1900: Poems of the Dispossessed.* Dublin: Dolmen Press.

Payne, Michael, and John Schad, eds. 2003. *Life after Theory: Jacques Derrida, Frank Kermode, Toril Moi and Christopher Norris.* London: Continuum.

Plato. 1978. *The Collected Dialogues of Plato Including the Letters.* Edited by E. Hamilton and H. Cairns. Princeton, NJ: Princeton Univ. Press.

Protevi, John. 2001. *Political Physics: Deleuze, Derrida, and the Body Politic.* London: Athlone Press.

Quinn, Justin. 2008. *The Cambridge Introduction to Modern Irish Poetry, 1800–2000.* Cambridge: Cambridge Univ. Press.

Rabaté, Jean-Michel. 2003. "Lacan's Turn to Freud." In *The Cambridge Companion to Lacan*, edited by Jean-Michel Rabaté, 1–24. Cambridge: Cambridge Univ. Press.

Rabinovich, Diana. 2003. "What Is a Lacanian Clinic?" In *The Cambridge Companion to Lacan*, edited by Jean-Michel Rabaté, 208–21. Cambridge: Cambridge Univ. Press.

Rancière, Jacques. 2004. *The Flesh of Words: The Politics of Writing.* Translated by Charlotte Mandell. Stanford, CA: Stanford Univ. Press.

Ricoeur, Paul. 2006. *On Translation.* Translated by Eileen Brennan. London: Routledge.

Ross, Raymond J., and Joy Hendry, eds. 1986. *Sorley MacLean: Critical Essays.* Edinburgh: Scottish Academic Press.

Russell, Richard Rankin. 2014. *Seamus Heaney's Regions.* South Bend, IN: Univ. of Notre Dame Press.

Said, Edward. 1990. "Yeats and Decolonization." In *Nationalism, Colonialism, and Literature*, edited by Terry Eagleton, Frederic Jameson, and Edward Said, 69–98. Minneapolis: Univ. of Minnesota Press.

Simon, Jules. 2011. *Art and Responsibility: A Phenomenology of the Diverging Paths of Rosenzweig and Heidegger.* London: Continuum.

Sinclair, Mark. 2006. *Heidegger, Aristotle and the Work of Art: Poiesis in Being.* London: Palgrave.

Smith, Anna Marie. 1998. *Laclau and Mouffe: The Radical Democratic Imaginary.* London: Routledge.

Smith, Stan. 1997. "The Distance Between: Seamus Heaney." In *Seamus Heaney*, edited by Michael Allen, 223–52. New Casebook Series. London: Macmillan.

Stevenson, Anne. 2001. "Stations: Seamus Heaney and the Sacred Sense of the Sensitive Self." In *The Art of Seamus Heaney*, edited by Tony Curtis, 129–38. 4th ed. Dublin: Wolfhound Press.

Synge, John Millington. 1992. *The Aran Islands, 1871–1909.* Edited by Tim Robinson. London: Penguin.

———. 1994. *The Playboy of the Western World.* London: Methuen.

Tobin, Daniel. 1998. *Passage to the Center: Imagination and the Sacred in the Poetry of Seamus Heaney.* Lexington: Univ. Press of Kentucky.

Tonner, Philip. 2010. *Heidegger, Metaphysics and the Univocity of Being.* London: Continuum.

Vendler, Helen. 2004. *Poets Thinking: Pope, Whitman, Dickinson, Yeats.* Cambridge, MA: Harvard Univ. Press.

Venuti, Lawrence. 1998. *The Scandals of Translation.* London: Routledge.

Vernant, Jean-Pierre. 1991. *Mortals and Immortals.* Edited by F. Zeitlin. Princeton, NJ: Princeton Univ. Press.

Viswanathan, Gauri. 1997. *Masks of Conquest: Literary Study and British Rule in India.* New York: Columbia Univ. Press.

Wagner, Erica. 2013. "Interview with Seamus Heaney." *Times*, Jan. 28.

Wallace, Nathan. 2015. *Hellenism and Reconciliation in Ireland: From Yeats to Field Day.* Cork: Cork Univ. Press.

Watkin, William. 2010. *The Literary Agamben: Adventures in Logopoiesis.* London: Continuum.

Whalen, Lachlan. 2007. *Contemporary Irish Republican Prison Writing: Writing and Resistance.* London: Palgrave Macmillan.

White, Barry. 1989. "Interview with Seamus Heaney." *Belfast Telegraph*, June 29.

White, Harry. 2008. *Music and the Irish Literary Imagination.* Oxford: Oxford Univ. Press.

Wilmer, Steven, and Audrone Žukauskaitė, eds. 2010a. *Interrogating "Antigone" in Postmodern Philosophy and Criticism*. Oxford: Oxford Univ. Press.

———. 2010b. Introduction to *Interrogating "Antigone" in Postmodern Philosophy and Criticism*, edited by Steven Wilmer and Audrone Žukauskaitė, 1–16. Oxford: Oxford Univ. Press.

Wilson, Ross. 2007. *Theodor Adorno*. London: Routledge.

Wrathall, Mark. 2002. *Heidegger Reexamined*. Vol. 2, *Truth, Realism, and the History of Being*. London: Routledge.

Yeats, W. B. 1965. *The Collected Poems of W. B. Yeats*. London: Macmillan.

Young, Julian. 1992. *Nietzsche's Philosophy of Art*. Cambridge: Cambridge Univ. Press.

———. 2001. *Heidegger's Philosophy of Art*. Cambridge: Cambridge Univ. Press.

Žižek, Slavoj. 1991. *Looking Awry: An Introduction to Jacques Lacan through Popular Culture*. Cambridge, MA: MIT Press.

———. 2005. *Interrogating the Real: Selected Writings*. Edited by Rex Butler and Scott Stephens. London: Continuum Press.

Zuidervaart, Lambert. 1991. *Adorno's Aesthetic Theory: The Redemption of Illusion*. Cambridge, MA: MIT Press.

Index

Eugene O'Brien is senior lecturer and head of the Department of English Language and Literature in Mary Immaculate College, Limerick. He is also director of the Mary Immaculate College Institute for Irish Studies. His publications include: *The Question of Irish Identity in the Writings of William Butler Yeats and James Joyce* (1998); *Examining Irish Nationalism in the Context of Literature, Culture and Religion: A Study of the Epistemological Structure of Nationalism* (2002); *Seamus Heaney—Creating Irelands of the Mind* (2002); *Seamus Heaney and the Place of Writing* (2003); *Seamus Heaney: Searches for Answers* (2006); and *Kicking Bishop Brennan up the Arse—Negotiating Texts and Contexts in Contemporary Irish Studies* (2009). He co-edited *La France et la Mondialisation / France and the Struggle against Globalization* (2007); *Reinventing Ireland through a French Prism* (2007); *Modernity and Postmodernity in a Franco-Irish Context* (2008); and *Breaking the Mould: Literary Representations of Irish Catholicism* (2010). His latest book, *From Prosperity to Austerity: A Socio-Cultural Critique of the Celtic Tiger and its Aftermath*, co-edited with Eamon Maher, was published in 2014 by Manchester University Press, and he is currently completing an edited book on the later poetry of Seamus Heaney, and another book about the cultural legacy of the Catholic Church in Ireland.